100 SCIENCE LESSONS

YEAR 6

Scottish

Published by Scholastic Ltd,
Villiers House,
Clarendon Avenue,
Leamington Spa,
Warwickshire CV32 5PR

© Scholastic Ltd 2001
Text © 2001 Karen Mallinson-Yates
(Introduction, Units 4 and 8),
Tom Rugg (Units 1–3), Clifford
Hibbard (Units 5–7)

67890   567890

Series Consultant
Peter Riley

Authors
Karen Mallinson-Yates
(Introduction, Units 4 and 8),
Tom Rugg (Units 1–3),
Clifford Hibbard (Units 5–7)

Editor
Joel Lane

Assistant Editor
David Sandford

Series Designers
David Hurley
Joy Monkhouse

Designer
Mark Udall

Cover photography
Martyn Chillmaid

Illustrations
Tony O'Donnell
Sarah Wimperis

British Library Cataloguing-in-Publication Data
A catalogue record for this book is available from the British Library.

ISBN 0-439-01807-2

The right of Karen Mallinson-Yates (Introduction, Units 4 and 8), Tom Rugg (Units 1–3), and Clifford Hibbard (Units 5–7) to be identified as the Authors of this work has been asserted by them in accordance with the Copyright, Designs and Patents Act 1988.

Teachers should consult their own school policies and guidelines concerning practical work and participation of children in scientific experiments. You should only select activities which you feel can be carried out safely and confidently in the classroom.

Acknowledgements
The National Curriculum for England 2000
© The Queens Printer and Controller of HMSO. Reproduced under the terms of HMSO Guidance Note 8.
The National Curriculum for Wales 2000
© The Queens Printer and Controller of HMSO. Reproduced under the terms of HMSO Guidance Note 10.
Wiring diagrams on page 139 reproduced by kind permission of Volkswagen Group United Kingdom Ltd.
Photographs on pages 181 and 187 © NASA.

Contents

Introduction

100 Science Lessons is a series of year-specific teachers' resource books that provide a wealth of lesson plans and photocopiable resources for delivering a whole year of science teaching, including differentiation and assessment.

The series follows the QCA *Science Scheme of Work* in the sequencing of topics. However, instead of having six or seven units as in the QCA scheme, the book for each year contains eight units. These units are the familiar topics: 1. Ourselves, 2. Animals & plants, 3. The environment, 4. Materials, 5. Electricity, 6. Forces & motion, 7. Light & sound, 8. Earth and beyond. They appear in the same order in every book, but have sub-titles which describe the emphasis of the work in that year. For example, in this book Unit 4 is Materials: Reversible and non-reversible changes.

By having eight units, this resource builds on the QCA scheme to accommodate the demands of the curricula for Wales, Scotland and Northern Ireland. It also creates opportunities to visit each topic in every year: after visiting a topic in synchrony with the QCA scheme, you can make a further visit the following year for extension or consolidation of the previous year's work. A grid showing how the topics map from one book in the series to the next is given on page 208.

Each unit is divided into a number of lessons, ending with an assessment lesson. The organisation chart at the start of each unit shows the objectives and outcomes of each lesson, and gives a quick overview of the lesson content (Main activity, Group activities, Plenary). The statements of the national curricula for England, Wales, Scotland and Northern Ireland (given in the grids on pages 196–207) provide the basis for the lesson objectives used throughout the book.

ORGANISATION (15 LESSONS)

	OBJECTIVES	MAIN ACTIVITY	GROUP ACTIVITIES	PLENARY	OUTCOMES
LESSON 1	● To sort objects into groups based on observable features.	Introduction to classification: the sorting of objects according to their features.	Complete two sorting tasks involving observation and logic.	Consider the need for classification of living things.	● Have experience of placing objects into groups based on observable characteristics. ● Understand that trying to sort things into groups can cause problems.
LESSON 2	● To know that living things can be arranged into groups according to observable features. ● To know that these groups can help in identifying unknown living things.	Explain that living things are divided into kingdoms. Break down the animal kingdom into invertebrates and the five classes of vertebrates.	Sort an assortment of pictures of living things into their correct vertebrate groups.	Discuss the classification of the duck-billed platypus.	● Can identify an animal appropriately as a vertebrate or an invertebrate. ● Can classify a vertebrate accurately as a bird, amphibian, reptile, mammal or fish using external characteristics.

LESSON PLANS

Each lesson plan is divided into four parts: Introduction, Main teaching activity, Group activities and Plenary. In many of the lessons, the introduction is supported by background information and a vocabulary list that will help in delivering the lesson and support assessment of the work. The lesson introduction sets the context for the work. The Main teaching activity features direct whole-class or group teaching, and may include instructions on how to perform a demonstration or an experiment in order to stimulate the children's interest and increase their motivation. There is then usually a choice of two activities to engage groups of children. (In those lessons where a whole-class investigation takes place, there may be a single group activity related to this, and occasionally a 'circus' of group work is suggested.) Advice on differentiation and formative assessment linked to this work is provided. Finally, there are details of a concluding plenary session.

About 60% of the lesson plans in this book, including those for the assessment lessons, are presented in full detail. Many of these are followed by outlines for closely related lessons on the same topics or concepts, using the same background information. To avoid repetition and allow you to focus on the essentials of the lesson, these plans are presented as grids for you to develop. They contain the major features of the detailed lesson plans, allowing you to plan for progression and assessment.

Detailed lesson plans

The lessons in this book have been designed to reflect the children's developing maturity and interest in the world around them. The investigations suggested assume increasing independence, with greater emphasis on the children deciding what to explore and how to approach the investigation, guided by their teacher, as they prepare for KS3/S1–2. Units 2 and 3 encourage a broader approach to enquiry, while Unit 4 concentrates on introducing a more 'conventional', systematic approach to experimental methods. Content is provided in Units 3 and 5 to support teachers in England looking to address QCA Unit 5/6H in Year 6.

Wider issues concerning the impact of science are also addressed. For example, Units 4, 5 and 6 all relate basic scientific ideas (to do with materials, electricity and forces) to large-scale industrial applications in the real world.

Objectives

The objectives of the lessons are derived from the statements in all the UK science curriculum documents. They are stated in a way that helps to focus each lesson plan and give a unique theme to each unit. At least one objective for each lesson is derived from the statements related to content knowledge. In addition, there may be one or more objectives relating to scientific enquiry; but you may choose to replace these with others to meet your needs and the skills you wish the children to develop. The relationship of the curriculum statements to the coverage of each unit's lessons is given in the grids on pages 196–207.

Wherever relevant, the focus and content of each unit coincides with that of the matching unit in the QCA *Science Scheme of Work*. However, we have not distinguished in the lesson objectives which content is specific to any one curriculum, and have left it to your professional judgement to identify those activities that are best suited to the age and ability of your class and to the requirements spelled out in your local curriculum guidance. If you wish to check whether a particular activity cross-references directly to your curriculum, please refer to pages 196–207.

Resources and Preparation

The Resources section provides a list of everything you will need to deliver the lesson, including any of the photocopiables presented in this book. Preparation describes anything that needs to be done in advance of the lesson, such as collecting environmental data. As part of the preparation for all practical work, you should consult your school's policies concerning the use of plants and animals in the classroom, so that you can select activities for which you are confident to take responsibility. The ASE publication *Be Safe!* gives useful guidance on what things are safe to use in the classroom.

Background

The Background section in each lesson plan provides relevant facts and explanations of concepts to support the lesson. In some cases, the information

provided may go beyond what the children need to learn at Year 6/Primary 7; but you may value this further knowledge in order to avoid reinforcing any misconceptions the children may have.

Vocabulary

Each fully detailed lesson plan has an associated vocabulary list, containing words that should be used by the children in discussing and presenting their work, and in their writing. The words relate both to scientific enquiry and to knowledge and understanding.

It is important that children develop their science vocabulary in order to describe their findings and observations and to explain their ideas. Whenever a specialist word is used, it should be accompanied by a definition, as some children in the class may take time to understand and differentiate the meanings of words such as 'habitat' and 'environment' (or 'force' and 'strength').

Introduction

The lesson introductions contain ideas to get each lesson started and to 'set the scene'. You may also wish to draw on the background information or make links with other lessons in your scheme of work.

Main teaching activity

This section presents a direct, whole-class (or occasionally group) teaching session to follow the introduction. This will help you to deliver the content knowledge outlined in the lesson objectives to the children before they start their group work. It may include guidance on discussion, or on performing one or more demonstrations or class investigations to help the children understand the work ahead.

The relative proportions of the lesson given to the Introduction, Main teaching activity and Group activities vary. If you are reminding the children of their previous work and getting them on to their own investigations, the group work may dominate the lesson time; if you are introducing a new topic or concept, you might wish to spend all or most of the lesson engaged in whole-class teaching.

Group activities

The Group activities are very flexible. Some may be best suited to individual work, while others may be suitable for work in pairs or larger groupings. In the detailed lesson plans, there are usually two Group activities provided for each lesson. You may wish to use one after the other; use both together, to reduce demand on resources and your attention; or, where one is a practical activity, use the other for children who complete their practical work successfully and quickly, or even as a follow-up homework task. Some of the Group activities are supported by a photocopiable sheet.

The Group activities may include some writing. These activities are also aimed at strengthening the children's science literacy, and supporting their English literacy skills. They may involve writing labels and captions, developing scientific vocabulary, writing about or recording investigations, presenting data, explaining what they have observed, or using appropriate secondary sources. The children's mathematical skills are also developed through number and data-handling work in the context of science investigations.

Differentiation

For each of the lessons, where appropriate, there are suggestions for differentiated work for the more able and less able children in the class. Differentiated group activities are designed so that all the children who perform these tasks can make a contribution to the plenary session.

Assessment

Each lesson includes advice on how to assess the children's success in the activities against the lesson objectives. This may include questions to ask or observations to make to help you build up a picture of the children's developing ideas and plan future lessons. A separate summative assessment lesson is provided at the end of each unit of work.

Plenary

This is a very important part of the lesson. It is important not to let it get squeezed out by mistiming other activities in the lesson. Suggestions are given for drawing the various strands of the lesson together in this session. If an investigation has been tried, the work of different groups can be compared and evaluated. The scene may be set for another lesson, or the lesson objectives and outcomes may be reviewed and key learning points highlighted.

Homework

On occasions, tasks may be suggested for the children to do at home. Tasks, such as collecting things to add to a display or observing the night sky, cannot easily be done in school time, while other lessons may offer opportunities for follow-up work, for example using the photocopiables provided at home, or to research a broader knowledge of the topic under discussion.

Lesson outcomes

These are statements related to the objectives; they describe what the children should have achieved through the lesson.

Links to other units or lessons

The lesson can usually be linked to other lessons in the same unit to provide progression or reinforce the work done. It may also be linked to lessons in other units in the book, and suitable links of this kind are suggested in the lesson plans. You may like to consider these links in planning your scheme of work – for example, lessons may be integrated from Units 3 and 4 to develop a coherent scheme of work looking at the recycling of materials in the natural environment.

Links to other curriculum areas

These are included where appropriate. They may include links to subjects closely related to science, such as technology or maths, or to content and skills in subjects such as art, history or geography.

Lesson plan grids

These short lesson plans, in the form of a grid, offer further activity ideas to broaden the topic coverage. As the example below shows, they have the same basic structure as the detailed lesson plans. They lack the Introduction, Background and Vocabulary sections, but these are supported by the previous and related detailed lesson plans. Notes suggesting ideas for the Main activity and group work are provided for you to develop. Generally, there are no photocopiables linked to these lesson plans.

LESSON 3

Objectives	● To know that plants need light, water and warmth to grow well. ● To design a fair experiment and make predictions that they can test.
Resources	Photocopiable page 48 (one copy per group); cotton wool, cress seeds, Petri dishes, sticky labels, measuring cylinders; storage sites (eg cupboard, fridge, window sill).
Main activity	Explain that in this lesson, you will be revising what plants need in order to grow healthily. Ask the children for suggestions, and brainstorm these around the words 'Healthy growth'. From these ideas, pick 'light', 'water' and 'warmth' (or 'the right temperature') as three factors for the children to investigate using cress seeds.
Differentiation	Some children may need additional guidance in planning their ideas; adapt the suggestions provided with the prompt questions in the previous lesson to help with this. More able children could be asked to find out more about *why* plants need light and water to grow. (Light provides the energy used to make food by photosynthesis.)
Assessment	Use the guide sheet as a reference to check that the children are able to take logical steps in forming the process of enquiry and in reviewing their observations.
Plenary	At the end of the investigation, all the groups should share their results. Was a common trend observed? Ask the children why it is important for scientists to share their observations and results. (It allows them to reach a greater understanding of the topic being researched.)
Outcome	● Know the importance of water, light and warmth for healthy plant growth.

RESOURCES
Photocopiable sheets

These are an integral part of many of the lessons and are found at
the end of the relevant unit, marked with the 'photocopiable' symbol:
They may provide resources, quizzes, instructions for practical work, information 'factfiles' or
written assignments, and so on.

Classroom equipment and space

A wide range of resources are needed for the lessons in this book. However, every attempt has
been made to restrict the list to resources that will be readily available to primary schools. You
may wish to borrow some items (such as a retort stand, boss and clamp, data-logger or
microscopes) from the science department of your local secondary school, though these would
be very useful permanent additions to your science resources.

Each lesson plan includes a resources list. When you have planned which lessons you wish to
use, you could make up your own resources list for the term's or year's work. Encourage your
colleagues to do the same for other years, so that you can compare lists, identify times when
there may be a high demand for particular resources and make adjustments as necessary.

ICT

Many of the lessons in this book can be enhanced by the use of ICT. As new products are
entering the market all the time, few are specified in this book. However you may like to
consider opportunities for ICT work under these headings:

Using the Internet

The children can learn to use very large sources of
information, such as those found on the Internet.
However, it is important to make sure that they do not
simply retrieve pages of information in answer to a
question. They need to learn how to skim, and how to
take in information, interpret it and use it for their own
needs. It is important that you spend some time in
advance searching the Internet for suitable sites. Without
this, the children may spend many hours searching
fruitlessly, and much of what they do find may be beyond
their ability to comprehend. Show the children how to use
websites (which you have previously sourced) and the
search facilities of your browser, how to follow hyperlinks
and how to download text or pictures to use in their work
(including appropriate referencing of copyright holders).

Data-logging

Data-logging equipment should have been introduced in
Year 5/Primary 6 (if not before) to record the change of
temperature, light or sound over a given length of time,
providing an instant record of the changes and a graphical
representation. The children should use this equipment
confidently with your support. That the computer can be
used to register changes in the environment (such as
falling light levels) might be linked to its capability for
control, in this case being programmed to switch on
lighting.

Presentations

The children should be taught to use a wide variety of
methods to present their results and conclusions. They
should be encouraged to use more standardised recording
methods for appropriate experiments and investigations,
in preparation for the formality of secondary science and
beyond. By Year 6/Primary 7, the children should be able
to assemble at least a page of a multimedia presentation
(using images, sound and text) such as might be found on
a CD-ROM.

Spreadsheets

The children should have been introduced to spreadsheets
by Year 5/Primary 6. Their use to explore scientific models,
for example to look for patterns in survey data, should be
encouraged.

ASSESSMENT

The assessments in this book indicate likely achievements for children in Year 6/Primary 7. The stated learning objectives relate specifically to the work in these lessons. In this book, it is expected that most children will achieve National Curriculum Level 4/Scottish Level C/D and many will progress further to achieve Level 5/Scottish Level D, or even Level 6/Scottish Level D/E in some aspects, in certain school settings. Achievement in primary science is a well-documented National Curriculum success story. Of course, some children may not progress so well and may be expected to achieve only Level 3/Scottish Level C. You may find it useful to devise a diagnostic test to use at the beginning of a new unit. Look at the previous books in the series, find the appropriate unit and check the work that has been covered with your colleagues. Devise a test and apply it at the beginning of the unit, then use the results to plan the use of differentiated activities and materials as you teach the unit.

The last lesson in every unit focuses on summative assessment. Its objectives are related to appropriate expectations. This lesson only samples the content of the unit, and its results should be used in conjunction with other assessments you have made during the teaching of the unit. The assessment lesson consists of two activities. One or both may be a photocopiable test that has a mark scheme. The mark scheme is not related to curriculum levels of attainment, but provides a way of assessing the children's performance. The other assessment activity may be a practical activity with suggested questions for you to use while observing the children at work, or an activity that allows the children to use what they know, for example to think up quiz questions to put to other children. Note who is able to ask appropriate questions and knows whether the answer given is correct.

Certain assessment lessons in this book provide opportunities to assess 'experimental and investigative science'. These activities may allow you to assess the children on all three skills (planning, obtaining evidence, considering evidence), or just on one skill. When assessing the children's work, you need to refer to the statements of attainment and determine from these which level a child is at for each of the skills. For example, a child might reach Level 3/Scottish Level C for planning but Level 5/Scottish Level D for obtaining evidence. The lessons that deal with this aspect of assessment are intended to lead the children gently into planning and carrying out an investigation. For example, in one lesson, the children might help the teacher to carry out an experiment and obtain results. They will then be shown how to analyse the results; as they do so, they will be encouraged to ask or answer further questions. These questions will form the basis of another scientific investigation, which the children should now be confident to plan using the knowledge they have gained from the previous lesson's experiment. This work can then be assessed according to the appropriate curriculum attainment guidance.

The children's work in the assessment lessons can be kept in a portfolio and used to form the basis of your teacher assessment scheme.

SUPPORT FOR PLANNING

Developing your scheme of work

This book is planned to support the QCA *Science Scheme of Work* and the statements of the UK national curricula. In planning your school scheme of work, you may wish to look at the units in this book or throughout the series along with those of the QCA scheme. You may also wish to relate the objectives in your curriculum planning more directly to those of the curriculum documents. The grids on pages 196–207 show how the statements of the national curricula for knowledge and understanding and science enquiry for England, Wales, Scotland and Northern Ireland provide the basis for the lesson objectives used throughout this book. In the tables, each statement is cross-referenced to one or more lessons to help with curriculum planning.

Planning progression

The Series topic map on page 208 shows the focus of each of the units in the books in this series, to help you work out your plan of progression. By looking at the charts of curriculum coverage and the organisation chart for each unit, you can plan for progression through the year and from one year to the next, covering the whole of the work needed for Reception and Key Stages 1–2/Primary 1–7.

You may choose to use all or most of the lessons from the units in this book in their entirety, or make a selection to provide a 'backbone' for your own curriculum planning and supplement it with lessons you have already found successful from other sources. The pages in this book are perforated and hole-punched, so you can separate them and put them in a planning file with other favourite activities and worksheets.

TEACHING SCIENCE IN YEAR 6/PRIMARY 7

The units in this book will help to consolidate work done in Years 3–5/Primary 4–6. They broaden some of the concepts that have already been introduced, and provide a firm base for science at KS3/S1–2 and, in England, the Key Stage 2 SAT in science. It is expected that most children will attain at least NC Level 4/Scottish Level C/D as they work through this book, though some may only attain Level 3 or firmly achieve Level 5 – Scottish Levels C and D respectively – in some areas.

An underlying theme of this book is the application of science knowledge to our everyday world. As the children are maturing, this approach allows them to consider issues in which the consequences of using science can alter our everyday life. This should help them see that it is important to know about science (to become scientifically literate) in order to form opinions which in future can help in the sensible development of their world. This notion is only introduced here, but it should help to prepare the children for work in later years on this topic.

A brief description of the unit contents follows, to show more specifically how the themes are developed. The authors recognise that the individual units in this book will reflect their various teaching and learning styles, but hope that this variety will enhance the repertoire of teachers using the materials and benefit any scheme of work developed from them.

● **Unit 1: Ourselves** takes a look at healthy lifestyles and brings together work from previous years on diet, exercise, hygiene and the dangers of smoking, alcohol, drugs and solvents. In relation to growing up, Unit 1 focuses on human reproduction. Children should develop a secure knowledge of the human reproductive system and what happens during and after fertilisation.

● **Unit 2: Animals & plants** looks at 'Variation': how living things can be arranged into groups according to their observable features, and how these groups can help in the identification of unknown living things. The children will also look at variation in plants and animals of the same species, and the conditions that are needed for plants to grow.

● **Unit 3: The environment** considers how, in 'The living world', living things on different scales survive. The unit starts by looking at habitats and feeding relationships, and how plants and animals have special features that enable them to survive in their habitat. The children are given opportunities to examine how plants can survive and grow in different conditions. Ideas for supporting QCA Unit 5/6H are provided. Finally, this unit looks in detail at micro-organisms and their positive and negative effects on human life.

● **Unit 4: Materials** looks at 'Reversible and non-reversible changes'. The children investigate how soluble and insoluble solids can be separated from water, and how the rate of dissolving is affected by temperature, stirring and size of solid particles. The unit goes on to look at irreversible changes such as rusting and burning. The children are also given the opportunity to consider some health and safety issues, and to look at the environmental implications of our use of the materials on Earth.

● **Unit 5: Electricity** builds on the work on circuits covered in previous years. It gives the children opportunities to find out what factors influence circuits by investigating the effects on a circuit of changing its various components. This unit also formally introduces how circuits can be represented by conventional symbols, and how this is useful in science outside the classroom. Ideas for supporting QCA Unit 5/6H are provided.

● **Unit 6: Forces & motion** links the concept of force to the concepts of gravity and weight. It allows the children to develop an appreciation of the fact that forces can be measured, and to consider the effects of paired forces on objects.

● **Unit 7: Light & sound** builds on previous work to consider how we see our environment, reinforcing the idea that the reflection of light is the key to this process and how a shadow differs from a reflection. The unit then goes on to consider how the sounds around us are made and how we hear them.

● **Unit 8: Earth & beyond** briefly revisits the motions of the Earth, Sun and Moon, and then explores the structure of the Solar System.

New beginnings

ORGANISATION (8 LESSONS)

	OBJECTIVES	MAIN ACTIVITY	GROUP ACTIVITIES	PLENARY	OUTCOMES
LESSON 1	• To construct a plan for a healthy lifestyle.	Examine aspects of a healthy lifestyle through discussion. Key points to be raised: diet, exercise, hygiene.	Construct their own lifestyle chart, including diet, exercise and sleep. Examine their lifestyle critically to consider improvements.	The class vote on who has the healthiest lifestyle. Discuss TV-watching habits.	• Can plan a regime for a healthy lifestyle. • Can explain the need for each item in such a regime.
LESSON 2	• To identify activities and substances that may be harmful to health. • To develop skills in collaborative research, discussion and presentation of ideas.	Discuss activities that are hazardous to health.	Use a range of sources to research different health risks and prepare a presentation. Deliver the talk. Make brief notes on each topic covered by the other groups.	Assess each presentation. Encourage the children to do the same thing.	• Understand that drugs, solvents, alcohol, loud music and overexposure to sunlight can damage their health.
LESSON 3	• To assess the healthy and unhealthy aspects of a lifestyle. • To suggest lifestyle changes to improve the health of an individual.	The children write about their lifestyle, then prepare and perform a doctor–patient role-play in which lifestyle changes are recommended.		The children choose three lifestyle changes to adopt as 'resolutions'.	• Can assess a lifestyle and suggest changes to improve the health of the individual. • Recognise that the decisions they make may affect the quality of their lifestyle.
LESSON 4	• To know the stages of the human life cycle.	Brainstorm the stages in human life and how these form a life cycle.	Draw an illustrated diagram of the human life cycle. Research the life cycle of another animal and compare with the human life cycle.	Discuss how advances over the past 1000 years have changed features of the human life cycle.	• Know the key stages in the human life cycle.
LESSON 5	• To know about the structure of the reproductive organs. • To know that changes in the body leading to sexual maturity begin at puberty.	Use large diagrams to consider the reproductive organs of the human male and female, and explain the function of each part.	Match the names of parts with their functions and place them on a diagram. Model sperm and egg cells and try to explain the differences between them.	A quick test on the changes that occur at puberty.	• Can describe the functions of the parts that make up the male and female reproductive organs. • Know that the changes that bring about sexual maturity begin at puberty.
LESSON 6	• To know how fertilisation occurs. • To know how the growing foetus develops and how the baby is born.	Explain fertilisation and the subsequent stages of development up to birth.	Match pictures of the developing baby with captions and place them in sequence. Draw life-sized pictures of a developing baby at different stages.	Relate this lesson to earlier work by discussing the dangers of smoking during pregnancy.	• Can describe the growth of the foetus. • Understand the birth process.

ORGANISATION (8 LESSONS)

	OBJECTIVES	MAIN ACTIVITY	GROUP ACTIVITIES	PLENARY	OUTCOMES
LESSON 7	● To know about the changes in lifestyle that are necessary during pregnancy and the skills and care required in parenting. ● To develop skills in listening, note-taking and asking questions. ● To recognise stages in their own development.	The mother of a small child gives an account of the pregnancy and the care required by the baby after birth. The children make notes, then they arrange photographs of their own early life, including scans, and write about their needs at each stage and the effects on their parents.		Discuss the responsibility and pressures of parenthood.	● Understand that a pregnant woman needs to take special care of her health. ● Understand that being a parent is a demanding task that requires many skills.

	OBJECTIVES	ACTIVITY 1		ACTIVITY 2	
ASSESSMENT 8	● To assess the children's knowledge of aspects of a lifestyle that may be regarded as healthy or as unhealthy. ● To assess the children's knowledge of the structures that support a baby during its development in the womb and the care a mother needs to take during pregnancy.	The children read a description of the life of an Indian girl and her family and identify the healthy and unhealthy aspects of her lifestyle, then consider the reasons for the increased frequency of heart disease in the UK.		The children answer questions about the development of a baby in the womb. They identify activities that the mother should avoid when pregnant, and explain why these activities are dangerous.	

LESSON 1

OBJECTIVE
● To construct a plan for a healthy lifestyle.

RESOURCES
Group activity: A3 paper, pens, pencils.

BACKGROUND
The lessons in this unit deal with sexual reproduction from a scientific perspective. You might like to use these lessons to set a health context for wider discussions in PSHE lessons, dealing with issues such as changes at puberty, emotions, risk, responsibility and making informed choices. You may find *Resource Bank: Healthy Living (KS2/P4–7)* by Dilys Went (Scholastic) a useful resource for this. The children will already be familiar with many aspects of what makes up a healthy lifestyle (see *100 Science Lessons: Year 5/Primary 6*), and this lesson is a chance to draw together the positive aspects ('things to avoid' will be covered in the next lesson).

The incidence of premature death through heart disease is alarmingly high in Britain – health awareness at a young age is vital. Aspects of diet, exercise and hygiene are targeted in this lesson. Good personal hygiene prevents the build-up of body odour – the sweat we produce provides an ideal breeding ground for microbes living on our skin, and these microbes can react with sweat to make us smell. 'Athlete's foot' is caused by a fungus that thrives on moist, sweaty skin between the toes; washing and drying thoroughly helps to prevent this. Microbes thrive on food deposits left between our teeth; they feed on sugars and produce acids that attack the enamel of the teeth and cause cavities to form. Regular brushing is important for keeping teeth healthy.

INTRODUCTION

Gather the children together. Ask them to imagine how their lives would have been different if they had lived 200 years ago. *Did people live as long as they do today?* Explain that people in Britain now live almost twice as long (on average) as they once did.

MAIN TEACHING ACTIVITY

Explain that this lesson is about looking at our lifestyles and trying to decide whether they are healthy. *What does 'healthy' mean?* Explain that for many people who live in relatively wealthy parts of the world, such as Britain, the quality of life has greatly improved; but that some diseases, including heart disease, have become more common as a result of an unhealthy lifestyle. *What things are important for staying healthy?* Hopefully, responses will include diet, exercise, getting enough sleep and good hygiene. Some children may refer to 'avoiding drugs', 'not smoking' and so on; explain that 'things to avoid' will be covered in more detail in the next lesson.

Ask the children what a healthy diet should and should not include. A healthy diet should include plenty of fresh fruit and vegetables, fish or lean meat (or beans), wholemeal foods containing fibre, foods rich in minerals (such as calcium) and vitamins, and so on. Foods to avoid should include foods that are high in fat, or that have added salt, sugar, colourings, preservatives and so on.

Now ask the children why exercise is important. Hopefully, answers will include: 'it makes your muscles and bones stronger'; 'it strengthens the heart and improves the circulation of the blood'; 'it reduces stress'; 'it helps to prevent obesity' (becoming overweight, which increases blood pressure and the strain on the heart); and 'it reduces the likelihood of developing many serious diseases later in life'.

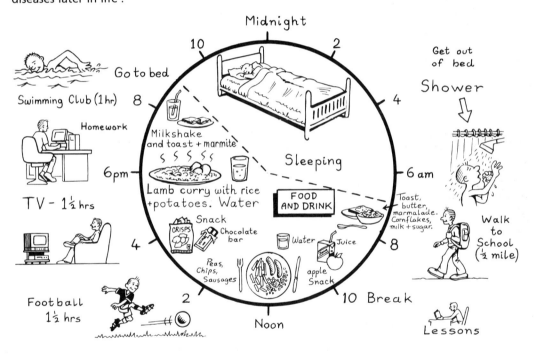

GROUP ACTIVITY

Using A3 paper, the children should each draw a circle to represent their day, showing what time they wake, wash, eat breakfast and so on. They can call this chart 'My Lifestyle' (see illustration above). Emphasise that they must show exactly what they eat – for example, not just 'sandwiches' but 'ham sandwiches (white bread) with butter, tomatoes and lettuce'. They must mention milk and sugar if these are added to cereals. They should also include whether (and for how long) they watch TV; what time they bath or shower, what time they go to bed and so on. At the bottom of the page, they should draw two boxes: one titled 'Good points' and the other 'Bad points'.

After completion, the children should swap their charts and look critically at each other's day, then discuss the good and bad points about each other's lifestyles. When they have agreed on the main points, they should write these ideas and some of their own in the boxes under the chart (still using the swapped copies).

Once the children have done this, ask them to compare their lifestyles and discuss (in groups) how they could improve the quality of their diet, their exercise routine and their lifestyle as a whole to become more healthy. They should add these suggestions to their charts. Perhaps they could suggest ways to improve the health of all the children in the school, the country or the world.

DIFFERENTIATION

Some children will need help with setting out their day as an A3 chart. You may want to give a rough guide on the board. Alternatively, you could draw the circles in advance with key activities (such as 'Eat breakfast') added at the bottom, allowing the children to sort out the events.

ASSESSMENT

Go through the charts as a class, checking the aspects of lifestyle that have been recognised as healthy and unhealthy. Check that each child recognises the importance of exercise, a balanced diet and hygiene as key aspects of a healthy lifestyle.

PLENARY

Have a class vote on who has the healthiest lifestyle based on their daily plan. Take care not to encourage comments that refer to children's upbringing or background. Tell the children that many national groups in the USA and in Britain are campaigning for measures that will lead children to watch less TV. *Can you think why this might be a good idea?* Perhaps you could use this opportunity to carry out a quick survey of the children's TV-watching habits. Generate discussion by asking: *Do any of you believe that TV should be abolished? What would the advantages and disadvantages be?*

OUTCOMES

- Can plan a regime for a healthy lifestyle.
- Can explain the need for each item in such a regime.

LINKS

Unit 3, Lessons 11, 12: microbes.
PSHE and citizenship: what makes a healthy lifestyle.

LESSON 2

OBJECTIVES

- To identify activities and substances that may be harmful to health.
- To develop skills in collaborative research, discussion and presentation of ideas.

RESOURCES

Group activity: A4 paper; access to the school library; CD-ROMs such as *Encarta* (Microsoft); young people's health advice booklets concerning drugs from your local health authority; photocopiable pages 24, 25 and 26.

PREPARATION

Make one copy per child of page 26. Copies of pages 24 and 25 will be needed for support (see Differentiation).

Vocabulary

medicines, symptoms, liver, brain, addicted, ozone layer, ultra-violet rays, decibels, hertz (Hz), mucus, cilia, cancer, toxic

BACKGROUND

Smoking claims many thousands of lives in the UK each year. Alcohol is linked to a high percentage of the accidents treated by hospitals, to violence in the home, to liver disease and to many other problems. Solvents and 'recreational' drugs ruin the health of many young people and are linked to avoidable fatalities. Overexposure to sunlight can lead to cancer and the premature ageing of unprotected skin. Prolonged exposure to very loud music damages the hearing.

INTRODUCTION

Gather the class together. Remind them that in the last lesson, they looked at their lifestyles to see how healthy they were. Explain that today, they are going to look at some activities that can be harmful to our health.

MAIN TEACHING ACTIVITY

Ask the children to name some activities that can damage our bodies. Focus on ones that are intrinsically harmful, rather than ones that carry a risk of accidental injury. Hopefully suggestions will include smoking, taking drugs and drinking too much alcohol; you may have to prompt the children to mention overexposure to the sun and listening to very loud music.

Now tell the class that they will be working in groups, and that each group will be looking at one topic and then presenting it to the rest of the class. They will have 30 minutes to write their ideas on a sheet of A4 paper, and the presentation by each group should last about two minutes. Say that you will give each group a mark out of 10, based upon how effectively they present their ideas.

GROUP ACTIVITY

Write the topic titles below on sheets of A4 paper and give one to each group. Each group should discuss and research their given topic. Advise them to share their ideas within the group. Suggest that they brainstorm ideas, with one person writing them down, then decide how they are going to present them. They can use reference materials to find information. Encourage them to try to be entertaining and imaginative when they present their ideas – perhaps they might like to present a role-play, or give their audience a quiz at the end of their talk. Tell them that they have 30 minutes to prepare.

Group 1: Avoid drugs!
Group 2: Avoid solvents!
Group 3: Avoid sunburn!
Group 4: Avoid alcohol!
Group 5: Avoid loud music!
Group 6: Don't smoke!

Provide a space at the front of the room and ask each group to come up in turn and present their talk. Give the 'audience' copies of page 26; after each talk, they should write down what they have learned in the appropriate space.

DIFFERENTIATION

More able groups should be able to carry out independent research using textbooks, CD-ROMs and so on. Less able groups can be given the appropriate section of the 'Factfile' on pages 24 and 25 to show them what they should include in their presentation. If any group is struggling, you may want to prompt them with some particular facts from the 'Factfile'.

ASSESSMENT

Ask the children to design a poster for children in Year 5/Primary 6 (perhaps for homework), telling them what they should do and what they should avoid to live a healthy life. This will provide a summary of what they have learned. This activity could be developed in a future lesson, using design software, and could be used to assess how well the children have grasped the key points.

PLENARY

Give each group a mark (out of 5) for the content of their talk, with higher marks for those who have used a number of information sources. Give them another mark (out of 5) for the style of their talk: was it engaging, humorous, imaginative, memorable? Share your marking with the children, as it will help them to develop their presentation skills. You could also ask the class to give each group's talk a mark out of 10 to help them develop their critical appreciation skills.

OUTCOME

● Understand that drugs, solvents, alcohol, loud music and overexposure to sunlight can damage their health.

LINKS

PSHE and citizenship: effects and risks of drugs.
Unit 2, Lesson 11, 12, 13.

LESSON 3

Objectives	● To assess the healthy and unhealthy aspects of a lifestyle. ● To suggest lifestyle changes to improve the health of an individual.
Resources	Paper, writing materials, notes from previous lessons, space for the children to perform sketches, a white coat (optional).
Main activity	Ask the children to put together a role-play in pairs: as a doctor and a patient. They should start by writing individually about their lifestyle: what they eat, how often they exercise, whether they listen to loud music and so on. They should try to balance the good and bad points. At the end of this, they should work in pairs: the doctor giving advice, the patient seeking advice. They should prepare and act out the consultation, then swap over. The 'doctor' should draw on the knowledge gained in previous lessons to provide a 'prescription' for a healthier life. Select pairs to act out their piece in front of the class (if you have a white coat, the 'doctors' can take turns to wear it). Check to see whether there is general agreement about the 'prescriptions' given by the doctors. If there is disagreement, explore the suggestions made and see what other alternatives there might be. Some of the role-plays could be repeated in an assembly.
Differentiation	For less able children, you may wish to provide extreme examples of poor lifestyle so that they can start to consider possible improvements – for example, someone who chain-smokes, eats nothing but chips and sausages, drinks heavily and so on (not necessarily a member of your school's staff).
Assessment	Note whether the children can identify healthy and unhealthy aspects of a lifestyle, and whether they can recommend appropriate changes to improve the quality of an individual's health.
Plenary	With the class, check the key issues that have arisen. Ask the children to choose three resolutions they can make to improve their health. These should be realistic! They shouldn't aim to give up all sweets, for example, but they could aim to eat one apple every day in place of one sugary snack. You can put up the children's names on a 'health promises' chart on the wall and give them a gold star for each week they keep up their resolution.
Outcomes	● Can assess a lifestyle and suggest changes to improve the health of the individual. ● Recognise that the decisions they make may affect the quality of their lifestyle.

LESSON 4

OBJECTIVE
● To know the stages of the human life cycle.

RESOURCES

Group activities: 1. A3 paper (one sheet per pair), coloured crayons. **2.** A3 paper (one sheet per pair), textbooks containing references to the life cycles of non-human animals (frogs, butterflies and so on); the *Encarta* CD-ROM (Microsoft) or similar.

BACKGROUND

A **life cycle** is the name we give to the key stages of an animal's (or plant's) life. The fact that the death of an individual does not lead to the eventual extinction of the species is the essence of the life cycle. Dying individuals are replaced by new individuals born into the population, and these in turn reach sexual maturity and are able to produce young before they die. The key stages in the human life cycle are **fertilisation** (the joining or fusing of an egg and a sperm cell), **birth** (about 9 months from fertilisation), **infancy** (lasting up to 1 year from birth), **childhood** (from 1 to 12 years), **adolescence** (from 11 to 18), **adulthood** (from adolescence to old age) and ultimately **death**. The **lifespan** of an individual is the number of years he or she lives for. The key event that completes the human life cycle is **reproduction**. In most models, death is not included in illustrations of the life cycle.

The timescale of the human lifespan is influenced by environmental factors. In 1900, the average age of girls starting their first period was 18 years; today, it is common for girls to have their first period before the age of 11. The average lifespan in Britain in 1900 was below 50 years, and the infant mortality rate was very high. Today the average lifespan is close to 80 years, and the infant mortality rate is very low.

INTRODUCTION

Gather the children together. Ask them: *What season are we in? How do you know?* They may refer to the temperature outside – or better still, the state of the trees outside. *In which season*

Vocabulary

life cycle, fertilisation, fuse, birth, infancy, childhood, adolescence, puberty, adulthood, reproduction, lifespan, mammals *do the trees shed their leaves and disperse their seeds?* (Autumn.) *When are the trees bare except for the closed buds?* (Winter.) *When do the buds start to open and the seeds start to germinate?* (Spring.) *When are the trees in full leaf and forming fruits and seeds?* (Summer.) Explain that the world we live in is full of patterns of life, such as the changes in plants brought on by the seasons. The life of animals also follows a pattern: the stages in an animal's life that make up its life cycle. Humans share certain stages in their life cycle with other mammals.

MAIN TEACHING ACTIVITY

Tell the children that they are going to look at the life cycle of humans. Ask them to help you sort through the most important stages in our lives. Brainstorm their ideas on the board or flip chart: write the words 'The human life cycle' in the middle, and add their suggestions for stages in a circle around it. Start at a random point and deliberately put the stages in the wrong order. The main stages you should aim to include are fertilisation, birth, infancy, childhood, adolescence and adulthood. If the children suggest death, give acknowledgement to this, but explain that it isn't usually included in pictures of the life cycle. Explain that fertilisation is when the sperm and egg cell fuse (join) inside the mother, and this moment marks the start of life; and that adolescence is the time when the body develops to become sexually mature, which means that it changes physically to prepare it for reproduction (having children).

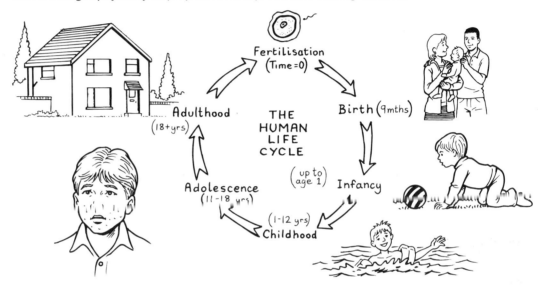

GROUP ACTIVITIES

1. The children should work in pairs, with a sheet of A3 paper, to draw the human life cycle by copying the stages you have listed and arranging them in the correct order. Next, they can try to write down an age (or age range) corresponding to each stage, then illustrate their life cycle diagram with a picture of each stage. The illustration above shows a typical answer.

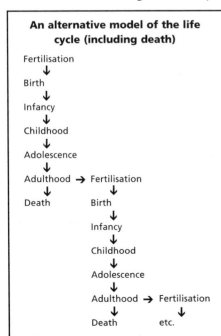

An alternative model of the life cycle (including death)

Fertilisation
↓
Birth
↓
Infancy
↓
Childhood
↓
Adolescence
↓
Adulthood → Fertilisation
↓   ↓
Death   Birth
          ↓
         Infancy
          ↓
        Childhood
          ↓
       Adolescence
          ↓
Adulthood → Fertilisation
     ↓   ↓
  Death   etc.

2. The pairs should now try to find out about the life cycle of another animal by referring to textbooks and the *Encarta* CD-ROM. They should record and illustrate this life cycle on another sheet of A3 paper. Encourage them to note similarities and differences between this life cycle and that of a human. For example, they could look at the life cycles of butterflies or frogs, which have a stage of metamorphosis. Many insects have a life cycle that goes egg → larva → pupa → adult → egg. Many animals (such as spiders and crabs) have distinct stages of growth when they shed their outer case, leaving behind the old case as a 'ghost'.

DIFFERENTIATION

Some children will need additional help with organising the stages of the human life cycle; you may want to provide a simple diagram on A3 paper for them to refer to. More able children could try to draw a 'step' version of the human life cycle that includes death, as shown opposite. Ask them: *How is this way of showing the life cycle more realistic than drawing a circle?*

ASSESSMENT

Check the children's understanding of the human life cycle from their diagrams. Are the stages in the correct order? Is the correct approximate age range given for each stage?

PLENARY

Ask the children to suggest how parts of the human life cycle have been changed by advances over the last thousand years or so. (We live longer because of better medical care; we tend to have children later in life; children are reaching puberty at a younger age, probably due to improvements in diet and lifestyle.)

OUTCOME

● Know the key stages in the human life cycle.

LINKS

Unit 3, Lesson 4: how species evolve to become adapted to their environment.

LESSON 5

OBJECTIVES
● To know about the structure of the reproductive organs.
● To know that changes in the body leading to sexual maturity begin at puberty.

RESOURCES

Main teaching activity: Enlarged copies of photocopiable pages 27 and 28 (or similar diagrams); a 3-D model of a human torso (if possible).
Group activities: 1. Copies (one of each per pair) of pages 27 and 28; A4 paper, scissors, adhesive, pencils. **2.** Plasticine. The *Human Body* CD-ROM (Dorling Kindersley) or similar will be useful for extension work.

Vocabulary

extinct, reproduce, penis, testes, sperm, egg, fertilised, ovary, vagina, oviduct, womb/uterus, puberty, periods, menstruate

BACKGROUND

The next couple of lessons develop the children's understanding of life cycles further by looking specifically at reproduction in humans and the changes that take place at puberty. This lesson is guaranteed to cause a few smirks and blushes – one or two of them from the children. The range of vocabulary with which the children will be familiar will vary greatly, so don't be surprised if you need to spend time double-checking that they really do know what is called what. It is worth sticking to terms that will be used consistently, though you will need to be aware that in some cases there is more than one correct name for an organ (for example, 'uterus' and 'womb'). Key words in the information that follows are shown in bold.

In order for a new human being to form, an **egg (ovum)** made in the **ovary** of the mother has to join with a **sperm cell** made in the **testes (testicles)** of the father. When this happens, we say that the egg has been **fertilised**. Humans reproduce using internal fertilisation. This means that the egg and the sperm cell have to join together inside the mother's body. The reproductive organs of humans are designed to bring the egg and sperm together, and to enable the mother's body to provide care for the growing baby.

The testes of the male are outside the body (so that they are cooler – this helps them to make sperm cells). The **penis** of the male becomes stiff and erect in order to enter the **vagina** of the female during **sexual intercourse**, when sperms made in the testes are released through the penis into the vagina.

The female has two **ovaries** that make eggs. The eggs are carried down tubes called **oviducts** (also known as **fallopian tubes**) to the **uterus (womb)**. If the egg becomes fertilised, it will be nourished and protected here as it completes its development into a baby. At birth, the baby passes out of the mother through the vagina (which is also known as the 'birth canal').

During **puberty**, male and female bodies start to become sexually mature (able to participate in reproduction). The testes of boys start producing sperms, and girls start to **menstruate** (or have **periods**). Periods occur about once every 28 days, when the lining of the uterus is shed together with the unfertilised egg. The lining is then renewed, ready for a new fertilised egg.

INTRODUCTION

Gather the class in a horseshoe shape so that they are all facing you. The first part of the lesson will be a discussion, and it is perhaps best if the children are not too aware of their peers. Remind them of the work they have previously done on life cycles (for further information and ideas, see Unit 2 in *100 Science Lessons: Year 5/Primary 6*). Explain that over the next few lessons, you are going to look specifically at the part of the life cycle that prevents living things from becoming extinct. *Which part of the life cycle is this?* (Fertilisation.)

MAIN TEACHING ACTIVITY

Explain to the children that the next few lessons will be about reproduction in humans, and that you will start by looking at the reproductive organs.

Ask the class whether they know why the female body has to be different from the male body. Hopefully this will lead on to the idea that the female body needs to be able to provide for a growing baby. Now say that the female can produce **egg cells**. If the egg (ovum) becomes fertilised, it can grow into a baby. *Do you know where the eggs are made? Where are sperm cells made? What does 'fertilised' mean? How does this happen? Where does the developing baby grow?* Refer to enlarged diagrams of the male and female reproductive organs, and talk through the function of each part. Guide the children towards an understanding that **sperm cells** are made by the male, and that one sperm cell needs to join with the egg cell inside the female to **fertilise** it. The baby develops in the **uterus (womb)** of the mother.

A fun way of getting the children familiar with the names of the different parts is to hold up unlabelled diagrams of the reproductive organs and ask them (as a class) to shout out the correct name for each part as you point to it. The security of a group response makes the children far less self-conscious – though it may surprise any staff or visitors passing in the corridor!

Explain to the children that the time when humans change to become sexually mature (able to parent children) is called **puberty**. Check whether they can remember the work on puberty they covered in Year 5/Primary 6.

GROUP ACTIVITIES

1. Give the children one copy per pair of pages 27 and 28 (you may find that they are more comfortable working in same-sex pairs) and A4 paper. Ask them to cut out the labels and diagrams, match the correct name of each part of the reproductive system with the job that it does, then stick the labels in place around each diagram (with label lines) on an A4 sheet.
2. Ask the children to look at the diagrams of the sperm and egg cells on page 28 and try to work out why they are so different. (The sperm cells have a tail to help them swim to the egg. The egg cells are large to store food that provides for the developing baby over the first few days.) Ask them to make a Plasticine model of each cell, using the scale suggested on the sheet.

DIFFERENTIATION

Help less able children to match up the names and functions of the organs, but leave them to place the labels accurately on the diagram. Ask more able children to work out the exact route that a sperm cell will need to take from the testes to reach and fertilise an egg cell. They could use a CD-ROM to help them. (The route is: testes, epididymis, vas deferens or sperm tube (through penis), vagina, cervix, uterus, oviduct, egg cell.)

ASSESSMENT

Try to talk to each pair. Can they confidently explain, in simple terms, the function of each part of the male and female reproductive systems?

PLENARY

To consolidate the vocabulary used and link it to the idea that sexual maturity begins at adolescence, ask the children to say whether the following changes happen in males or females at puberty: the testes make sperm (boys); periods start (girls); an egg is released from the ovaries once every 28 days (girls); the penis grows larger (boys); the body gets bigger (boys and girls); breasts start to grow (girls).

OUTCOMES

● Can describe the functions of the parts that make up the male and female reproductive organs.
● Know that the changes that bring about sexual maturity begin at puberty.

LINKS

PSHE: understanding periods; responsible relationships.

LESSON 6

OBJECTIVES

● To know how fertilisation occurs.
● To know how the growing foetus develops and how the baby is born.

RESOURCES

Main teaching activity: A ruler, a large diagram of the female reproductive system (from photocopiable page 27), a diagram of a baby in the womb showing the key features (foetus, umbilical cord, placenta, uterus, amniotic sac).
Group activities: 1. Photocopiable page 29, A4 paper, scissors, adhesive. **2.** Paper, coloured pencils, sugar paper.

PREPARATION

3-D models of the unborn child at each stage of its development, as well as useful posters, are available from Philip Harris Education, Novara House, Excelsior Road, Ashby Park, Ashby de la Zouch, Leics. LE65 1NG. If you can obtain these, or other similar examples, they will make an invaluable contribution to your lesson and emphasise the 'Wow!' factor of the topic.

BACKGROUND

This lesson touches on a fascinating subject, and the children will probably be bursting with wonderful (and weird) questions to ask you. The 'Did you know?' section below is added in anticipation of a few of these questions!

Hundreds of millions of sperm cells are released by the male during intercourse, and they begin their journey through the **uterus (womb)** and up the **fallopian tubes (oviducts)** of the female. Here, they might just meet an **egg** on its journey down from one of the **ovaries**, swept along by millions of tiny waving hairs called cilia. Only one sperm cell can succeed in penetrating the egg (in *very* rare cases, two can – but the baby does not develop healthily); when it does so, it triggers a lightning-fast reaction preventing any others from doing the same. This is **fertilisation**: the fusing together of a sperm cell and an egg cell. The combined genetic material from the two cells (the fertilised egg) is now called the **zygote** – the first stage in its development into a young human being. The zygote passes into the womb and may be successful in settling into the lining. This is called **implantation**, and is the true beginning of **pregnancy**; it triggers many dramatic changes in the body of the mother.

In its earliest stages of development, the growing individual is called an **embryo** – up to the point at which the organs are fully developed (which happens after only nine weeks) and it begins to show a recognisably human form. It is now called a **foetus**. While it is developing, the growing baby receives **oxygen** and **nutrients** from the mother's blood, which also carries away carbon dioxide and other **wastes** (including urea, which is usually filtered out by our kidneys and forms part of our urine – the mother's body has to do this for the baby). This exchange of materials happens in the **placenta**, which is rooted to the mother's womb. The materials are then carried along the **umbilical cord** to and from the body of the baby. While the baby is growing, it is protected within a fluid-filled bag called the **amniotic sac** (which acts in a similar way to airbags in cars, protecting the baby from bumps).

Pregnancies usually last 39 weeks, though **premature** babies born up to three months before this date are now routinely cared for in Special Care Baby Units and have a good chance of survival. When the 'waters break' (the amniotic sac tears, releasing fluid), powerful contractions of the abdomen increase in intensity until the baby is forced down the birth canal and out of the body. In some cases (particularly if the baby is stressed), the baby may be withdrawn by surgery through an incision made in the abdomen of the mother – this is called a Caesarean birth.

Did you know?

● The mother and baby have separate blood systems – the baby's blood vessels are very delicate and would soon rupture if the mother's blood, which is at a much higher pressure, entered them.
● The mother doesn't just 'eat for two', she breathes for two and removes waste for two. The growing baby even strips calcium from her bones to make up the supply it needs for its own growing bones!
● Giving birth is probably more painful and hazardous for humans than for any other animal, due to the large skulls of human babies (if you are a mother reading this, I'm sure it didn't need pointing out to you).

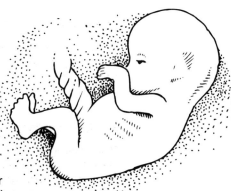

Vocabulary

uterus (womb), fallopian tubes (oviducts), fertilisation, zygote, pregnancy, embryo, foetus, umbilical cord, placenta, amniotic sac, premature

● The umbilical cord has no pain receptors; it doesn't hurt the baby or mother when it is cut.
● Identical twins form from one egg, fertilised by one sperm cell. The egg has then, for some reason, divided to make two zygotes – each with identical genetic information.
● Non-identical twins are formed from two separate eggs that have been fertilised by different sperm cells and have then implanted in the womb.

INTRODUCTION

Gather the children together. Revise some of the ideas from the previous lesson – in particular, the changes that occur at puberty and how this prepares the male and female bodies for reproduction.

MAIN TEACHING ACTIVITY

Describe in simple terms how sperm cells are released inside the body of the female during intercourse, and go on to describe the journey the sperm cells have to make. The distance they have to cover is comparable to a swimmer setting off from Blackpool across the Irish Sea to Dublin! Ask: *How are sperm cells designed for swimming?* (They have a moving tail.)

Explain the meaning of the word 'fertilisation', and go on to put the key events of the baby's life in order. Use a ruler to demonstrate the size at each stage.

Time = 0
One sperm out of the millions released joins with the egg. This is **fertilisation**.
Time = 1 week
The fertilised egg (called a **zygote**) settles into the cosy lining of the uterus. It is smaller than a grain of rice.
Time = 4 weeks
The zygote has grown to become an **embryo**. It is 6mm long and has some of its most important organs.
Time = 9 weeks
The growing baby is about 25mm long and has all of its organs. It is now called a **foetus**.
Time = 12 weeks
The foetus is now 56mm long and appears far more like a human baby.
Time = 20 weeks
The foetus is now 160mm long and is busy exercising its limbs. Its movements can be felt by the mother. (Sorry Mum – were you sleeping?).
Time = 28 weeks
The growing baby would have a good chance of surviving if it were born now. It is about 370mm long.
Time = 39 weeks
The baby is ready to be born! It is now about 520mm in length. Powerful **contractions** of the abdomen squeeze the baby out of the uterus and through the birth canal or vagina. Happy birthday, baby!

GROUP ACTIVITIES

1. Working in pairs, the children should cut out the pictures and boxes of text from page 29, match them and arrange them in sequence before sticking them on a sheet of A4 paper.
2. Using the illustrations and measurements given on page 29, the children should work in their table groups to draw life-sized pictures of the developing baby at each stage. These can be coloured, cut out and stuck onto a large sheet of sugar paper, with an appropriate caption for each stage.

DIFFERENTIATION

Some children will need additional guidance to sequence the stages on the worksheet. Children who complete the tasks ahead of the others could be encouraged to find out the difference between the ways in which identical and non-identical twins form (you will need to provide reference materials for this).

ASSESSMENT

Read through page 29 as a class. Check that the children have grasped the main developmental stages of the baby. Write these stages on the board and see whether the children can place them in order confidently: A. birth; B. attachment to lining of womb; C. fertilisation; D. zygote; E. embryo; F. foetus. (Correct order: C, D, B, E, F, A.)

PLENARY

Link this lesson to previous work on healthy lifestyles by asking: *Why is it a bad idea for pregnant mothers to smoke?* (The amount of oxygen received by the baby from the mother's blood is reduced, and the levels of nicotine and other toxic chemicals received by the baby increase. The health of the child, as well as that of the mother, suffers.)

OUTCOMES

- Can describe the growth of the foetus.
- Understand the birth process.

LINKS

PSHE and citizenship: safety and responsibility.

LESSON 7

Objectives	● To know about the changes in lifestyle that are necessary during pregnancy and the skills and care required in parenting. ● To develop skills in listening, note-taking and asking questions. ● To recognise stages in their own development.
Resources	A3 or sugar paper, adhesive, coloured pens or pencils, a new mother who is willing to talk to the children about the experience of being pregnant and caring for a baby. The children need to bring in **labelled** pictures of themselves at various times from ante-natal scan to two years old. Scans could be photocopied for inclusion in displays. Five photographs of each child at different stages will be enough.

Main activity	The issue of parenting may be a sensitive one in cases where family splits have occurred, so use your judgement as to the best way to tackle each situation. Ask the children, a week in advance, to request parental permission to bring in pictures of themselves at different stages from scans to their second birthday. Remember that childhood photos will be priceless to the parents of the children – so make sure that they are clearly labelled with the child's name and protected from damage. Invite a parent who has recently had a baby to visit the school, show their child and talk to the children about the pregnancy: the preparation needed leading up to the birth, the birth itself, and the subsequent care of the child.
	  Start the lesson by asking how the children's families would cope if they had to look after a new-born baby. *What would the baby need? How would their lifestyle have to change?* Introduce the mother and baby. Emphasise that you are fortunate in having this visitor, as she is going through the experience of being a mother to a new child. Explain to the children that you want them to make rough notes while your visitor speaks (make sure you share the questions in advance with the mother, so that she feels prepared). Ask questions about:
	● What the pregnancy itself was like. What special food did the mother have to include in her diet? Did she have to change her lifestyle, eg her exercise routine? What checks were carried out by the health visitor or hospital before the birth?
	● What the birth was like. How long did the mother and baby stay in hospital? What special help did the nurses give to help the mother care for the baby?
	● How the lifestyle of the mother changed in caring for the baby. How often does the baby cry, sleep, feed, need its nappy changing, need bathing? Has the house had to be rearranged to suit the needs of the baby? What check-ups is the baby having? When will/did the baby start eating solid food?
	  Give each child a sheet of A3 paper headed 'Looking after a baby'. Ask them to arrange some photographs of themselves in order of increasing age. Now ask them to write something next to each picture about the care they needed at that stage, and how this might have affected their parents' lives.

Differentiation	Less able children may benefit from having key questions/headings written out for them before the visitor starts to speak so that they have only to fill in the blanks.
Assessment	From the children's display work, check whether they have grasped the main points of the visitor's talk and have arranged the pictures with relevant, informative captions.
Plenary	Ask one or two of the children to read out their accounts. Ask: *Is being a parent easy? Has it made you think a little differently about your own parents?* If they have younger brothers or sisters, perhaps they can understand why their parents sometimes need a little help around the home. Mention that sometimes girls become pregnant while only in their young teens. *Do you think this is a good thing to happen? How might it be difficult for the girl to cope?* Take care not to sound judgemental – you could be talking about a sister or a parent of one of the children!
Outcomes	● Understand that a pregnant mother needs to take special care of her health. ● Understand that being a parent is a demanding task that requires many skills.

LESSON 8

OBJECTIVES

● To assess the children's knowledge of aspects of a lifestyle that may be regarded as healthy or as unhealthy.
● To assess the children's knowledge of the structures that support a baby during its development in the womb and the care a mother needs to take during pregnancy.

RESOURCES

Photocopiable pages 30 and 31, writing materials.

INTRODUCTION

You may want to give the children advance warning of the assessment, so it is not a shock to them. Gather the class together and, in general terms, remind them of the work they have covered on healthy lifestyles, the human life cycle, the human reproductive organs and the development of a baby. Explain that they are going to have a short assessment test on these ideas, and that they must work silently and on their own. Advise them not to panic if they are struggling with a question, but to leave it and come back to it if they have time at the end.

Arrange the children so that none are too tempted to look at another's work. Distribute the sheets, asking the children to write their names clearly at the top of each.

ASSESSMENT ACTIVITY 1

Ask the children to read the text on page 30, examine the graph and answer the questions.

Answers

1a. Traffic fumes, polluted drinking water, mosquitoes (risk of malaria). 1b. Active lifestyle (looking after brothers and sisters), healthy diet (milk, fresh fruit). 1c. Lack of money to pay for medicines; 2a. 590*; 2b. 360* (*per 100 000 males). 2c. Avoid smoking, avoid fatty food, exercise frequently, eat plenty of fresh fruit and vegetables. 2d. Heart disease is linked to lack of exercise, being overweight and consumption of fatty foods; in developing countries manual labour is more common, being overweight is less common and the diet tends to contain less fatty food.

Looking for levels

All the children should be able to recognise harmful and healthy aspects of Fatima's lifestyle. Most of the children should be able to suggest key guidance for avoiding heart disease: regular exercise, a healthy diet and not smoking. More able children should be able to suggest why heart disease is a greater killer in the UK than in India.

ASSESSMENT ACTIVITY 2

Using page 31, ask the children to match words to labels on the diagram, then to try and answer the questions.

Answers

1. A = uterus, B = placenta, C = umbilical cord, D = amniotic sac, E = foetus. 2. Sperm released by the male, fertilisation of egg cell, zygote, embryo, foetus, birth. 3a. Smoking, drinking alcohol; 3b. These activities result in poisons building up in the mother's blood which will be transmitted to the baby and can harm its development. 4. The placenta in the mother's womb transmits blood, containing oxygen and nutrients, to the baby through the umbilical cord.

Looking for levels

All the children should be able to label most of the parts accurately. Most of the children should be able to name activities that the mother should avoid during pregnancy and give a reason for their choices. More able children should be able to explain how the baby receives the nutrients it needs for its development, referring to the role of the placenta in exchanging materials with the mother's blood and of the umbilical cord in carrying these materials to the foetus.

PLENARY

Use the children's answers to Assessment activity 1 as the basis for a discussion linking together aspects of health covered in the topic. Ask them to consider whether Fatima is able to control all aspects of the healthiness of her lifestyle. *Why not?* (Some aspects are affected by her environment, such as the abundance of mosquitoes, poor quality of drinking water and air pollution.) Ask whether they think poverty can influence someone's health. *How?* (Poverty can lead to malnutrition, which has a significant impact on the health and development of children.) Go over the answers to Assessment activity 2; explain anything the children have misunderstood.

FACTFILE 1: Things to avoid!

DRUGS

Medicines are drugs that are given by doctors to treat illnesses. They have been **tested** and are given in **safe doses** (to prevent harm to your body). Medicines have their chemical ingredients written on the packets. Other types of drugs, sometimes called **recreational drugs**, are not recommended by a doctor or chemist. They have often **not been tested**, so there is **no safe dose** (except avoiding them altogether). Sadly, many deaths are caused by these types of drugs each year. Even drugs that have been tested should never be taken unless a doctor has prescribed them for you.

Many drugs are **addictive**, and when addicts stop taking them they suffer from **withdrawal symptoms** such as fevers and cramps. Many people who rely on these drugs lose their jobs and so have to find other ways to pay for their expensive drug habit (such as stealing). Drugs can cause **damage** to the **liver**, the **brain** and other organs. Diseases can spread through the sharing of infected needles.

Does taking drugs seem like a good idea to you?

SOLVENTS

When people talk about 'solvents', they often mean the liquid that keeps glue runny. Glue dries because the liquid part **evaporates** (turns to a gas). The gas is what people call the 'fumes' or 'vapour'. The fumes from some glues cause a kind of dizziness when breathed in. This is hardly surprising, because they are **toxic** (poisonous) and also allow less oxygen to reach the lungs. Some people, including many of the homeless street children of Guatemala, become **addicted** to sniffing these fumes. Sadly, the fumes cause **brain damage** and **liver failure**, and many children die young because of this habit.

In Britain, it is illegal for shops to sell glues containing harmful solvents to children under the age of sixteen. Do you think this is a good idea?

ALCOHOL

Alcohol is found in many drinks that are sold in pubs, such as lager, wine and beer. It is a type of **drug** that is legal for people over the age of 18. Alcohol causes problems because, like many other drugs, it is **addictive**. People who are addicted to alcohol are called **alcoholics**. Taking large quantities of alcohol causes damage to many organs, including the liver and the brain. One of the most worrying things about alcohol is the way it changes behaviour. Some hospitals have found that **over half** of the **accidents** they deal with are linked to alcohol, and the police say that over 80% of **violent incidents** in the home and on the streets are connected with alcohol. Accidents are more common after drinking alcohol because of the way it affects co-ordination: drinkers are slower to react and more clumsy.

Driving after drinking alcohol is particularly dangerous – why do you think this is?

If you compared a man and a woman of the same size, you would find that the man's body contained 25% more water. Doctors recommend that men drink less than 28 **units** (1 unit $=\frac{1}{2}$ pint of beer or 1 glass of wine) per week. What should the limit for women be?

SUNBURN

High up around the Earth is a layer of gas called the **ozone layer**. This gas does an important job: it stops some of the invisible (ultraviolet) rays from the Sun reaching the Earth. **Ultraviolet (UV)** rays can harm the skin – if you have ever had **sunburn**, you will know this! UV rays pass through the top layer of our skin and damage the cells underneath. As well as causing sunburn, overexposure to the Sun (being out too long without protecting your skin) can cause the skin to **age** more quickly because it loses its elasticity or stretchiness.

Most worrying, though, has been the huge recent increase in the number of cases of **skin cancer** reported each year. The bad news is that the ozone layer is getting thinner each year, and already has large holes in it, so more harmful rays are getting through. The good news is that we now know more about avoiding cancer. Here are some top tips for sun-seekers:

- Avoid the Sun during the hottest part of the day (11am–3pm), but if you can't...
- Cover all exposed skin with a high factor (20+) suncream.
- Wear a hat to protect your nose and neck.
- Wear a long-sleeved shirt.
- Get a doctor to check any moles or unusual spots if they start to itch or bleed – the doctor won't mind, and it is far better to be safe than sorry.

Everyone loves having a tan, but be sensible. Don't forget that the tan will wear off after a few weeks, but the effects of too much sunlight will stay with you for far longer.

FACTFILE 2: More things to avoid!

LOUD MUSIC

We lose the sensitivity of our hearing as we grow older (but this doesn't mean your teacher can't hear you whispering). Listening to very loud music damages the way our ears work. Listening to loud music in headphones for a long period of time reduces the sensitivity of the ears and can lead to early **deafness**. Workers who use noisy machinery, such as pneumatic drills, wear ear defenders to protect their hearing. Some people suffer from a distressing problem later in life when they can 'hear' a sound that isn't really there. This problem is called **tinnitus**. Take care of your hearing – avoid loud music near the speakers at discos or on headphones.

    Loudness is measured in **decibels (dB)**. The sound level at which you can only just hear a sound is 0dB. Passing lorries produce a sound of about 90dB, and a jumbo jet makes about 120dB (if you are standing close to it). The sound level in discos is usually around 110dB.

    Hearing range (the range of different notes you can hear) is measured in **hertz (Hz)**. The higher the frequency of a sound is (in hertz), the more high-pitched the note will sound. Humans can hear between 20Hz and 20 000Hz. Cats can hear between 20Hz and 70 000Hz. Porpoises can hear between 50Hz and more than 130 000Hz.

SMOKING

Sadly, smoking claims many thousands of lives each year. It greatly increases the likelihood of dying through a blood clot in the brain (a stroke), heart disease or lung cancer. Smoking not only leads to an early death, it also reduces the quality of life for smokers. Here's why:

● Our lungs produce **mucus** all the time to trap dust and germs. Cigarette smoke **irritates** our lungs and makes them produce extra mucus, which clogs up the airways (cough cough).

● Delicate hairs called **cilia** line our airways and sweep the mucus towards the mouth. Cigarette smoke paralyses the cilia, and **coughing** destroys them. The mucus settles in the airways, making breathing wheezy and giving germs time to breed (ouch, my chest).

● Germs **inflame** the lining of the airways, making them even **narrower** (hold on while I catch my breath). Smoking if you already have **asthma** would be seriously dangerous.

● The tiny **air sacs** at the end of each delicate branch of our lungs are torn apart by constant coughing, leading to **emphysema** (which is very bad news).

● The thousands of chemicals contained in cigarettes produce a sticky **tar** that settles inside the lungs, irritating the lining and harming the cells around it. This increases the risk of **cancer**.

● **Nicotine** is the **addictive** drug in cigarettes that makes smokers want to keep smoking. Giving up smoking is difficult because of this drug.

● Mothers who smoke when they are **pregnant** can cause problems for their unborn children: chemicals in the mother's blood pass on to the child. (And you thought smoking was illegal until you were sixteen!)

● Smoking is expensive, and makes your clothes and breath smell. Enough facts to be going on with? Think about it. Top athletes and footballers don't smoke – what does that tell you? And remember: you are bound to have friends who try smoking when they are older to 'look cool' – it takes character to say no. What will you do? Why not share some facts with them?

Name

How to stay healthy

Topic	What I learned
Avoid drugs!	
Avoid solvents!	
Avoid sunburn!	
Avoid alcohol!	
Avoid loud music!	
Don't smoke!	

The female reproductive system

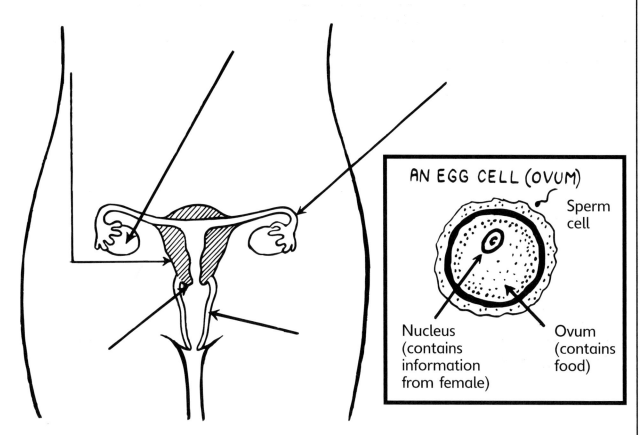

AN EGG CELL (OVUM)

Sperm cell

Nucleus (contains information from female)

Ovum (contains food)

1. Cut out the labels below and try to match up the name of each part with its function. Cut out the diagram. Put the labels around the diagram on a sheet of paper. Check with your teacher that they are in the right places, then stick them down.

2. Use coloured arrows to show the route the egg (ovum) takes on its journey from the ovary to the uterus.

3. Under the labelled diagram, write down why you think the ovum (egg cell) is so much larger than the sperm cells that try to fertilise it.

labels					
	uterus	ovary	oviduct (fallopian tube)	vagina	cervix

functions		
Releases an egg (ovum) into the oviduct once every 28 days.	A special sac that provides nutrients and protection for the fertilised egg as it develops. If the female is not pregnant, the lining is shed once every 28 days during her period.	
The penis releases sperm here during intercourse. The baby is born through this tube.		
The narrow entrance to the uterus through which the sperm have to travel.	The tube down which the egg is moved after it is released from the ovary. Sperm may reach and fertilise the egg here on its journey to the uterus.	

The male reproductive system

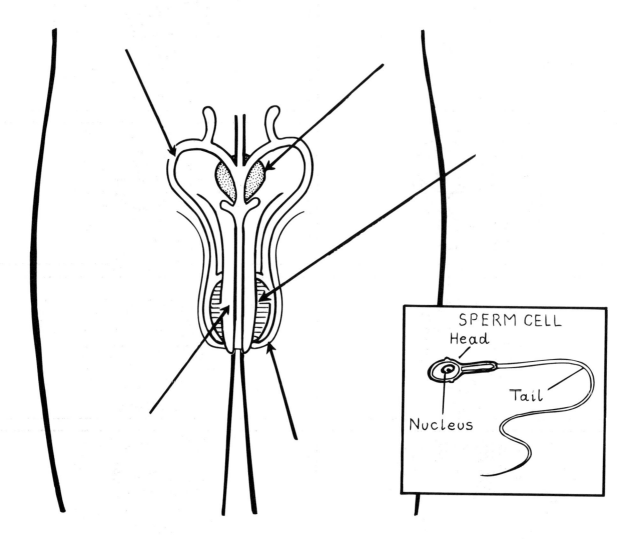

1. Cut out the labels below and try to match up the name of each part with its function. Cut out the diagram.

2. Put the labels around the diagram on a sheet of paper. Check with your teacher that they are in the right places, then stick them down.

3. Under the labelled diagram, write down why you think each sperm cell has a tail.

labels

testes	penis	prostate gland	sperm tube	scrotum

functions

Becomes erect as blood rushes into it. During intercourse it enters the vagina of the female and releases sperm.	This and other glands add special chemicals to the sperm cells to make them active before they are released.
Special organs that produce millions of sperm cells.	The sac that contains the testes.
	The tube down which sperm cells travel from the testes.

Name

Life before birth

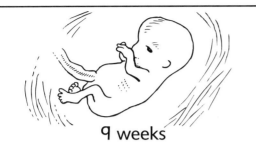
9 weeks

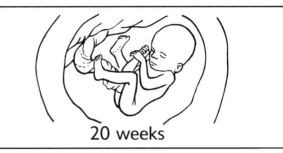
20 weeks

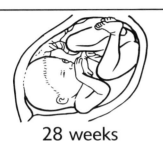
28 weeks

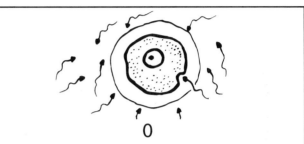
0

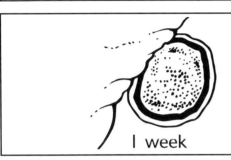
I week

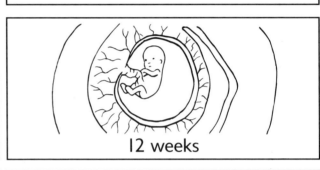
12 weeks

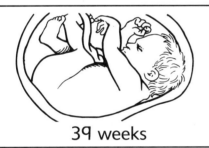
39 weeks

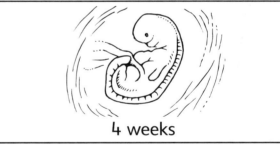
4 weeks

Time = **9 weeks**
The growing baby is about 25mm long and has all of its organs. It is now called a **foetus**.

Time = **12 weeks**
The foetus is now 56mm long and appears far more like a human baby.

Time = **1 week**
The fertilised egg (called a **zygote**) implants itself in the lining of the uterus. It is smaller than a grain of rice.

Time = **39 weeks**
The baby is ready to be born! It is now about 520mm in length. Happy birthday, baby!

Time = **20 weeks**
The foetus is now 160mm long and is busy exercising its limbs. Its movements can be felt by the mother. (Sorry Mum – were you sleeping?)

Time = **4 weeks**
The zygote has grown to become an **embryo**. It is 6mm long and has some of its most important organs.

Time = **28 weeks**
The growing baby would have a good chance of surviving if it were born now. It is about 370mm long.

Time = **0**
One sperm out of the millions released joins with the egg. This is **fertilisation**.

New beginnings

1. Read this information about Fatima and then answer the questions below on another sheet of paper.

Fatima is 10 years old and lives in New Delhi in India. Her parents have six children and live in a poor part of the city. She shares a room with three brothers and a sister – the youngest sleeps in the room next door with her parents. Fatima is the oldest child and does not go to school: she is needed to care for the children while her mother works at a textiles factory and her father drives a motor rickshaw.

The streets are busy during the day, often choked with traffic. The fumes from the traffic leave the buildings dirty and cause problems for one of Fatima's brothers, who suffers from respiratory (breathing) problems and coughs through the night. In the dry season, water is pumped from the river to supply her area of the city. After the monsoons, the sewers flood the streets and often pollute the drinking water. Mosquitoes are common, and her youngest sister has malaria. Paying for medicines to treat the disease is a struggle for her parents. Fatima's family live near the market, so one of her jobs is to collect rice, milk, and fresh fruit.

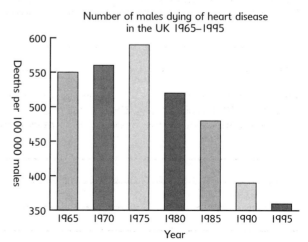

Though her life is hard, Fatima loves her family and has an ambition: she wants to go to secondary school full-time when her brothers and sisters are older, and eventually to university.

a. Name three things that are unhealthy in Fatima's lifestyle.
b. Name two things that are healthy aspects of her lifestyle.
c. In what way does poverty (lack of money) cause a health problem for Fatima's family?

2. This graph shows the number of people who have died from heart disease in the UK each year. Use the graph to answer the questions below on another sheet of paper.

a. How many people died of heart disease in the UK in 1975?
b. How many people died of heart disease in the UK in 1995?
c. Name three things that people can do (or avoid doing) to reduce the risk of developing heart disease.
d. Why do you think heart disease is more common in the UK than it is in India?

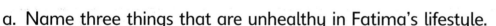

Number of males dying of heart disease
in the UK 1965–1995

Deaths per 100 000 males

1965	1970	1975	1980	1985	1990	1995

Year

New beginnings

1. Look at the picture and choose the right word from the list below to go with each letter.

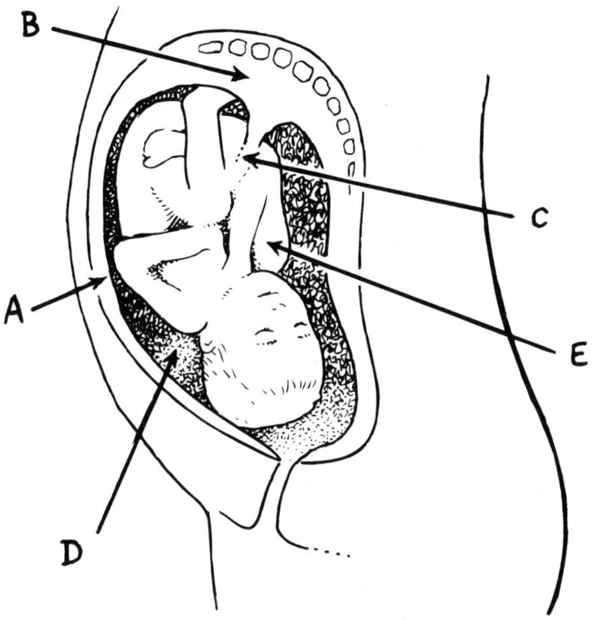

B

A = _____

B = _____

C = _____

D = _____

E = _____

A

C

E

D

**umbilical cord   ovary   uterus
placenta   zygote
amniotic sac   foetus**

2. Put these events in the development of a baby into the right order.

**fertilisation of egg cell   sperm released by male   zygote
foetus   embryo   birth**

Correct order: _____

_____

3a. Which of these activities are pregnant mothers asked to avoid? You can choose more than one.

walking   smoking   cycling   drinking milk   drinking alcohol   swimming

Answer: _____

_____

3b. Give a reason for your choices in question (a).

_____

_____

4. Explain the purpose of the placenta and the umbilical cord.

_____

_____

_____

_____

Variation

ORGANISATION (9 LESSONS)

	OBJECTIVES	MAIN ACTIVITY	GROUP ACTIVITIES	PLENARY	OUTCOMES
LESSON 1	● To sort objects into groups based on observable features.	Introduction to classification: the sorting of objects according to their features.	Complete two sorting tasks involving observation and logic.	Discuss problems encountered. Consider the need for classification of living things.	● Have experience of placing objects into groups based on observable characteristics. ● Understand that trying to sort things into groups can cause problems.
LESSON 2	● To know that living things can be arranged into groups according to observable features. ● To know that these groups can help in identifying unknown living things.	Explain that living things are divided into kingdoms. Break down the animal kingdom into invertebrates and the five classes of vertebrates.	Sort an assortment of pictures of living things into their correct vertebrate groups.	Discuss the classification of the duck-billed platypus.	● Can identify an animal appropriately as a vertebrate or an invertebrate. ● Can classify a vertebrate accurately as a bird, amphibian, reptile, mammal or fish using external characteristics.
LESSON 3	● To use branching and numbered keys to identify an organism.	Introduce the idea of keys and work through an example of a branching key and a numbered key.	Collect various leaves and make a key for them. Make a key for pictures of leaves and twigs.	Discuss the children's keys.	● Can use a key to identify an organism.
LESSON 4	● To know that plants and animals of the same species vary.	Discuss variations between individuals in the class. Introduce the ideas of continuous and discontinuous variation.	Complete a table of variations within their group. Draw a bar graph of grouped height data.	Discuss the results recorded, and whether the variations are continuous or discontinuous.	● Recognise how living things of the same species vary.
LESSON 5	● To use their knowledge of keys to identify plant species in the field.	Carry out fieldwork on identifying trees by their leaves and twigs.		Discuss the need to conserve trees and wild flowers.	● Can use keys to identify plant species in the field.
LESSON 6	● To investigate variation in plant growth. ● To design a fair experiment, make a prediction and test it.	Set up a group investigation into the relationship between the measured size of seeds and the rate of seedling growth.	Record measurements and make a prediction about the growth of the seeds.	Draw together the observations of the class and look for common trends. Share conclusions and evaluate the investigation.	● Know that growth in a plant species is subject to variation. ● Can design an experiment, test predictions, make observations, interpret results, draw conclusions and evaluate the investigation.

ORGANISATION (9 LESSONS)

	OBJECTIVES	MAIN ACTIVITY	GROUP ACTIVITIES	PLENARY	OUTCOMES
LESSON 7	● To know that plants need light, water and warmth to grow well. ● To design a fair experiment and make predictions that they can test.	Use cress seeds to plan and carry out an investigation into factors that affect plant growth.		Share results and look for common trends. Discuss the importance to scientists of sharing results.	● Know the importance of water, light and warmth for healthy plant growth.
LESSON 8	● To know that plants need nutrients from the soil for healthy growth. ● To know that farmers and gardeners often add nutrients to the soil in the form of fertiliser.	Discuss the need for fertilisers in gardening. List the main nutrients needed by plants, and the symptoms of deficiency.	Assess the nutrient deficiencies of some unhealthy plants. Design an advertisement for a fertiliser.	Discuss hydroponic cultivation and crop rotation.	● Know that plants need nutrients for healthy growth, and that fertilisers can provide these. ● Can recognise unhealthy plants.

	OBJECTIVES	ACTIVITY 1	ACTIVITY 2
ASSESSMENT 9	● To assess the children's understanding of branching keys. ● To assess the children's ability to consider the reliability of evidence.	Use a branching key and create a numbered key to identify fictitious creatures.	Criticise an investigation into variation in height and design an investigation to obtain more meaningful results.

LESSON 1

OBJECTIVE
● To sort objects into groups based on observable features.

RESOURCES

Main teaching activity: Assorted objects including a plant, a rock, iron nails, shells, woodlice (in a pot).
Group activities: 1. Paper, writing materials. **2.** One tray for each table containing these objects mixed up: a knife, a spoon, a fork, a paper clip, staples, paper fasteners, a glue stick, a roll of sticky tape, two sea shells, two pebbles, some gravel, a pencil sharpener, two coloured crayons, a biro, two potted plants, some dead leaves and petals, some coins (10p, 5p, 2p, 1p), a screwdriver, a pair of pliers, some nails, some screws, five playing cards, two dice, a chess piece, a battery, a bulb. (These are just some ideas – others may grab your attention.)

Vocabulary

classification, groups, classes, features

BACKGROUND

Many criteria can be used for organising objects into groups. This lesson requires the children to decide on a sensible way of arranging a wide variety of materials into groups or classes. They may wish to use formal criteria such as 'living' and 'non-living', or 'solid', 'liquid' and 'gas', or less formal criteria such as colour, size or shape. Whichever criteria they choose, the activity will start them thinking about alternative ways of classifying objects; this will lead nicely into the next few lessons, which go on to look at the classification of organisms in the living world.

INTRODUCTION

Gather the children together. Ask them to imagine that they are moving house. *The lorry turns up ready to take everything to the new house. Imagine if all the cupboards, drawers and wardrobes were just emptied out and everything tipped into the back of the lorry, along with the contents of the fridge and freezer, the oven, the toolbox, the goldfish bowl... what a mess! We wouldn't really do this – but why not?* (Because of the confusion it would cause.) *To prevent this, we sort things before we pack.*

MAIN TEACHING ACTIVITY

Explain that this lesson is about sorting things into groups: making decisions about what should go with what, and being able to explain this organisation. Explain that organising objects based on their features is common in science, and is known as **classification**. Explain to the group that when they go back to their places, they will have two tasks to do. The first will be to imagine they are moving house and sort out which objects will go in which box when they move. The second will be to place objects on a tray into groups based on their characteristics (what they look like or the type of object they are).

GROUP ACTIVITIES

1. Each table group should spread five sheets of A4 paper on their table. Explain that each sheet of paper represents a box. They have 15 minutes to decide and write on each 'box' what it will contain when they move house. At the top of the sheet, they should write 'Box containing...' and add a short description of the contents (such as 'electrical things'). Ask the children to keep their ideas secret from the other groups. Stop the class after 15 minutes and ask each group in turn to explain the decisions they made. There will be a wide range of suggestions – all valid, though some may be more practical than others. It will be interesting to see how the children explain their ideas.

2. In the same groups, the children should look through the contents of the tray on their table and decide how to sort them into groups. Try not to guide the children: just prompt them to explain to you how they are making their decisions. They can place the objects on separate sheets of A4 paper and write the name of the group at the top of each (for example, 'Objects that are used as tools'). Give them another 15 minutes to do this, then ask each group in turn to share their ideas with the class.

DIFFERENTIATION

1. Help children who are struggling by asking whether they could group things according to how they are used: things we wear, things we eat and so on. **2.** Some children will need additional guidance to organise the groups they place objects into. You may want to prompt them with questions such as: *Is this object useful as a tool? Are any of the others?* Hopefully, less able children will be prompted by others in the group to help them organise their ideas.

ASSESSMENT

The feedback from each group will serve as a useful reference in gauging the children's ability to take logical steps in their organisation of the objects. It will also help you to decide which children you will choose to help you when you next move house.

PLENARY

Draw the children's attention to the different approaches they have used in sorting the objects; ask them to share the problems they encountered. Explain that deciding how to sort things into groups has been a common problem for scientists over the ages – particularly for biologists who have had to sort living organisms into groups. Ask the children to find out the special name for a biologist who studies the groups into which organisms are placed. (A taxonomist.)

OUTCOMES

● Have experience of placing objects into groups based on observable characteristics.
● Understand that trying to sort things into groups can cause problems.

LINKS

Unit 2, Lesson 2: sorting and classifying.

LESSON 2

OBJECTIVES

● To know that living things can be arranged into groups according to observable features.
● To know that these groups can help in identifying unknown living things.

RESOURCES

Main teaching activity: A non-fiction book from a local library.
Group activity: Photocopiable page 45 (one A3-sized copy per group or pair), scissors, adhesive, A3 paper.

Vocabulary

classification,
kingdom,
vertebrate,
invertebrate,
species, mammal,
reptile, amphibian,
bird, fish

BACKGROUND

The living world is divided into five main groups, or 'kingdoms', the most familiar of which are the animal and plant kingdoms. This lesson gives the children some experience of looking at the features of different organisms and placing them in their correct kingdom. The plant kingdom can be divided into flowering and non-flowering plants (non-flowering plants include mosses and ferns; flowering plants include most of the rest). The animal kingdom is divided into vertebrates and invertebrates. A vertebrate is an animal with a backbone. There are five vertebrate groups (classes): mammals, reptiles, amphibians, birds and fish. There are five major invertebrate groups (phyla): molluscs, jellyfish, arthropods, worms and starfish (the children don't need to know these).

INTRODUCTION

Gather the class together. Show them the spine label on a non-fiction book from a local library. Explain that libraries use something called 'classification' to decide what goes where. Ask what 'classification' means. *You are in a 'class' – what does that mean?* Explain that biologists need to be able to sort living things into groups that everyone recognises and agrees on, and that this is known as 'classification'.

MAIN TEACHING ACTIVITY

Ask the class for ideas about how living things should be sorted. It may be useful to write the names of some organisms on the board – for example: 'oak tree', 'daffodil', 'ant', 'elephant', 'slug', 'crocodile', 'dolphin', 'kestrel', 'frog', 'shark'. *What groups can these living things be put into?* Hopefully, the classification as either 'plant' or 'animal' will be suggested.

Explain that living things are divided into five kingdoms; you are going to look at two of them, the plants and the animals. The plant kingdom includes living things that make their own food (mushrooms can't, so they are not plants – they belong to the fungus kingdom), and is divided into 'flowering plants' (such as roses and apple trees) and 'non-flowering plants' (such as mosses and ferns). Ask them to suggest the names of the two main parts of the animal kingdom. *Aristotle, an Ancient Greek philosopher, suggested that animals should be grouped according to whether they live on land or in water. Was this a good idea?* Some may already know the terms 'vertebrate' and 'invertebrate'. Introduce these and explain what they mean.

Tell the children that vertebrates belong to five main groups. Draw a table on the board:

The animal kingdom		
Vertebrates		
Name of group	Special features	Examples

Brainstorm the class to see whether they can name the groups and fill in appropriate details. (Birds have feathers; mammals provide milk for their young, and usually have hair or fur; amphibians have moist skin and lay eggs in water; reptiles have scales and lay eggs on land; fish have gills and scales.)

GROUP ACTIVITY

Give each group or pair a copy of page 45, preferably enlarged to A3 size. Ask them to cut out the animals and arrange them into the five vertebrate groups on an A3 sheet of paper, giving each group its correct name. Underneath each group, they must write down what the animals in that group have in common. Can they spot the odd ones out that don't belong to any vertebrate group? The answers are:
● Mammals – humpback whale, giraffe, human, duck-billed platypus.
● Reptiles – python, iguana, crocodile, turtle.
● Fish – hammerhead shark, plaice, stickleback, salmon.
● Birds – golden eagle, sparrow, swallow, heron.
● Amphibians – common frog, salamander, great crested newt, natterjack toad.
● Odd ones out – Portuguese man o' war (jellyfish – invertebrate), tarantula (arthropod – invertebrate), oak tree (flowering plant), bumble bee (arthropod – invertebrate), fern (non-flowering plant).

DIFFERENTIATION

Some groups may need further help with deciding how to classify organisms. You could guide them with questions such as: *Do you think the organism is a plant or an animal?* (Animal.) *Do you think it has a backbone?* (Yes.) *OK, so it must be a vertebrate. Which one?* You could leave the names of the five main groups on the board, with one key clue for each group as a guide (for example, 'Birds: feathers').

ASSESSMENT

Check the accuracy with which each group has sorted the vertebrates. Did they spot the odd ones out? Can they explain why these are not vertebrate animals?

PLENARY

Look at a picture of a duck-billed platypus. Point out that it has a bill (a rounded beak), webbed feet and fur. It lays eggs on land, but it provides milk for its young. Explain that when biologists first saw a platypus (in the form of a dead specimen), they thought it was a hoax: parts of different animals stitched together. *How would you have decided which group to place it in?* (It is a mammal.) Ask the children to explain their reasons.

OUTCOMES

- Can identify an animal appropriately as a vertebrate or an invertebrate.
- Can classify a vertebrate accurately as a bird, amphibian, reptile, mammal or fish using external characteristics.

LINKS

Unit 2, Lessons 5 and 6.

LESSON 3

OBJECTIVE

- To use branching and numbered keys to identify an organism.

RESOURCES

Main teaching activity: A copy of photocopiable page 46 enlarged to A3 size or (preferably) copied onto an OHT.
Group activities: 1. Access to plants in the local environment; plain paper, pencils, reference books on plants. **2.** Plain A4 paper, rulers, pencils, coloured pencils.

PREPARATION

Collect a range of leaves from common British trees.

Vocabulary

branching key,
numbered key,
identification

BACKGROUND

Two different types of key are commonly used by biologists to work out the identity of an organism: branching keys and number keys. The children should be aware of both methods. Branching keys are useful for identifying organisms from a limited selection. Numbered keys (also known as dichotomous keys, word keys or 'Go to' keys) are useful when a larger number of organisms are being studied; most field reference keys are of this type. A simple example of each type is shown below. Try to match up A, B, C and D with the lion, worm, tarantula and dolphin, using the key to help you.

Branching key
Animal

vertebrate   invertebrate

legs   no legs   legs   no legs

A   **B**   **C**   **D**

Numbered key
1. Does the animal have a backbone?

Yes   Go to 2.
No   Go to 3.

2. Does the vertebrate have legs?

Yes   It's a lion.
No   It's a dolphin.

3. Does the invertebrate have legs?

Yes   It's a tarantula.
No   It's a worm.

INTRODUCTION

Explain to the children that scientists in the Amazon rainforest, and other rainforests around the world, are working hard to identify the rich variety of colourful plants and animals they find. Keys guide them step by step towards classifying a specimen and finding its name (or being able to give it a name if it is a new discovery). Tell the children that they are going to find out about two different types of key.

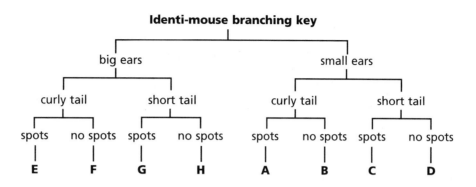

MAIN TEACHING ACTIVITY

Display the OHT or enlarged version of page 46. You may want to give the mice the names of children in the class to make the activity more fun. Ask the children to say how a stranger would be able to tell the mice apart. Use this information to draw the branches of your key. Hopefully the children will have identified mice with straight and curly tails, big and small ears, spots and no spots. Once you have drawn the key, fill the blanks with the letters A–H and ask the class to copy the key, replacing each letter with the name of a mouse (see illustration). Now show the children how to set out a 'Go to' or numbered key:

Identi-mouse numbered key

1. Does the mouse have big ears?   Yes Go to 2.   No Go to 5.

2. Does the mouse have spots?   Yes Go to 3.   No Go to 4.

3. Does the mouse have a curly tail?   Yes It's E.   No It's G.

4. Does the mouse have a curly tail?   Yes It's F.   No It's H.

5. Does the mouse have spots?   Yes Go to 6.   No Go to 7.

6. Does the mouse have a curly tail?   Yes It's A.   No It's C.

7. Does the mouse have a curly tail?   Yes It's B.   No It's D.

Talk the class through this key. Usually keys of this kind are quite easy to follow, but the children may have difficulty in making their own (see below), as fairly logical sequencing is needed.

GROUP ACTIVITIES

1. Take the children out, a group at a time, to collect leaves from up to eight different trees. Next, ask them to make rubbings or drawings of the leaves and then find the name of the plant they belong to by using reference books. Now ask them to make a key to distinguish these plants, so that other classes will be able to identify them from their leaves.
2. Ask the children to have a go at making their own key for the specimens drawn at the bottom of photocopiable page 46. You may want them to work in pairs as they organise their ideas and draw out the keys.

DIFFERENTIATION

In the Main teaching activity, some children may benefit from having copies of a blank identi-mouse key (see page 46) onto which they can add the branch labels and the letters for the mice. Many children may struggle with making their own numbered keys, but encourage more able children to have a go at producing their own.

ASSESSMENT

Can the children follow a numbered key to identify organisms? Can they produce a logical branching key?

PLENARY

Talk through examples of the keys the children have drawn, and check for any problems. Ask the children to draw a branching key of their family (they might like to include the goldfish and budgie) or their friends as homework.

OUTCOME

● Can use a key to identify an organism.

LESSON 4

OBJECTIVE

● To know that plants and animals of the same species vary.

RESOURCES

Group activities: 1 and 2. Rulers, graph (or squared) paper, coloured pencils, a height chart; a computer and data-handling software; reference books with details about blood groups.

Vocabulary

species, variation, continuous, discontinuous

BACKGROUND

Classification of living things starts with the main divisions into kingdoms and branches into the smallest categories, which scientists call **species**. A species is a group of living things that can successfully reproduce together. Differences between organisms of the same species are called **variations**. Offspring inherit genetic features from their parents. As humans, we have all (with the exception of identical twins) inherited different combinations of genetic features from our parents: we show genetic variation. Differences in experience and lifestyle contribute to physical variation between people. There are two main types of variation: **continuous** variation (differences that are difficult to place in distinct groups, such as hand span, height, body mass or foot length) and **discontinuous** variation (differences that are easy to group people by, such as blood group, gender or whether you can roll your tongue).

INTRODUCTION

Ask the class: *Can you roll your tongue from the sides inward? Can everyone?* Explain that this is an example of variation between individuals, and this lesson is about such variations.

MAIN TEACHING ACTIVITY

Ask: *What do you think 'variation' means?* Agree on a definition, then ask the children what variations they can see within the group (ask for general observations rather than personal comments). Brainstorm suggestions on the board around the title 'Variations in our class'.

Explain the two types of variation. Ask the group to look at the board and to decide which type of variation each is (you may want to treat eye colour as discontinuous, though there are subtle variations between shades). To demonstrate that height is an example of continuous variation, get the class to stand in order from shortest to the tallest. Then stand them in two groups: males on the left, females on the right. *What kind of variation is this?* (Discontinuous.)

GROUP ACTIVITIES

1. Ask the children, working in groups of six or more, to complete a table like the one shown opposite – draw this on the board, or prepare it on the computer as a worksheet for the children to complete. For each variable, they should note whether it is continuous (C) or discontinuous (D). They should go on to plot a bar chart of the discontinuous variations in their class.
2. Write some height categories on the board, spanning the interval from the shortest to the tallest child (see example opposite). Ask each child to put a tally mark in the height class that he or she belongs to. On another sheet of graph paper, they should draw a bar chart of the data recorded for the class and label this as 'Continuous variation in Class …'. If possible, ask some more able children to input this data into a spreadsheet so that they can plot graphs of the results.

DIFFERENTIATION

Blanks of the two tables can be photocopied to help less able children keep up with the others. Children who complete the tasks could calculate the average height of the children in the class (this is easy if the results are in a spreadsheet). These children could also use reference books to find out the names of the different blood groups. *What kind of variation is this?* Ask them to find out their own blood group. This data can be added to the chart for the next lesson.

Name of child	Height (cm)	Sex (male/female)	Shoe size	Roll tongue?	Handspan (cm)
Mary					
Joe					
Kulvinder					
Andy					
Zaidi					
Liz					
C or D?					

ASSESSMENT

See Plenary.

PLENARY

Talk through the charts and check that there is common agreement as to which variations are continuous.

OUTCOME

● Recognise how living things of the same species vary.

LINKS

Maths: discrete and continuous data.

Height class (cm)	No. of children
110–114.9	
115–119.9	
120–124.9	
125–129.9	
130–134.9	
135–139.9	
140–144.9	
145–149.9	
150–154.9	

LESSON 5

Objective	● To use their knowledge of keys to identify plant species in the field.
Resources	Copies (one per pair) of photocopiable page 47, a field reference guide to trees of the British Isles, a photograph of a car from a magazine.
Main activity	This lesson will support teachers in England seeking to address QCA *Science Scheme of Work* Unit 5/6H, especially when linked to Unit 3 of this book. If your school grounds are not suitable for fieldwork, you may wish to organise a trip to a local park or canal, or the hedgerows on nearby farmland. Warn the children that they may need wet weather clothing. You will need to organise the work with the children's safety in mind, and may need another teacher to help with supervision. Remind the children to treat the living things in a habitat with respect: *Take nothing but photographs, leave nothing but footprints.* Taking a single leaf from a tree is acceptable, but uprooting or picking wild flowers is against the law. Remind the children of their previous work on keys. Check whether they remember the names of the two types of key (branching and numbered). Tell them that the kind most commonly used 'in the field' (for outdoor work) is the numbered key. Explain that they will be working in pairs, using keys to identify common trees. Hold up a picture of a car from a magazine and ask the children to identify its make and model. Point out that makes and models of cars change every year, but that the plants they will be identifying have been around for hundreds of thousands of years – so we should be able to identify them! Give each pair the guide key copied from page 47. Take them to an appropriate site. They should use the keys to identify as many tree species as possible.
Differentiation	If children are struggling, you may want to provide a sample of leaves (from common British trees) for them to fit to the examples given on the sheet. More able children could try to find out the identity of species not recorded on the guide sheet; encourage them to take samples of leaves (from trees only), and to make sketches of the arrangement of the buds, the texture of the bark (for trees) etc.
Assessment	Back in class, describe various plants you have found to the children. Use their responses to judge how easily they recognise the most common species in their local environment. Alternatively, play a game using the guide keys: the children are only allowed to ask you four questions to work out the identity of a tree you have thought of. This will require them to use the keys as a reference. Allow each table one question in turn (they will need to confer) and disqualify teams who shout out.
Plenary	Why do the class think picking wild flowers is against the law? In Britain, many trees have Tree Preservation Orders put on them so that permission from the county council is needed before they are cut down. *Is this a good idea? Why?* Herbicides (sprays used to kill unwanted plants) are used by farmers on their crops. *Why might this be bad news for wild flowers?*
Outcome	● Can use keys to identify plant species in the field.

LESSON 6

OBJECTIVES
● To investigate variation in plant growth.
● To design a fair experiment, make a prediction and test it.

RESOURCES
Main teaching activity: Bean seeds; photocopiable page 48 (one copy per child).
Group activity: Accurate weighing scales (ideally a top pan balance), a selection of broad or runner bean seeds, cotton wool, measuring cylinders, sticky labels, beakers or jars. You will need somewhere warm and sunny to place the beans while they germinate and grow.

PREPARATION
Don't forget that most beans need soaking overnight before they will germinate.

BACKGROUND
Variations between individuals in a plant species are as marked as those in an animal species. Leaf size and shape, root length, diameter of stem and other factors will vary between individuals. This lesson provides an opportunity to examine the seeds of one species of plant, record the differences and make predictions based on these observations. The children may well predict that the largest seeds will grow most quickly – but as with all biological investigations, the actual outcome is influenced by a complex interaction of factors (including the genetic variation between the seeds). Never mind: this is a good starting point to get the children forming questions and making predictions that they can test. It is important to check, before the children start, that they have understood the concept of fair testing (that is, only changing the variable they aim to test).

> **Vocabulary**
> variation, fair test, prediction, investigate, observe, results, conclusion, evaluation

INTRODUCTION
Give out bean seeds for the children to look at. Point out that these are all slightly different. *What is the correct name to describe differences between individuals?* ('Variations'.) Remind them of the story of *Jack and the Beanstalk*. Which beans would grow fastest for Jack? *Should Jack choose big beans to grow his beanstalk?*
Refine the question you want them to find the answer to: *Do bigger beans grow into beanstalks more quickly than smaller beans?*

MAIN TEACHING ACTIVITY
Ask the children to look carefully at the seeds and name variations they can see (colouring, shape, size, mass). Explain that they will be working as a group on each table. Their task is to examine the beans and predict which will grow the tallest if planted and left to grow for two weeks. They should place the beans in order according to how quickly they think each will grow. Point out the apparatus available for them to use if they feel they need it: top pan balances, rulers, graph paper (to draw around the seeds on) and so on.
Ask for ideas about how the experiment could be set up; brainstorm the ideas on the board. Using measurable variations between beans, guide the children to set up an experiment to find out which bean plant will grow the tallest. The treatment of the beans during the experiment will need to be thought out by the children. *How will you make sure it is a fair test? How long will you leave the beans growing for? How will you measure the speed of growth? Will the number and size of leaves be taken into account, or just the height?* Introduce the guide sheet (page 48) as a way for the children to structure their planning. Talk through each point, giving guidance in the following ways:
● What I aim to find out. (What is the problem that has been set? This could just be a title, such as 'Should Jack choose bigger beans to grow his beanstalks more quickly?')
● How I plan to do this. (Describe the basic idea of the plan – for example, 'Find the mass of the beans (or measure them) and plant them, leaving them to germinate.')
● Measurements I will need to take. (Mass of the beans in grams or width/length of the beans in millimetres, time the beans have been growing for in days, amount of water added to each bean in millilitres, height the bean shoots have grown to in millimetres after a set time, temperature (°C) the beans germinate in.)
● What I need to keep the same to make the test a fair one. (Amount of water added, the temperature and amount of light the growing beans are exposed to.)
● What I think will happen and why. (I think the bigger beans will grow more quickly, because they have more food stored inside them for the developing plant.)
● How I will make sure the test is SAFE. (Take care with glassware.)

● Results (tables and graphs can be attached on separate sheets of paper.)
● Do my results show a pattern or trend? What is it? (Is there an obvious pattern in the results? If not, that's OK – but the children still need to draw attention to this. Did the rest of the class get similar results? What can I learn from what they found out?)
● Do my results support my prediction? (If not, the results are still useful. Encourage the children to be objective: the experiment has not necessarily 'gone wrong' just because the results are not those predicted.)
● Can I trust my results? Why? (Are there enough results to provide convincing evidence? Remember that drugs companies have to test their products many hundreds of times before they are considered safe for the public to use.)
● What I have learned from this investigation. (Are there conclusions the children can draw from their results? Which beans would you choose if you were Jack?)
● If I were to carry out this investigation again, how would I change it to make the results more reliable? (Were the beans used genetically identical? Could the experiment be repeated to see whether the same results are achieved?)
● Other ideas I could investigate are. (Think of related factors that are relevant – for example, how does temperature affect the speed at which bean shoots grow?)

GROUP ACTIVITY

The groups may choose to measure the mass, length or width of the seeds – it is up to them to decide on the best strategy. Encourage them to record their observations (provide paper for this). Prompt any children who are struggling, but don't be afraid to let children go off at a tangent even if you know the experiment will probably 'fail'. They will learn by their mistakes – and if necessary, they can always look at the results of another group.

DIFFERENTIATION

Children who are advancing quickly in their ideas could try to observe which part of the seedling breaks through the seed coat (testa) first: the radicle (root) or the plumule (shoot). They could try to draw the first few stages of growth. Ask them: *Why do many seeds only grow after they have been chilled?* (The chilling is a cue that the worst of the winter weather has passed – if seedlings germinated in the autumn, they would perish in the winter frosts.)

Children who really are struggling could be guided towards finding the mass of each seed and helped to draw a table for their results. Ask them to decide which seed they think will grow the fastest and to write this down as a prediction.

ASSESSMENT

Use the criteria outlined in the investigation guide above to check that the children are able to form a clear plan and follow the process of enquiry.

PLENARY

Draw together the observations of the class and see whether there are any common trends or patterns in their results. Share conclusions. Ask the children to suggest possible improvements to the investigation.

OUTCOMES

● Know that growth in a plant species is subject to variation.
● Can design an experiment, test predictions, make observations, interpret results, draw conclusions and evaluate the investigation.

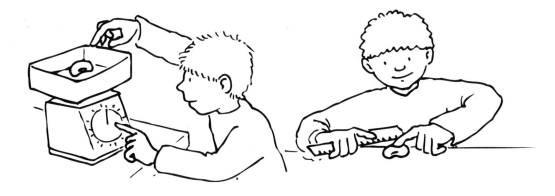

LESSON 7

Objectives	● To know that plants need light, water and warmth to grow well. ● To design a fair experiment and make predictions that they can test.
Resources	Photocopiable page 48 (one copy per group); cotton wool, cress seeds, Petri dishes, sticky labels, measuring cylinders; storage sites (eg cupboard, fridge, window sill).
Main activity	Explain that in this lesson, you will be revising what plants need in order to grow healthily. Ask the children for suggestions, and brainstorm these around the words 'Healthy growth'. From these ideas, pick 'light', 'water' and 'warmth' (or 'the right temperature') as three factors for the children to investigate using cress seeds. The children should work in groups to plan their ideas for the investigation, using page 48 as a guide. Each group may choose to investigate just one factor (eg how well the seedlings grow at different temperatures) or more than one factor – but they must remember to keep their tests fair.
Differentiation	Some children may need additional guidance in planning their ideas; adapt the suggestions provided with the prompt questions in the previous lesson to help with this. More able children could be asked to find out more about *why* plants need light and water to grow. (Light provides the energy used to make food by photosynthesis. Water is one of the raw materials that plants use to make sugars in this reaction, and is also necessary to keep plant cells firm and so enable the plant to stand upright.)
Assessment	Use the guide sheet as a reference to check that the children are able to take logical steps in forming the process of enquiry and in reviewing their observations.
Plenary	At the end of the investigation, all the groups should share their results. Was a common trend observed? Ask the children why it is important for scientists to share their observations and results. (It allows them to reach a greater understanding of the topic being researched.)
Outcome	● Know the importance of water, light and warmth for healthy plant growth.

LESSON 8

OBJECTIVES
● To know that plants need nutrients from the soil for healthy growth.
● To know that farmers and gardeners often add nutrients to the soil in the form of fertiliser.

RESOURCES

Main teaching activity: A bottle of children's multivitamins; a pot plant with food colouring added to the soil; a glass beaker big enough to hold the plant pot.
Group activities: 1. Labelled bottles of indoor plant fertiliser (including Baby Bio), a range of different unhealthy pot plants, paper, pencils. **2.** Paper, coloured pencils.

PREPARATION

Ask at a garden centre for some unhealthy pot plants, explaining what they are for. Make sure that all the bottles of indoor plant fertiliser are tightly sealed. For safety, do **not** allow children to handle fertilisers.

Vocabulary

photosynthesis, nutrients, trace elements, deficiencies, leach

BACKGROUND

Green plants use the energy of sunlight to combine simple materials (water and carbon dioxide) in the process of photosynthesis to make sugar in their leaves. However, there are other nutrients that plants need in order to grow healthily (just as we need vitamins and minerals in our diet). Sometimes the plants need only tiny quantities of particular chemical elements – these are known as **trace elements**. The three main substances needed by plants are nitrates (used for making proteins), phosphates (used for a number of purposes, including an important role in photosynthesis) and potassium (also involved in photosynthesis). Iron and magnesium are needed as trace elements in order for plants to grow healthily: they are used in the formation of the essential green pigment chlorophyll in the leaves.

Nutrient	Symptom of deficiency
Nitrates	Stunted growth, older leaves turn yellow
Phosphates	Poor root growth, purple younger leaves
Potassium	Yellow leaves with dead spots

INTRODUCTION

Show the children a bottle of children's multivitamins. Ask whether any of them have ever taken vitamin tablets. *Why did you take them?* Explain that if we lack a particular vitamin, we are said to be **deficient** in it (we have a **deficiency**). We need the correct balance of vitamins in our diet in order to stay healthy.

MAIN TEACHING ACTIVITY

Ask the children where plants get their nutrients from. Hopefully some will suggest 'the soil'. If they suggest 'photosynthesis', explain that this process only makes sugars in the leaves. *Does anyone know what farmers and gardeners do to help improve the growth of their crops?* (Add compost, manure or fertiliser.) Explain that house plants also sometimes need to be given extra nutrients to stay healthy. Place the pot plant with food colouring in its soil inside the large glass beaker and pour water into the pot. As the water drains through, it will wash out the colouring. Explain that rain will wash or 'leach out' nutrients from the soil in this way.

Write on the board the names of the main nutrients that plants need for healthy growth, and explain how the plants show particular symptoms if they are lacking any of these. The children will need to refer to this list of visible symptoms when carrying out the Group activities.

GROUP ACTIVITIES

1. Ask the children to examine the labels of some liquid fertiliser bottles and list the contents they find. They should work in pairs to assess the health of three unhealthy plants on their table, referring to the deficiency symptoms on the board, then fill in a chart like the one shown below. Pairs on the same table can check to see whether they agree with the other pairs' observations.

Plant	Observation	Treatment needed
Geranium	No purple leaves. Some dead spots on leaves.	Might need more potassium.

2. The children can work individually to design an advertisement for a fertiliser, explaining why their product is the best for healthy plant growth and showing what plants will look like without it! Alternatively, they could design an information booklet called *Look After Your Plants!* telling plant owners how to check whether their plants are healthy – and what to do if they are not.

DIFFERENTIATION

Less able children may benefit from having a blank copy of the recording table prepared for them.

ASSESSMENT

At the start of the Plenary session, show the children examples of plants that appear to be suffering from a lack of one or more of the nutrients discussed. Check to see whether there is general agreement between the children in their assessment of these plants.

PLENARY

Tell the children that tomato plants in many greenhouses are grown directly from water that has all the essential nutrients added to it; the roots trail directly into the solution. Growing crops in this way is called **hydroponic cultivation**. Ask: *Where else have you heard the prefix 'hydro'? What might it mean?* ('Water.') *What are the advantages of growing the plants in this way?* (It is possible to check the nutrient levels in the water continually and so make sure that all the plants are getting exactly what they need – this is not so easy if they are all in individual pots.) *Any disadvantages?* (The growers need to make sure they get the levels right, or else the whole crop suffers.)

Farmers who grow the same crop on their land year after year eventually find that the quality (yield) of their crop starts to fall. Why is this? (The plants are using up the same nutrients year after year, so the crop begins to suffer from nutrient deficiencies.) *What might the solution be?* (The farmer can add fertilisers to the soil.) Explain that farmers usually do this, though leaching of fertilisers into rivers and streams by rain can harm the environment. Another solution is to change ('rotate') the type of crop grown – bean and pea plants actually add nitrates to the soil, because of special microbes living in their roots.

OUTCOMES

● Know that plants need nutrients for healthy growth, and that fertilisers can provide these.
● Can recognise unhealthy plants.

LINKS

Unit 3 Lesson 10: microbes in the soil.

LESSON 9

OBJECTIVES
● To assess the children's understanding of branching keys.
● To assess the children's ability to consider the reliability of evidence.

RESOURCES
1. Photocopiable page 49, writing materials. **2.** A4 paper, writing materials.

INTRODUCTION
You may want to gather the children together and remind them of the work they have covered on keys and variation. Encourage them to think about the quadrat method they used in fieldwork for looking at vegetation.

ASSESSMENT ACTIVITY 1
Give the children a copy each of photocopiable page 49 and let them complete it individually.

Answers
A = spots; B = no spots; C = legs; D = no legs; E = legs; F = no legs; G = Fip; H = Zy;
I = Chuck; J = Zak; K = Peep; L = Vodo; M = Teepee; N = Dibble.

1. Antennae?	Yes	Go to 2.				
	No	Go to 3.	5. Legs?	Yes	It's Teepee.
2. Spots?	Yes	Go to 4.		No	It's Dibble.
	No	Go to 5.	6. Legs?	Yes	It's Fip.
3. Spots?	Yes	Go to 6.		No	It's Zy.
	No	Go to 7.	7. Legs?	Yes	It's Chuck.
4. Legs?	Yes	It's Peep.		No	It's Zak.
	No	It's Vodo.			

Looking for levels
All the children should be able to identify the missing alien names in the branching key. Most children should be able to add the missing labels to the branches of the key. More able children should be able to devise a logical numbered (Go to) key to help people identify the aliens.

ASSESSMENT ACTIVITY 2
This activity is concerned with an aspect of variation. It also looks at the children's ability to question the results of an investigation and suggest ways of obtaining more reliable results. Write this task on the board. Give the children up to 20 minutes to write down their answers.

> Caroline and Tom are in the playground, watching the other children. Caroline says she has noticed that the girls are taller than the boys. She says she has proved this by measuring the height of some boys and some girls, and the girls were taller. Tom says he isn't convinced.
> 1. What questions should Tom ask about the results?
> 2. How should the investigation be planned to provide reliable results?

Looking for levels
All the children should ask questions about the age of the children chosen for the survey, and suggest that they should all have been taken from the same age group. They should refer to this in their answer to question 2. Most children should ask how many boys and girls were measured in Caroline's survey, and explain that the smaller the number chosen the less reliable the results will be. An ideal survey will include as many individuals as possible. More able children should ask questions about the range of children chosen (for example, were they all from the same ethnic background?). The survey may need to be carried out across the whole country, or even across the world, to see whether the results are consistent. Perhaps diet and lifestyle will have an effect? In answer to question 2, the children should refer to the importance of collecting results from as wide a variety of situations as possible in order to gain reliable results.

PLENARY
Go through the answers to Assessment activity 1, checking that the children understand their mistakes and are clear about how to make corrections; encourage them to write their corrections on the sheet. Discuss Caroline's idea about the height of boys and girls, and check whether the children share Tom's uncertainties. Ask them to think about the claims made by TV adverts: *Should we just accept what they tell us? What would a good scientist do?*

All creatures great and small

Cut out the pictures below and sort them into these groups:

Mammals	Reptiles
Amphibians	Fish
Birds	Odd ones out

Why don't the 'odd ones out' fit into any of your other groups?

Identi-mouse

A   B   C   D   E   F   G   H

Identi-mouse branching key

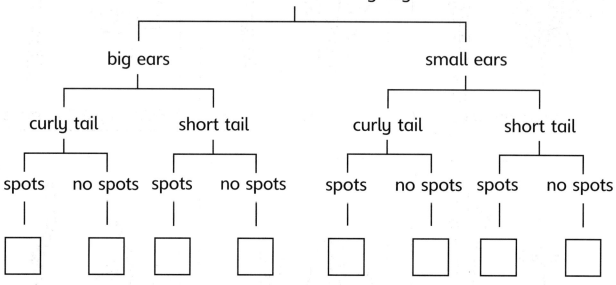

big ears   small ears

curly tail   short tail   curly tail   short tail

spots   no spots   spots   no spots   spots   no spots   spots   no spots

1. Write the correct letter for each mouse in the blank boxes at the bottom of the key.

2. Look at these bugs and make your own branching key to help identify them. Start by spotting the differences.

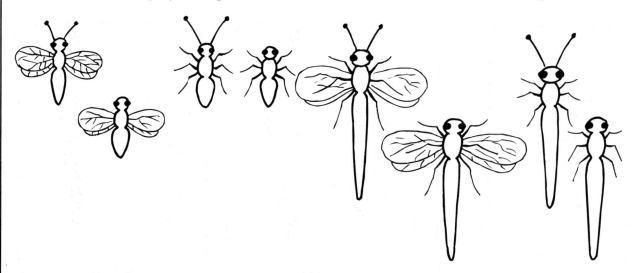

3. Now make a numbered 'Go to' key for the bugs.

Common trees

Use this sheet to help you identify trees around your school.
See how many types of tree you can learn to recognise in one week.

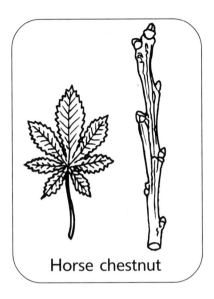

Horse chestnut

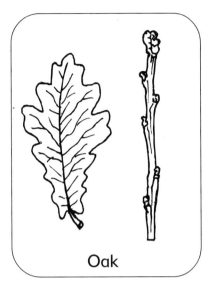

Oak

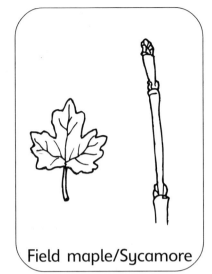

Field maple/Sycamore

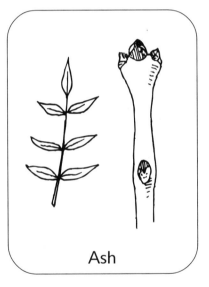

Ash

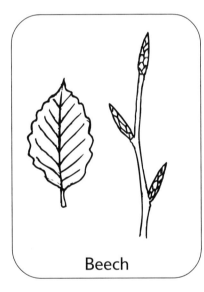

Beech

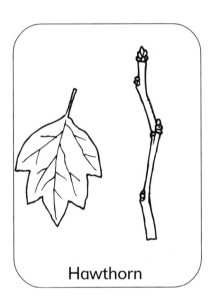

Hawthorn

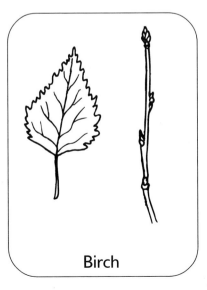

Birch

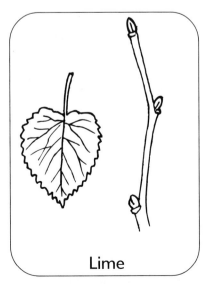

Lime

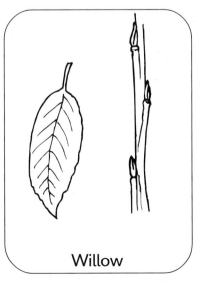

Willow

Investigation guide

What I aim to find out: _____

_____

How I plan to do this: _____

_____

Measurements I will need to take: _____

_____

What I need to keep the same to make the test a fair one: _____

_____

What I think will happen and why: _____

_____

How I will make sure the test is SAFE: _____

_____

Results (tables and graphs can be attached on a separate sheet of paper)

_____

Do my results show a pattern or trend? What is it? _____

_____

Do my results support my prediction? _____

_____

Can I trust my results? Why? _____

_____

What I have learned from this investigation: _____

_____

If I were to carry out this investigation again, how would I change it to

make the results more reliable? _____

_____

Other ideas I could investigate are: _____

_____

Name

Variation

This branching key has not had all its branches labelled. Fill in the blanks (A–F). Now use the key to fill in the names of the aliens in boxes G–N.

Peep   Fip   Teepee   Chuck

Vodo   Zy   Dibble   Zak

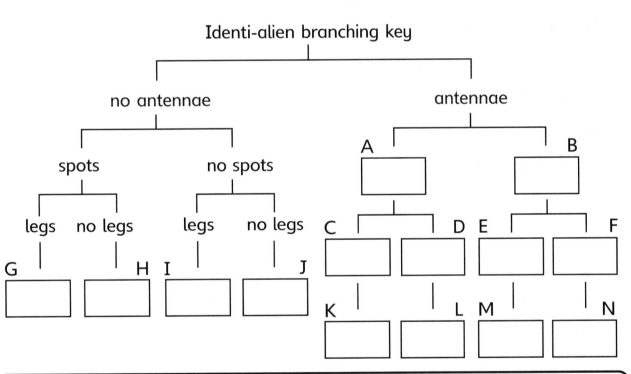

Identi-alien branching key

Now make a 'Go to' (numbered) key to help someone recognise these aliens. The first part has been done for you.

1. Antennae?   Yes   Go to 2.

   No   Go to 3.

2. Spots?   Yes   Go to ___.

   No   Go to ___.

The living world

ORGANISATION (16 LESSONS)

	OBJECTIVES	MAIN ACTIVITY	GROUP ACTIVITIES	PLENARY	OUTCOMES
LESSON 1	● To know that animals and plants in a habitat depend on each other in a variety of ways.	Discuss the hedgerow as an example of a habitat in which many different plants and animals coexist.	Study of a hedgerow – the children link the different living components.	Consider the environmental value of hedgerows and the damaging effects of their removal.	● Can describe ways in which plants and animals in a habitat depend on each other. ● Have some awareness of the environmental value of hedgerows.
LESSON 2	● To know that food chains are used to describe feeding relationships in a habitat.	Introduce the key terms and show the children how to construct a food chain.	Construct food chains. Make mobiles of food chains.	Introduce the role of decomposers in the food chain.	● Know that the Sun provides the energy for food chains. ● Can construct food chains. ● Can use the words 'producer', 'consumer', 'herbivore', 'carnivore', 'predator' and 'prey' correctly.
LESSON 3	● To know that unfamiliar habitats can be studied in the same way as familiar habitats.	Read out the text for a comprehension exercise; the children answer questions.	Construct an illustration of the feeding relationships in an Arctic environment.	Consider the threats posed by industry to a fragile ecosystem.	● Can describe the features of an unfamiliar habitat. ● Can construct food chains from information about an unfamiliar habitat.
LESSON 4	● To know that plants and animals have special features that help them survive in a habitat.	Brainstorm ideas about how a cactus is suited to life in the desert. Introduce the concept of adaptation.	Choose a picture of an animal or plant and label the special adaptations it possesses.	Introduce the idea of behavioural adaptation in relation to humans.	● Recognise features of plant and animal species that help them to survive in their habitats.
LESSON 5	● To use simple environmental survey techniques.	Introduce the use of a quadrat and line transect to estimate the abundance of plant species.	Set up their own line transects and carry out quadrat studies.	Consider what other information could be collected along a line transect.	● Can use quadrats and line transects as a way of collecting environmental data.
LESSON 6	● To develop their investigative skills. ● To develop their understanding of environmental survey techniques.	The children plan and carry out an investigation, using survey techniques to identify changes in the distribution of plant species.		Discuss the need for environmental surveys to be carried out before new roads are built.	● Can carry out a line transect and quadrat study. ● Are aware of the use of these as environmental survey techniques.
LESSON 7	● To know that different soils can be compared.	Explain the main soil types and their drainage characteristics.	Work in pairs to examine the settling of soil into layers.	Discuss ways of maintaining soil drainage.	● Can compare features of different soil types. ● Can interpret a model of the soil.
LESSON 8	● To be aware of the variety of animal life found in soil.	Introduce techniques for looking at soil animals. The children collect and identify soil invertebrates and draw a cross-section of life in the soil.		Consider the roles of animals and plants in maintaining the soil, and the need to protect soil from erosion.	● Can describe different methods for collecting invertebrates. ● Are aware that soils support a variety of life.

ORGANISATION (16 LESSONS)

	OBJECTIVES	MAIN ACTIVITY	GROUP ACTIVITIES	PLENARY	OUTCOMES
LESSON 9	● To know that different plants grow better in different soil conditions.	Demonstrate how to prepare dandelion roots for examination under a microscope, and how to test the pH of soil. Discuss plants that live in difficult conditions.	Examine the fine structure of dandelion roots and record their observations. Solve some gardening problems.	Consider the impact of acid rain on plant life and the use of lichens as indicators of air quality.	● Know that different plants are adapted to living in different types of soil. ● Can describe the functions of roots.
LESSON 10	● To know that the decay caused by micro-organisms is useful in the environment.	Introduce the term 'decomposers' and explain their role in the recycling of organic materials.	Interpret a diagram of a compost heap and answer questions about it.	Consider biodegradable and non-biodegradable materials and the need for recycling.	● Understand that the decay caused by micro-organisms allows nutrients to be recycled.
LESSON 11	● To know that micro-organisms cause many diseases.	Explain the idea that microbes are the causes of communicable diseases.	Work in groups to dramatise discoveries about the prevention of diseases. Perform the sketches to the class.	The children place these events on a timeline. Discuss the need for scientists to share their findings.	● Know that many diseases are caused by micro-organisms. ● Can describe how a scientific theory is based on evidence.
LESSON 12	● To know about the range of diseases caused by micro-organisms.	Use models to explain the nature of bacteria, viruses and fungi and the diseases they cause.	Complete a table listing types of microbe and diseases they cause. Complete a chart showing the growth of a bacterial population.	Briefly introduce the idea of the body's specific defence system.	● Can describe some diseases and identify their causes.
LESSON 13	● To know that mould on food is caused by micro-organisms. ● To plan and carry out a fair test.	Brainstorm ideas for an investigation into the conditions that favour mould. The children set up an investigation.		Review the children's findings. Discuss food preservation techniques.	● Can describe good practice for food hygiene. ● Can explain why food hygiene is necessary. ● Can plan and carry out a fair test.
LESSON 14	● To know that yeast is a useful organism.	Explain the nature of yeast. Describe the experiment the children will carry out.	Carry out an experiment with yeast and record their observations.	Consider the role of yeast in the baking of bread.	● Can identify the conditions needed for yeast to grow and reproduce. ● Know the function of yeast in bread-making.
LESSON 15	● To know that micro-organisms are used in food production.	Explain the use of microbes to produce a variety of foods. The children use these facts to complete a summary grid and make a poster.		Link this lesson to the role of microbes in causing decay and the recycling of nutrients.	● Can describe how micro-organisms are used in food production.

	OBJECTIVES	ACTIVITY 1	ACTIVITY 2
ASSESSMENT 16	● To assess the children's understanding of food chains and of adaptations. ● To assess the children's ability to plan an investigation and apply environmental survey techniques.	Answer questions about food chains and adaptations.	Plan an investigation involving a survey of dandelion growth (using a quadrat). Explain how the methods used will produce reliable findings.

LESSON 1

OBJECTIVE

● To know that animals and plants in a habitat depend on each other in a variety of ways.

RESOURCES

Main teaching activity: A picture of a song thrush.
Group activities: 1. Plant and bird identification guides or keys, hand lenses, clipboards or notebooks, pencils. **2.** Photocopiable page 72, trowels, plastic cups, an insect identification guide, hand lenses. **3.** Photocopiable page 72, paper, pencils.

BACKGROUND

Ideally, you should teach this topic in the late spring or early summer, when the hedgerows are in bloom and you and the children will be able to get out and about.

The place where a living thing (organism) is found is called its **habitat**. A habitat is often named after the type of plants that are found there – for example, woodland, hedgerow, grassland, rainforest. The animals depend on the plants for shelter, nesting sites and food. The plants benefit from the animals, which pollinate their flowers and disperse their seeds. (See Unit 2 of *100 Science Lessons: Year 5/Primary 6* for more information on this.) Most animals breathe oxygen, and this gas is produced by green plants when they make their food by photosynthesis. So the relationship between plants and animals is a very close one – the children need to appreciate this.

Hedgerows provide a habitat for a rich web of life. They are also vital 'corridors' of movement for many species, which use the cover of hedgerows to move between woodlands and other habitats. Removing the hedgerows leaves some animals and plants isolated, which can lead to their local extinction.

INTRODUCTION

Tell the class that these lessons are about the environment, the relationships between living things in an environment and how living things get the energy they need to survive. Explain that in the first lesson, you will be looking at how the animals and plants in a habitat depend on each other.

MAIN TEACHING ACTIVITY

Ask: *What is a habitat?* Ask the children to name some examples. Elicit the idea that different habitats are home to different types of animals and plants, which all need certain things to survive. *What do all living things need to survive?* Hopefully, the children will suggest that animals need food, water, the right temperature and shelter; and that plants need light, water and nutrients from the soil.

Now say that you are going to look at hedgerows as an example of a habitat. Explain that many birds are found living in hedgerows. Show a picture of a song thrush. (See Unit 2 of *100 Science Lessons: Year 5/Primary 6* for more information on the song thrush as an endangered species.) Ask why the hedge is a good habitat for a thrush. Responses should include: 'it provides somewhere to nest'; 'it contains insects, snails and berries to eat'; 'it gives shelter from predators'. *The thrush benefits in many ways from the plants – but does anyone know whether the thrush helps the plants?* Explain that the thrush feeds on invertebrates that could harm the plants, and that it carries the seeds of fruits such as blackberries in its gut as it flies away, and so helps to disperse them. *Do other animals help these plants?* Guide the children towards thinking about the role of bees and other insects in pollinating flowers. (See Unit 2 of *100 Science Lessons: Year 5/Primary 6* for more on plant life cycles and interdependence.)

GROUP ACTIVITIES

1. If possible, organise a trip to take the children to a nearby hedgerow and ask them to find and name four species of plant found there, using keys or guide books to help them. Can they identify two different types of bird seen nearby? Ask them to make a note of the insect life they see.
2. Each group can build their own pitfall trap, using the guidance given on page 72. They should check its contents each day for several days, identify any insects caught using reference materials, and then release them.
3. Each group can use the information on page 72 to complete the 'web of life' chart by showing the links between each animal and the animals and plants around it. An example is shown opposite. (Note that this is not a 'food web'.)

DIFFERENTIATION

3. Children who are struggling could be given a 'web of life' chart with the plants and animals that have a relationship already linked. Ask them to find the statement on the sheet that shows how each pair are related. Ask more able children to try to find out about other relationships in the same environment that are not shown on the chart.

ASSESSMENT

Check through the photocopiable sheet as a class to see whether the children have identified the key relationships between the organisms. Note whether the children can suggest other relationships that are not shown.

PLENARY

Thousands of miles of hedgerow are torn up by farmers each year. Ask the class why is this a problem for wildlife. Explain that hedgerows are both habitats and 'corridors' (see Background) for many species. Ask them to imagine that a hedgerow near the school is about to be torn up. Ask the children to design a poster (perhaps as homework) telling local people why they should try to protect it, or construct a joint letter to the local newspaper in order to model writing.

OUTCOMES

● Can describe ways in which plants and animals in a habitat depend on each other.
● Have some awareness of the environmental value of hedgerows.

LINKS

History: changes in local land-use.

LESSON 2

OBJECTIVE

● To know that food chains are used to describe feeding relationships in a habitat.

RESOURCES

Main teaching activity: A pot plant, a worksheet (see Preparation), an OHP (optional).
Group activities: 1. A3 paper, coloured pens. **2.** Cotton thread, wire coat-hangers, card, scissors, coloured pens, wildlife magazines or reference books.

PREPARATION

Write the following on the board or an OHT. Prepare it as a worksheet with a word bank of the missing words for less able children to complete.

> **Food chains**
> All green plants use energy from the _____ to make food in their leaves. Plants are called _____ because they can make food for themselves. Animals cannot make food for themselves: they have to eat plants or other animals to get the energy they need for life. Animals are called _____. An animal that eats only plants is called a _____. An animal that eats only other animals is called a _____. In a food chain, arrows are used to show which way the _____ is going.

BACKGROUND

The energy from the Sun is harnessed in a complex reaction, photosynthesis, that takes place in the leaves of plants. Using sunlight, water and the gas carbon dioxide, plants make their own sugars. Green plants are called **producers** because they can make their own food. Animals cannot make their own food, and so are known as **consumers**: they obtain their energy by eating other animals or plants. Almost all life on Earth depends on the producers.

Food chains are used to show feeding relationships: what eats what. The producer (plant) is always the first step in the food chain. Next come the consumers:

Producer → primary consumer → secondary consumer (predator) → tertiary consumer

The tertiary consumer is often the 'top predator': nothing else preys on it. Not all food chains are this long, however; producers might be eaten by the top predator – for example, brown bears sometimes eat berries. The arrows are very important: they show the direction of flow of **energy** through the food chain. (The Sun is not usually included as part of the food chain.)

An animal that eats only plants is called a **herbivore**. Such animals are often eaten by (are the **prey** of) other animals, called **predators**. An animal that eats only other animals is called a **carnivore**. Some (such as pigs and humans) eat plants and animals. They are called **omnivores**.

INTRODUCTION

Tell the children that this lesson links the work they have done on the interdependence of plants and animals in their habitats to understanding how energy is passed through living communities. They have already looked at how the living things in a hedgerow rely on each other for survival – but how do all living things get the energy they need to survive?

Explain that almost all life on Earth depends on energy that has come from the Sun. Invite the children to prove you wrong. For example, a child might say that a chocolate bar doesn't contain energy from the Sun – but explain that the chocolate bar contains sugar that was produced by a plant called the sugar cane, which got its energy from the Sun. If a child suggests that he or she got energy from a bacon sandwich at lunchtime, explain that bacon comes from pigs, and that pigs eat plants that got their energy from the Sun.

MAIN TEACHING ACTIVITY

Hold up a plant and ask the children: *What do most plants have in common? What colour is most of the countryside when seen from above?* The idea that plants are mostly green should emerge. *Why green? Why is green so important?* Explain that it is because of the green chemical in plants that we are alive. This green chemical, **chlorophyll**, is used by plants to catch the Sun's energy and turn simple materials into sugars in its leaves. This energy is passed on to animals when they eat the plant. Explain that we call plants 'producers' because they can make their own food, and animals 'consumers' because they have to eat other organisms to stay alive.

Write the word 'Sun' in a circle in the middle of the board. On one side of this, write 'Grass'. Then ask the children to name an animal that eats grass (such as 'Rabbit'). Write this down next to 'Grass' and draw an arrow going **from** the grass **to** the rabbit. Ask for the name of a **predator** of rabbits (if they are unfamiliar with this word, explain that a predator is an animal that hunts other animals for its food – the animal it hunts is called its **prey**). Write down the name of this animal (such as 'Fox'). Now draw an arrow going **from** the rabbit **to** the fox. Explain that this is called a **food chain**. Explain that the arrows show the direction the energy is going in through the food chain. *Do you know which animal is a herbivore?* Check that the children know what 'herbivore' means. *Can you name a carnivore in this food chain?* Check that they know what 'carnivore' and 'omnivore' mean.

Talk through the paragraph on the board or OHP, or ask the children to copy it and fill in the blanks. The missing key words are: Sun, producers, consumers, herbivore, carnivore, energy.

GROUP ACTIVITIES

1. Ask the children, working in groups, to draw a circle in the middle of a sheet of A3 paper and write the word 'Sun' in it, then copy the example of a food chain that you have done as a class. Now ask the groups to each think of five more food chains and add these, radiating outward from the Sun. They should write 'P' next to each producer and 'C' next to each consumer. *Who can make the longest sensible food chain?*

2. Ask the children to make mobiles of food chains, using cards (with words, drawings or pictures cut from magazines) hung from coat-hangers on cotton threads, or just linked together with cotton and hung on the wall.

DIFFERENTIATION

Main teaching activity: Give less able children a worksheet with the paragraph and a word bank to choose answers from. **Group activity 1.** Suggest some food chains to less able children, but leave them to draw the arrows in the correct direction.

ASSESSMENT

Can the children identify a producer and a consumer? Can they draw arrows appropriately to show the flow of energy through the food chain?

PLENARY

Ask the children to read out examples of their food chains. Check to see whether everyone agrees. *What happens to top predators when they die?* Explain that their bodies are broken down by **decomposers**, such as fungi and bacteria. These form the start of a new food chain. Decomposers are covered in more detail later in this unit.

OUTCOMES

- Know that the Sun provides the energy for food chains.
- Can construct food chains.
- Can use the words 'producer', 'consumer', 'herbivore', 'carnivore', 'predator' and 'prey' correctly.

LINKS

Unit 1, Lesson 1.

LESSON 3

OBJECTIVE

- To know that unfamiliar habitats can be studied in the same way as familiar habitats.

RESOURCES

Main teaching activity: Photocopiable page 73 (a copy for yourself and/or one copy per group), paper, pencils.
Group activity: Coloured A2 sugar paper (blue and white), adhesive, scissors, coloured pens, rulers, the Encarta CD-ROM (Microsoft) or similar.

PREPARATION

You may want to carry out this exercise as a comprehension quiz with groups in competition, in which case the children could be arranged in mixed-ability groups for a more even distribution of ability. Alternatively, you may prefer to distribute copies of page 73 for the children to complete individually.

Vocabulary

Arctic, habitat, predator, prey, producer, consumer, temperature

BACKGROUND

All habitats on Earth share basic features: an energy source (usually, but not always, the Sun), producers and consumers. This lesson deals with the Arctic environment and the feeding relationships between species that inhabit it.

Did you know? Many people mistakenly believe that polar bears eat penguins. They don't – not just because they can't get the wrappers off, but because polar bears are found in the Arctic (near the North Pole) and penguins are found in the Antarctic (near the South Pole).

INTRODUCTION

Ask the children to remind you what organisms that can make their own food are called (producers). Ask them where most producers get their energy from (the Sun). Explain that almost all habitats on Earth share certain features. They are going to hear a description of a habitat they are not familiar with. They will need to be detectives: to listen to the details of the habitat and try to spot the different parts of a food chain. Explain that you will be quizzing the class at the end to see which group can get the most questions right. (Obviously you would not want a group of less able children to be made to feel self-conscious, so you may want to redistribute the children into balanced teams before you begin.)

MAIN TEACHING ACTIVITY

Read out the information on page 73 after explaining that there will be a quiz at the end. Ask each table group a question on which to confer before their spokesperson answers, or distribute copies of the page so that the children can work through them at their own pace. The answers are: 1. Tundra; 2. Heather, lichen; 3. Deer, Arctic hares; 4. Polar bear; 5. Thick coat for warmth, white for camouflage, claws to grip ice, powerful jaws to kill prey, broad legs to use like paddles when swimming, small ears to reduce heat loss, hibernating during the coldest months; 6. Ringed seals, walrus; 7. From the Sun; 8. Plankton → fish or crabs → ringed seal or walrus → polar bear.

GROUP ACTIVITY

Ask each group to produce an illustration of the habitat, the different species found there and the food chain (using arrows to show the flow of energy). They can use blue and white sugar paper as backgrounds. They may wish to find out more about each species by referring to a CD-ROM such as *Encarta*). Ask them to label the energy source, producer, consumers, herbivores, carnivores and top predator on their drawings.

DIFFERENTIATION

Less able children may need help with reading through the information sheet if this is how you decide to use the sheet. It may be better for each group to read through the sheet together.

ASSESSMENT

Check that the children have successfully identified a producer, a primary consumer and a predator in the Arctic habitat. Can they construct an appropriate food chain, using arrows to indicate the flow of energy?

PLENARY

Explain that many Arctic regions have oil reserves buried under the sea bed that could be developed in the future. Ask: *What problems could building and using oil rigs cause for this habitat?* Many people believe that the Antarctic should be preserved as an unspoiled sanctuary for wildlife – do the class agree?

OUTCOMES

● Can describe the features of an unfamiliar habitat.
● Can construct food chains from information about an unfamiliar habitat.

LINKS

Geography: polar regions.

LESSON 4

OBJECTIVE

● To know that plants and animals have special features that help them survive in a habitat.

RESOURCES

Main teaching activity: A cactus and a geranium (or similar).
Group activity: Sugar or A3 paper, coloured pencils, scissors, adhesive; a tray of wildlife pictures (see Preparation); reference books and CD-ROMs on world wildlife; sources of wildlife pictures (such as exotic plant catalogues, old infant reference books, wildlife park visitor resources).

PREPARATION

Prepare a resource tray with pictures of animals (such as a camel, lion, shark, eagle, owl, crocodile, jellyfish, mosquito, polar bear, hedgehog, seal) and plants (such as a cactus, Venus fly-trap, water lily). The pictures can be stuck on card and laminated.

Vocabulary
survive, adaptation, adapt, environment, habitat

BACKGROUND

To survive, every living thing must possess features that make it suited to its environment. For example, a seal has a streamlined body and powerful flippers to help it move quickly through the water, sharp teeth for grasping and eating its prey (fish, crabs and so on), blubber to keep it warm, and a clear skin (membrane) that covers its eyes when it is swimming. When a living thing has developed a special feature to help it survive, this feature is called an **adaptation** (since it enables the organism to **adapt** to its environment).

INTRODUCTION

Ask the children to imagine that they are going scuba diving off a coral reef in the Caribbean. What will they need? They will probably mention air cylinders for breathing, a wetsuit to keep them warm, flippers for swimming, goggles to protect their eyes, and perhaps a knife to use for protection or as a tool. Now ask them to think of a shark living in the same ocean. *How does it survive?* Humans need special equipment to prepare themselves for new environments, but the animals already living there have their own special adaptations.

MAIN TEACHING ACTIVITY

Explain that this lesson is about surviving in the wild. Show the group a cactus and a geranium (or similar plant). Ask them which they think would survive better in a desert. Write the word 'Cactus' in the middle of the board, and ask them to suggest what about it suits it to a life in the desert. Write the suggestions as a brainstorm around the word 'Cactus'. Ideas might include: no true leaves (the leaves of cacti have changed to become spines, reducing water loss); a thick fleshy stem for storing water; long roots that can reach down to water trapped in the rocks; furrows in the stem to channel water and hold the tiny breathing pores; spines to ward off grazing animals. Tell the children that all the special features they have mentioned are called **adaptations**, which means special features that help a plant or animal to survive in its habitat. Write the word 'Adaptations' under the cactus brainstorm.

Now suggest a seal as another example of an organism that is suited to its environment. Ask the children to tell you what special adaptations the seal displays. (See 'Background' for ideas.)

GROUP ACTIVITY

The children should work in pairs to choose an animal or plant from the resource cards. On a sheet of sugar paper or A3 paper, they should draw a picture (or stick one cut from an old book or magazine) of the animal or plant they have chosen. Make this more fun by including dangerous animals such as the great white shark, piranha fish, golden eagle or Portuguese man o' war. Among the plants, include the Venus fly-trap or another 'carnivorous' plant – if you have specimens available, so much the better! Around each drawing, the children should label the special adaptations.

DIFFERENTIATION

You may want to give the more able children a brain-teaser: *Which animal is responsible for the greatest number of human deaths on Earth?* Perhaps they will be surprised when you tell them it is the mosquito. *What special features does it have?* Leave them to find this out, using reference books or a CD-ROM such as *Encarta*. Less able children may benefit from prompts such as: *How does the animal feed/move/defend itself?*

ASSESSMENT

You may want to ask each pair to present their chosen example to the group. Check that they can name appropriate adaptations and explain how they help the organism to survive.

PLENARY

Ask the class: *Humans are relatively defenceless, lacking claws and sharp teeth – so why have we been quite successful as hunters?* (Because of our behavioural adaptations: we can work and communicate in teams, and invent weapons. Also, our hands are physically suited to holding and using tools.)

Discuss how 'carnivorous' plants such as the Venus fly-trap, sundew and bladderwort are able to survive in nutrient-poor soils. They still make their own food by photosynthesis; but by snacking on small insects, they obtain the additional nitrates they need for healthy growth.

OUTCOME

● Recognise features of plant and animal species that help them to survive in their habitats.

LINKS

History: early humans.

LESSON 5

OBJECTIVE
● To use simple environmental survey techniques.

RESOURCES

Main teaching activity: Samples of the leaves of the most common plant species found in your study area; a quadrat frame, photocopiable page 74.
Group activity: Quadrat frames (one per pair, ideally 25cm × 25cm); record sheets (one per pair), with six 5 × 5 squares drawn on squared paper; long tape measures, field identification guides for wild flowers, squared paper, clipboards.

PREPARATION

Before going into 'the field', you may want to familiarise yourself with the most common plant species the children are likely to encounter. It would be useful to photocopy page 74, which provides space for children to record their observations, and also shows how to make percentage calculations). The children will need to be suitably dressed for outdoors.

BACKGROUND

This lesson and Lesson 6 provide ideas to help teachers in England looking to address QCA Unit 5/6H in Year 6 through an environmental fieldwork project.

A **quadrat** is a square frame (which can be a wire coathanger bent into a square approximately 25cm × 25cm) that is placed on the ground. The observer has a sheet of squared paper with boxes drawn on it (for example, a 5 × 5 square), and on this draws a sketch of the ground inside the quadrat showing the proportion covered by each type of vegetation. For example, of 25 squares, 5 might be bare ground, 9 moss, 7 broad-leafed plantain and 4 grass. It is now possible to estimate the percentage of the quadrat covered by each type of vegetation. If your grid on the paper is 5 × 5, then each square is 4% of the total (since 4 × 25 = 100). So, in our example, bare ground occupies 5 × 4 = 20% of the total – and even a biologist can work that out, so the children should have no trouble. They can design a key for their quadrat sketches, using symbols to represent each type of plant found. Quadrats are widely used for habitat surveys: the author has used them in the mountains of Guatemala, ecologists use quadrats to study the ocean floor, and researchers have dropped huge frames onto the rainforest canopy from hot air balloons.

Quadrats can be used in a number of ways. They can be thrown randomly onto the ground to take a 'sample', or they can be used along a line (which is called a **line transect**). Line transects are useful for looking at trends in vegetation – for example, how the plant species change as you move from a sand dune into adjacent heathland, or from a meadow into a nearby woodland. A tape measure can be laid on the ground along the line to be studied. At regular intervals (such as every 2m), a quadrat is laid on the ground and the vegetation is recorded. The changes in the abundance and distribution of species recorded in this way can then be studied.

INTRODUCTION

Ask the children to imagine hot air balloons above the Amazon rainforest, lowering a huge square frame onto the trees. Explain that scientists have done this to study small sections of the rainforest in detail, in order to learn more about this fragile habitat. Say that the frames are called quadrats, and that smaller quadrats can be used to study habitats around the school.

MAIN TEACHING ACTIVITY

Show the children one of the quadrats and explain how it is used. Draw a 5 × 5 grid on the board and explain that when they look down on the quadrat, they will have to use the grid to help them sketch the quadrat, with different areas covered by different types of plant. Talk them through making a key and using different shadings to indicate different plant species. Explain how the use of quadrats along a line (making a line transect) can be useful in learning about changes in vegetation between different areas. Perhaps they can suggest reasons why the plants found on the ground might be different in different places (changes in soil type, level of acidity or alkalinity, water content, degree of sunlight or shade, whether the plants are regularly cut by a lawnmower or grazed by sheep, and so on).

GROUP ACTIVITY

Give each pair a record sheet and ask them to carry out a line transect, placing a tape measure across the field (you will probably want different pairs to use the same tape measure, perhaps starting at either end). They will need to place the quadrat at 2m intervals. Ask them to try to identify the plant species they find, using reference guides.

Ask the children to work out the percentage of ground covered by each plant species in each quadrat. They can do this by counting each of the 25 squares as 4% of the total – so they multiply the number of squares covered by 4. If only half a square is covered, it can be counted as 2%. If more than half a square is covered, it is usually rounded up as being a whole square. The children should check that their total for each quadrat is 100%. Give each pair a copy of page 74 to help them with their calculations.

Ask: *Which type of plant is most common? Which is least common?* The children should draw a sketch of the leaves and/or flower of the most common species they find. On a school field, the grass species will be difficult to identify, but it may be possible on the uncut margins.

DIFFERENTIATION

Less able children could record three common plant species by name and record all others as 'other'. More able children could draw bar charts showing the abundance of different species.

ASSESSMENT

Check that the children have understood how to estimate the abundance of different plants by using their quadrat work as a reference.

PLENARY

What other information could be collected along a line transect? Elicit suggestions such as: soil samples for analysis, water content, variety of invertebrates (caught in pitfall traps).

OUTCOME

● Can use quadrats and line transects as a way of collecting environmental data.

LINKS

Maths: estimates, percentages.

LESSON 6		
Objectives	● To develop their investigative skills. ● To develop their understanding of environmental survey techniques.	
Resources	Wildflower identification guides or keys; long tape measures, quadrats, photocopiable page 74.	
Main activity	There are a number of possible options for this lesson; the investigation you choose will depend on the environment around the school. If you have access to an area of land where the grass is often allowed to grow to full height, the children can carry out a transect from the trampled ground near a path to the uncut grass. Two common types of plantain are found in grassland. The ribwort plantain (*Plantago lanceolata*) has thin leaves and grows tall in long grass; it competes well for light and is not easily outshaded. The greater plantain (*Plantago major*) has shorter, broader, rounded leaves that grow flat to the ground. It is very resistant to trampling and thrives near footpaths; but in long grass it is soon shaded out due to its flat leaves, and so is far less common. The children could develop an investigation and predict how the frequency of each species will change as they move from short trampled grass to longer grass along a line transect. 　Alternatively, they could carry out a line transect from an open area of a field into the shade and see how the abundance of moss changes. Can they explain their observations? If it is possible to organise (perhaps by contacting an outdoor education centre), the children could investigate how plant species change as you go from meadowland to woodland, or from marshland to forest.	
Differentiation	Less able children could use page 74 to help them develop their planning.	
Assessment	Can the children make clear predictions and draw conclusions from their fieldwork?	
Plenary	Before the construction of a new road, a number of possible routes are considered. Ask the children why environmental surveys are needed to help in the decision-making process. (They provide data on the abundance and distribution of plant and animal species in an area, so that its conservation value can be assessed.) The most important sites in terms of conservation value are called Sites of Special Scientific Interest, or SSSIs. Do the children know of any of these sites in the local area?	
Outcomes	● Can carry out a line transect and quadrat study. ● Are aware of the use of these as environmental survey techniques.	

LESSON 7

OBJECTIVE

● To know that different soils can be compared.

RESOURCES

Main teaching activity: A piece of rock (sandstone would be ideal), a hammer, a bucket of clay-rich soil (labelled A), a bucket of sandy soil (labelled B), a bag of composted material (such as a growbag) or peat, 1p and 2p coins, sand, dry peas, a bag of flour, two beakers, newspaper, rubber gloves, an apron, spatulas or spoons, water.
Group activity: A bucket of loamy soil (labelled C); boiling tubes (ideally) or test tubes, test tube racks, spatulas (these may be borrowed from your local secondary school); water in beakers (or access to taps), hand lenses (one per pair), a bucket, paper, writing materials.

PREPARATION

Draw a copy of the soil settling diagram (see opposite) on the board, without labels. Cover desks and tables with newspaper.

> **Vocabulary**
>
> rock, fragments, air spaces, particles, sandy, clay, humus, nutrients, texture, loam

BACKGROUND

Soils are made from weathered rock fragments and decayed plant and animal remains (called **humus**). In between the grains or particles of soil are **air spaces**. Water is an additional and very important component of soils. The texture of a soil depends on the size of the grains. **Sand** is made from large grains and holds little water. Sandy soils feel dry and gritty. **Silt** is the name given to smaller mineral particles found in soils. The smallest kind of soil particles are **clay**. When they are dry, the particles in clay soils clump together, making it feel lumpy. When they are wet, they make the soil feel sticky. In water, clay particles make the water cloudy and take time to settle (they are called **suspended particles**). Clay is important in helping a soil to keep some of its water, and so helping plants to grow after rains have passed. Ideal soils are a combination of sand, clay, silt and humus, with spaces for air to enter the soil – these are usually called loams (there are different types). Small invertebrates play an essential role in giving soil its structure and in recycling nutrients (this process will be looked at in more detail later).

NB Tell the children not to handle the soil if they have open cuts on their hands. They must wash their hands at the end of the lesson. Also, make sure the children don't flush waste soil down the sinks at the end of the investigation – or your school caretaker may take you off his or her Christmas card list.

INTRODUCTION

Gather the children around a table that has been covered with newspaper and on which there is a piece of rock and a container filled with sand. Explain that you are going to look at soil. *What is soil?* If they suggest that it is just dirt or mud, explain that some of the bits in soil come from rocks that have been broken up by ice and water; the small bits are carried by the wind or water until they settle in layers. If you have a piece of sandstone, tap it gently with a hammer to show particles crumbling off. Now display the sand. *This is made out of bits of rock – but is it soil?* Explain that soils contain **humus** – the name given to bits of plant remains, such as rotting leaves. If you have a growbag handy, take some out and show it to the children, explaining that the peat is made from partially decomposed plant remains that are full of the nutrients plants need to survive. Mix some sand and peat, and ask the class whether *now* you have made soil. Explain that the missing final ingredient is water, which is vital for all plant and animal life. Air trapped in the larger spaces in the soil is also needed to support life. Check that the children know the main ingredients of soils: rock particles, humus, water and air.

MAIN TEACHING ACTIVITY

Lift up two buckets: one labelled A (sandy soil) and another labelled B (clay soil). Explain that there are different types of soil. The different sizes of particles mean that the soils look and feel very different. For the next part, you may need an apron or lab coat (and gloves if you have any open cuts.) Lift some soil out of bucket A and ask what the children notice. (It is grainy.) Say that the feel of a soil is called its **texture**. Add some water to it and try to roll it into a ball. *Does it* *hold its shape?* Now lift some dry soil out of bucket B and crumble it in your fingers. At first, it appears to be made from bigger particles than the other soil – but wet it, and show what it looks like in your hands. Try to mould the wet soil into a ball shape. Tell the children that one of the soils is a clay soil and one is a sandy soil. Which do they think is which? Explain that the clay soil is made from microscopic particles that clump together when the soil is dry, but that when wet make the soil very heavy and sticky. Have they ever walked in a clay soil and nearly lost their wellies in the mud?

Now show the class two beakers: one full of peas, the other full of flour. Pour some water into each. *Which lets the water drain through more easily?* (The peas.) *Why?* (There are bigger gaps between the particles.) *Which holds more water?* (The flour.) *Which do you think behaves more like a sandy soil?* (The peas.) *Why?* (Sandy soils drain quickly.)

Explain that to farmers, the texture of a soil is very important: clay soils can become waterlogged, whereas soils that are too sandy dry out quickly. Ideal soils are a mixture of sand and clay, and are called **loams**. Show the class bucket C (a loamy soil). Tell them that they will now look at this soil.

GROUP ACTIVITY

Working in pairs, the children quarter-fill a test tube with loam using a spatula. They then fill the test tube up to about the three-quarters mark with water. With the palm of one hand (or a thumb) over the end of the tube, shake it a few times and then leave it to stand in a test tube rack. When they have done this, they can use what they observe and what has been discussed in the lesson to copy the diagram from the board and fill in the labels (working as a pair or individually). The diagram below shows what they will observe.

At the end, remind the children to tip the contents of their test tubes into a spare bucket – not down the drain. Remind them to wash their hands.

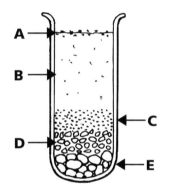

Settling of soil
A – floating humus
B – suspended clay particles
C – fine silt
D – sand particles
E – small stones

DIFFERENTIATION

Less able children could be given a copy of the soil diagram with some labels provided and some blanks left for them to complete. Alternatively, you may want to set up a larger version of the soil experiment so that you can point out the layering. Arrange 1p and 2p coins on a desk to illustrate the air gaps between soil particles.

ASSESSMENT

Read through the children's completed photocopiable sheets, correcting any mistakes or misunderstandings as they arise.

PLENARY

Heavy machinery or trampling can squash the soil, reducing the number of air spaces. Ask why this might cause a problem. (It makes it more difficult for the water to drain away, and there is less air available to support soil organisms that are essential for the breakdown of plant material. This is one reason why farmers use tractors with wide back wheels, so that the soil is less compressed.) Ask what a gardener should do if their soil is a heavy clay and is poor at letting water drain away. (Add some sand.)

OUTCOMES

● Can compare features of different soil types.
● Can interpret a model of the soil.

LINKS

Unit 2, Lesson 8.

LESSON 8

Objective	● To be aware of the variety of animal life found in soil.
Resources	A clamp and stand, a gardening sieve, a lamp on a stand, a funnel, a beaker, leaf litter, freshly collected soil; a 'wormery' made from a glass tank (at least 30cm in depth) containing soil interspersed with layers of chalk and sand, with leaves on the top; hand lenses, brushes, Petri dishes, an invertebrate identification guide, insect pitfall traps (see Lesson 1), plastic margarine tubs, trays, white paper, a microscope, fresh topsoil.
Main activity	This lesson gives children an opportunity to explore the rich variety of life found on and within soils. Take the children outside with margarine tubs (one per pair) to collect leaf litter and soil. (Make sure they have no open cuts on their hands, and that they wash their hands before they next eat.) If possible, encourage them to explore under stones or rotten wood for larger invertebrates. They could use pitfall traps to collect larger insects living on the soil. Back in the classroom, they can spread the leaf litter and soil onto white paper in a tray and brush any small invertebrates into a Petri dish. They can use an identification guide to name their specimens, draw a sketch of each one and explain where it was found. Ask them to try to find out which are herbivores and which are carnivores. As a class demonstration, set up a 'Tullgren funnel' to collect small invertebrates. Place topsoil and leaf litter in a gardening sieve and clamp it with a funnel underneath leading to a glass beaker. Set up a lamp above the sieve. The heat and light produced by the lamp should cause the animals in the soil to move downwards until they fall through the sieve, down the funnel and into the beaker. The children can attempt to identify them later. Set up a wormery (see Resources). This will enable the class to observe over the following weeks the important role of worms as mixers and fertilisers of the soil: they pull leaves down into their burrows to feed. To collect worms, add 50ml of washing-up liquid to 10 litres of water and pour it gradually onto 1m² of soil. As the worms come up to the surface, rinse them in water and place them in the wormery. Leave a microscope set up with a fresh sample of topsoil in view. Ask the children to look and try to spot more soil organisms. Ask them to draw a cross-section picture of 'The busy world of the soil'.
Differentiation	Less able children could name and sketch just one example of an animal that lives on or in the soil, and add this to their cross-section. More able children could use library reference books or CD-ROMs to find out more about earthworms: *How do they feed, move through the soil, reproduce? Why do farmers and gardeners think they are vital for a healthy soil?*
Assessment	Each child should be able to describe three ways of collecting invertebrates. Can they name an example of an invertebrate found using each method?
Plenary	Ask the children to give you a summary of the different invertebrates they have found. Explain that along with decomposers, they play a vital role in recycling nutrients. Plants also play a vital role in binding the soil and protecting it from erosion (being washed or blown away). Ask the children to suggest why it is so important for farmers to try to reduce soil erosion.
Outcomes	● Can describe different methods for collecting invertebrates. ● Are aware that soils support a variety of life.

LESSON 9

OBJECTIVE
● To know that different plants grow better in different soil conditions.

RESOURCES

Main teaching activity: A dandelion (pulled up with roots intact), a heather, a Venus fly-trap, a cactus, a marram grass, some lichen (from a stone surface), some moss, a bag of peat, a beaker of sand, a bag of lime.

Group activities: 1. Slides of dandelion roots (or dandelions, tiles, knives and slides), hand lenses and/or microscopes, paper, pencils. **2.** Paper and pens or a computer and DTP software.

PREPARATION

Collect the plants, peat, sand and lime from a garden centre. The scientific equipment could be borrowed from your local secondary school. If possible, prepare a number of microscope slides with dandelion roots. Make sure the children take care when handling knives or slides; they will need close supervision. Warn them never to reflect the image of the Sun in a microscope mirror.

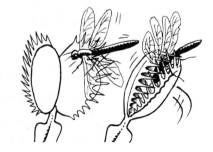

Vocabulary

surface area, absorb, root hairs, acid, alkaline, minerals, anchor

BACKGROUND

The roots of plants provide anchorage and a large surface area over which the plant can absorb water and essential nutrients. The swollen roots of some plants are used as food storage depots.

Plants have different tolerances of soil conditions. Lichens grow on bare rock (though strictly speaking, they are not true plants but a fungus and an alga in partnership). Marram grass grows well in sand. Cacti survive in drought-stricken landscapes. Willows grow on waterlogged riverbanks. The Venus fly-trap thrives in nutrient-poor soils, obtaining the nutrients it needs from invertebrate snacks. Mosses can only survive in damp conditions. Heather grows well in acid soils, which are unsuitable for many other species. Plants are as varied as animals in their needs.

The factors that vary between soils include pH (how acid or alkaline they are), temperature, water content, humus content and texture (size of grains). The pH can be found by adding a sample of soil to a test tube, adding water, shaking it and then adding drops of universal indicator. Peaty soils are acid; soils rich in lime are alkaline. Find out the pH of the soil around the school. If you have any hydrangeas, find out whether these are also good indicators of the pH of a soil. Do the petals grow red or pink in acid soils and blue in alkaline soils?

INTRODUCTION

You may want to divide this into two different lessons if time is short. Show or remind the children how to set up a microscope ready to view a specimen.

MAIN TEACHING ACTIVITY – PART 1

Ask the children: *How do plants take in the water and nutrients they need?* Hopefully, they will refer to the roots. *Plants use their roots to absorb what they need from the soil, but the roots do another job – what is this?* (They anchor the plant to the ground, and can act as a storage site for food.) Show the children the dandelion with its roots intact. Explain that the branches give the roots a large **surface area** to absorb water and minerals. Show the children how to cut off one of the fine branches of the roots on a tile and then sandwich it between two slides, ready to be viewed under a microscope.

A simple way to explain surface area is to ask the children to hold out their hands in front of them, palms and fingers together. Ask them how much of their hands would be covered if they dipped them in paint. Now ask how much would be covered if they opened their hands and dipped them in the paint. What would happen if they opened up their fingers and dipped again? The roots of plants need as large a surface area as possible to take in water and dissolved minerals, so they divide into fine branches.

GROUP ACTIVITY 1

Let the children view the prepared microscope slides, prepare and view their own slides and/or use hand lenses to look at the roots close up. They should draw what they see. *What do you notice about the roots?* (They are covered in hairs, which further increase the surface area.)

MAIN TEACHING ACTIVITY – PART 2

Gather the children together and remind them of the work they have done on soils. Explain that plants are sensitive to soil conditions, and that different plants grow in different soils. One way that soils vary is in their pH (how acid or alkaline they are). To demonstrate this, add some peaty soil to a beaker of water and give it a swirl, then do the same to a sample of soil from the school grounds. Add universal indicator and match the colour formed to the indicator colour chart. *What does it show?* Explain that a pH of 1–6 is acidic, 7 is neutral and 8–14 is alkaline. Add some lime to a separate beaker of water and test this with the indicator. *What does it show? Why do you think gardeners add lime to acidic soils?* (The lime neutralises the acidity of the soil, making it more favourable to plants.)

Show an example of each plant as you explain the following: *Some plants (such as heather) thrive in acidic soils, but many others cannot survive there. Cacti survive in dry conditions – how is this possible?* (Long roots, spines instead of leaves to reduce water loss, a fleshy stem to store water.) *Venus fly-traps can survive in soils that are very poor in nutrients because of their ability to trap and consume insects. Lichens grow on bare rock, absorbing minerals from dissolved rock and moisture from the air. Mosses tend only to grow in damp conditions. Marram grass has a curled leaf to reduce water loss and strong roots that bind sand together.*

GROUP ACTIVITY 2

The children can pretend that they are answering questions on the problem page of a gardening magazine, such as *My soil is very sandy. What plants could I grow?* They should invent and answer a question about each soil type that the lesson has dealt with. They could use a DTP program to present their work in a magazine format.

DIFFERENTIATION

Less able children could be given a list of soil types and asked to name one plant that is adapted to each soil type (for example, 'Nutrient-poor soil – Venus fly-trap').

ASSESSMENT

Can the children describe ways in which soils may vary; name a plant that may suit a particular soil type; explain clearly why plants have roots?

PLENARY

Explain that fumes from burning fossil fuels (coal, oil and natural gas) combine with rainwater to make it more acidic. Rainwater is naturally slightly acidic because carbon dioxide from the air dissolves in it. *Why might this 'acid rain' cause problems for plants?*

As an extension, the children could find out how many different types of lichen are growing on old stonework around the school. Lichens are good indicators of local air quality: the cleaner the air is, the greater the number of different types of lichen there will usually be.

OUTCOMES

- Know that different plants are adapted to living in different types of soil.
- Can describe the functions of roots.

LESSON 10

OBJECTIVE

- To know that the decay caused by micro-organisms is useful in the environment.

RESOURCES

Group activity: Photocopiable page 75 (one copy per child), pens.
Plenary: Assorted rinsed litter (cans, bottles, crisp wrappers, newspaper, half an apple) in a tray, for demonstration.

BACKGROUND

Vocabulary

decomposers, decay, nutrients, microbes, recycling, biodegradable, non-biodegradable

In 25–30g of soil, there are estimated to be over 4000 million tiny organisms. These micro-organisms (or microbes) play a vital role in breaking down organic substances and freeing nutrients that are needed by plants. In rainforests, the soils are particularly poor because the rain quickly leaches away the nutrients. **Decomposers** breaking down dead plants and animals provide the main source of important soil nutrients, and the buttress roots of the forest spread wide to take in these nutrients. Decomposers include fungi and bacteria that can travel easily through the air and settle on dead material. Both release **enzymes**: special organic chemicals that help to break apart the remains. The rain washes the released nutrients into the soil, while the bacteria and fungi form the start of new food chains. Decomposers are vital in keeping the cycle of life going.

Did you know?

- Compost heaps get very hot inside, and in the winter they sometimes appear to be steaming. The heat is a result of the activity of billions of decomposers.
- Decomposers work best when the compost is well ventilated – just like us, most microbes need oxygen to stay alive.
- Water treatment works rely on microbes to break up the organic material in sewage. The microbes are encouraged to reproduce inside warm tanks that have oxygen bubbled through.
- Microbes are also used to clean up oil spills. In delicate coastal environments, fertilisers are sometimes sprayed on to the rocks to encourage bacteria to feed on the oil and break it up.

INTRODUCTION

Gather the children together. Begin by saying: *The world is not littered with the dead bodies of pterodactyls and mammoths, dodos and sabre-toothed tigers. Why not?* Hopefully, the suggestions offered will include the idea that dead things rot or decay.

MAIN TEACHING ACTIVITY

Explain that this lesson is about decomposers – it is going to be a rotten lesson. Ask the children whether they have a compost heap at home. *Do you know what one is? Can you describe it?* Remind them of the work they have done on soils. *What is the plant material found in soils called?* (Humus.) Explain that when this material decomposes, it releases important nutrients into the soil. **Decomposers** (like the mould on stale bread) play a vital role in recycling the nutrients that are locked up in the dead bodies of animals and plants. These nutrients are released into the soil, and can be taken up through the roots of plants. Plants need nitrates, phosphates, iron compounds and potassium compounds for healthy growth. Decomposers help to provide these.

GROUP ACTIVITY

Give the children a copy each of page 75. They should label the diagram to show how decomposers return nutrients to the soil, then answer the questions about the action of microbes in a compost heap.

DIFFERENTIATION

Remind less able children that the decay in a compost heap is caused by microbes, which are living things. *What do they need to stay alive?* Ask more able children to explain why compost heaps sometimes steam in the winter. (Heat produced by the activity of microbes.)

ASSESSMENT

Check that the children understand that microbes are living things, and that they need oxygen, moisture and warmth to be active.

PLENARY

Explain that 'biodegradable' is the term used for materials that can decay within a few years. Non-biodegradable materials are those that either do not decay or take a very long time to decay. *Which of these two types of material is a good food for microbes? Some manufacturers have made plastic bags that are biodegradable – what is the advantage of this?*

With the children contributing suggestions, sort a collection of litter into 'biodegradable' and 'non-biodegradable' materials. Ask the children to complete page 75 by sorting the litter in the picture. (Non-biodegradable: soft drink can, jam jar, plastic drink bottle, burger container (compressed polystyrene), crisp packet, sweet wrapper. Biodegradable: matches, chip wrapper, apple core.) *What can we do with items of litter that are non-biodegradable, such as glass bottles or steel cans?* (Recycle them.) *What materials do your family recycle?*

OUTCOME

● Understand that the decay caused by micro-organisms allows nutrients to be recycled.

LINKS

Unit 2, Lesson 8: nutrients in the soil.

LESSON 11

OBJECTIVES

● To know that micro-organisms cause many diseases.

RESOURCES

Group activity: Photocopiable page 76, photocopied onto card and cut up (one section per group); paper, writing materials. The books *Horrible Science: Deadly Diseases* and *Suffering Scientists* and *Horrible History: The Measly Middle Ages*, published by Scholastic, will be entertaining and useful sources of reference material for yourself and the children.

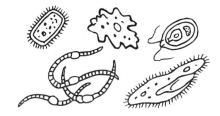

BACKGROUND

Micro-organisms are often called 'microbes' – a convenient name for any living thing that is too small to be seen clearly by the human eye. The category is huge, and the children only need to be aware that it includes fungi, bacteria and viruses. Before micro-organisms could be seen under a microscope, the causes of many diseases remained a mystery and were the basis of many superstitions. The first bacteria observed under a microscope were seen in 1676 by a Dutch scientist called Leeuwenhoek, who was looking at food samples taken from between his teeth. (Don't try this at home.) A combination of microscopic observation and experiment enabled scientists to demonstrate and explain how contagious illnesses spread. This lesson will help the children to see how ideas about microbes and diseases have developed through history.

INTRODUCTION

Ask the children: *Why is it considered a good thing to cover your mouth when you cough?* You may wish to ask them why we are taught to wash our hands after going to the toilet. Both questions should lead to the idea of germs. *What are germs?* Make it clear that germs are too small to be seen by the human eye, and so they are known scientifically as **micro-organisms**. They can also be called microbes. Our hair, skin, mouths and even intestines have microbes living inside them – most cause us no harm, and many are helpful to us. However, some microbes can cause illness and even death.

MAIN TEACHING ACTIVITY

Explain that people haven't always known about microbes. People were once very superstitious about the causes of diseases – for example, 'flu is short for influenza, which is derived from the old belief that the illness was caused by sleeping outside under the influence of the stars! Today, we know about how diseases spread and how to reduce the harmful effects of certain microbes.

Tell the children that they are going to work in groups to find out something about the history of our knowledge of microbes and diseases. You may wish to read through the whole factfile on page 76 as a class before you begin, or to keep the paragraphs separate until the children present their sketches.

GROUP ACTIVITY

Divide the children into seven groups and give each group a card copied from page 76. Each group should develop a role-play sketch to show one of the discoveries that have helped us to understand microbes and how diseases are spread. Encourage them to take roles and to make their sketch entertaining. When they are ready (after 20 minutes, or however long you feel they need), call each group in order of date to present their sketch. They may want to prepare scripts.

DIFFERENTIATION

Some groups will need help with reading through the text and dramatising it. Prompt them with questions such as: *What was the idea? How was it tried out? Did it work?*

ASSESSMENT

At the start of the Plenary session, ask the children to place the key events in the understanding of diseases on a timeline. Note whether they understand and can sum up these events.

PLENARY

Explain that our understanding of diseases is based on the research and evidence accumulated by scientists over hundreds of years. This process has enabled scientists to develop ideas that we call 'theories', which may explain what is known. Once a theory has been put forward, scientists try to prove or disprove it.

OUTCOMES

● Know that many diseases are caused by micro-organisms.
● Can describe how a scientific theory is based on evidence.

LINKS

History: the Black Death.
PSHE: immunisation.

LESSON 12

OBJECTIVE
● To know about the range of diseases caused by micro-organisms.

RESOURCES

Main teaching activity: A red balloon, split pins, beads, cotton wool, a football.
Group activities: 1. A worksheet (see Preparation), writing materials. **2.** Photocopiable page 77 (one copy per child), writing materials, graph paper (or a computer and data-handling program).

PREPARATION

Fill a red balloon with as many split pins as you can, then inflate it. Make a worksheet for Group activity 1 (see below).

BACKGROUND

Vocabulary

virus,
bacteria,
fungus,
disease

What we call 'germs' are usually viruses, bacteria, fungi and protists (one-celled organisms) that can cause diseases. Fungi only cause a few diseases in humans, but they cause many diseases in the crops that humans grow. The destruction of potatoes by a fungus caused the Irish potato famine, and a fungus known as 'brown rust' has wiped out whole crops of wheat. In this lesson, the children will learn the names 'virus', 'bacteria' and 'fungus' and the name of a disease caused by each. (For further information, see the Main teaching activity below.)

INTRODUCTION

Ask the children: *Has anyone here had chicken-pox? Hands up!* Next, ask whether anyone has had a sore throat; then whether anyone has had athlete's foot. Explain that these three diseases are caused by different kinds of microbes. Following on from Lesson 11, ask them to remind you what a microbe is. (A living thing too small to see with the naked eye.)

MAIN TEACHING ACTIVITY

Explain that you are going to talk about three kinds of microbe: bacteria, viruses and fungi.
1. Bacteria. Explain that our bodies are covered in bacteria! We are walking bacteria hotels. Ask the children to suggest reasons why we are a good habitat for bacteria. (We are warm; our skin is sometimes moist; and best of all, when we sweat we release salts and the chemical urea – not so good for someone sitting close to us, but a feast for bacteria!) Most of the bacteria covering us are harmless; some living deep in our intestines are actually very helpful, providing vitamins that our bodies need. Some bacteria are not so useful, however. Bacteria living in the mouth produce acid as they feed on leftover sugars, and this can cause tooth decay. Explain that in the right conditions, one bacterium can divide to make two bacteria every 20 minutes (you will return to this idea later in the lesson). Bacteria cause food poisoning, sore throats, tetanus and many other infections. They can be seen under a normal microscope. Many bacteria are destroyed by antibiotics: drugs derived from moulds (and other sources) that can attack bacteria.
2. Fungi. Explain that fungi can cause terrible devastation to crops, but only cause a few diseases in humans – the most common example being athlete's foot. *Have any of you had this? How did you get rid of it? Why are conditions between the toes so good for this?* (Warm, moist, dark conditions.) Fungi can cause some types of throat infection. They can usually be seen easily – for example, mould on stale bread. Some moulds are very useful, such as yeast in bread or the veins in blue cheeses.
3. Viruses. The word 'virus' comes from the Greek word for poison. Viruses are not, strictly speaking, alive. They are little bags of trouble that inject their genes into cells, tricking them into making more copies of the virus. Eventually they burst out of the cell. Present the balloon full of split pins and pop it dramatically to show the damage that viruses do to our cells. Viruses are bad news – except that sometimes, they kill harmful bacteria. Antibiotics will not work against them: we have to wait for our body to learn how to fight the invasion! Viruses cause colds, 'flu, German measles, chicken-pox and polio. The HIV virus causes a loss of immunity that can lead to the syndrome known as AIDS.

To reinforce the contrasts of size and appearance, present the following models: a football as a bacterium; a ball of cotton wool as a fungus; a split pin as a virus.

GROUP ACTIVITIES

1. Give the children a worksheet with the table shown overleaf and the following list of words and phrases, which they can use to fill in the blanks: fungus, bacteria, athlete's foot, rust on wheat, reproduces inside cells, pneumonia, sore throat.

Type of microbe	Features	Examples of diseases caused
A	Can be treated with antibiotics	B
Virus	C	AIDS, chicken-pox
D	related to the mould found on old bread	E

The answers are: A = bacteria; B = pneumonia, sore throat; C = reproduces inside cells; D = fungus; E = athlete's foot, rust on wheat.

2. Explain that in the right conditions, one bacterium can divide to make two bacteria every 20 minutes. *If one bacterium causing sore throats lands in your throat at 10pm, how many could there be at 7am the next morning?* Give the children copies of page 77 and ask them to put their calculations into the chart. If possible, ask them to put these results onto a spreadsheet and generate a graph showing the growth of the colony of bacteria.

DIFFERENTIATION

2. Less able children could be asked to make calculations for a two-hour timespan only. Encourage them to use mental doubling techniques from numeracy work. More able children could carry out research (using reference books) to find out how our bodies fight infection.

ASSESSMENT

Have the children filled in the microbes and symptoms table accurately? Check to see how they have got on with the chart on page 77 – do they understand the principle?

PLENARY

Go through the answers to the Group activities. Relate the rate of growth of a bacterial colony to the fact that bacteria (like one-celled organisms) reproduce by dividing in half. Explain that our body has a system of specific defences or 'antibodies' that can halt most harmful intruders.

OUTCOME

● Can describe some diseases and identify their causes.

LINKS

Maths: doubling and halving.

LESSON 13

Objectives	● To know that mould on food is caused by micro-organisms. ● To plan and carry out a fair test.
Resources	Bread, small plastic self-sealing freezer bags, sticky tape, sticky labels, pens, beakers; photocopiable page 48 (the investigation guide sheet).

Main activity	Ask the children whether they have ever gone to eat a slice of bread and found it mouldy. *What kind of microbe is mould?* (A fungus.) Explain that eating some kinds of microbes is not dangerous: the acid in our stomachs kills most microbes before they can cause a problem. However, some kinds of microbe cause food poisoning, which can make us very sick – it can even be fatal. One type of bacteria, botulism, can reproduce *inside* tinned foods and is very dangerous indeed.
	    Tell the children that they are going to set up an investigation to look at what conditions are best for mould to grow in. Explain that once they are set up, the bags will be sealed and not reopened. Brainstorm ideas for designing fair tests. Ideas to investigate could include the temperature the bread is left at, whether the bread has been exposed to the air before the experiment and whether the bread is wet or dry.
	    Let the children work in groups to design and set up their experiments. Afterwards, make sure that they dispose of all samples carefully.

Differentiation	Some children will need additional guidance in setting out their ideas and forming a prediction based on what they know about microbes.
Assessment	Ask the children questions about their investigation, using the guidelines on photocopiable page 48.
Plenary	You may wish to leave the Plenary until the results have been collected, several days later. Review the children's experiments and findings. Ask them how to prevent food spoilage. They should suggest keeping food covered up and refrigerated.
Outcomes	● Can describe good practice for food hygiene. ● Can explain why food hygiene is necessary. ● Can plan and carry out a fair test.

LESSON 14

OBJECTIVE
● To know that yeast is a useful organism.

RESOURCES
Introduction: A bottle of beer, a loaf of bread.
Group activity: (For each group) six test tubes, six balloons of the same size, a test tube rack, fresh or dried yeast, sugar, teaspoons, a timer, thermometers, a kettle, measuring cylinders, a copy of photocopiable page 78. You may need to borrow some resources from a local secondary school, or to present the activity as a demonstration with one set of apparatus.

PREPARATION
Blow up the balloons and let them down again before the lesson, so that they will stretch easily. You may want to set up a microscope with some fresh yeast for the children to look at.

Vocabulary

yeast, fungus, fermentation, budding, carbon dioxide, alcohol, respire

BACKGROUND
Yeast is the name given to a particular type of single-celled fungus. It is often associated with brewing, as it has the ability to react with sugar to produce carbon dioxide and alcohol. We call this process **fermentation**. The production of carbon dioxide is also useful in bread-making, as it makes the bread rise.

INTRODUCTION
Put out a bottle of beer and a loaf of bread. Ask the children to guess what these have in common (this may prompt some interesting answers). Help them by saying that the answer is a type of microbe. If necessary, reveal the answer: yeast.

MAIN TEACHING ACTIVITY
Explain that yeast is a fungus, and that the children are going to find out what conditions are best for its growth and reproduction. Show them the apparatus they will need, and talk them through the experiment described on page 78.

GROUP ACTIVITY
Explain that when yeast is growing and multiplying, it **respires** – that is, it uses up sugar and oxygen to make energy, and releases the gas carbon dioxide. In this experiment, they are going to test in what conditions yeast is most active (and so makes the most carbon dioxide. Let the children set up, or demonstrate setting up, the experiment shown on page 78.

Encourage the children to record and explain their findings. These should be as follows. In tube A there is no change, because the yeast lacks water and remains inactive. In tube B there is no change, because the yeast is still inactive. In tube C a little carbon dioxide is produced, because the yeast slowly becomes active but lacks the sugar it needs to respire (make energy) and divide. In tube D carbon dioxide is rapidly produced (the balloon inflates), because the yeast has everything it needs to become active and reproduce. In tube E there is no change, because the yeast has been killed by the boiling water (if the balloon expands, it is probably because of the heated gas). In tube F a little carbon dioxide is produced, because the yeast becomes active more slowly – most living things become more active as the temperature reaches about 37°C.

DIFFERENTIATION
Prompt less able children by reminding them that yeast is a living organism. *What do all living things need to survive?* (Water, oxygen, warmth, a food source.)

ASSESSMENT
At the bottom of page 78, the children should write what conditions seem best for yeast to grow and reproduce, giving a reason for their answer. Use their answers in discussion to assess their understanding of the experiment and their ability to use their scientific knowledge.

PLENARY

Discuss the experiment and the children's answers (see Assessment). Ask the children to think why the yeast used in bread-making is left for a few hours in the bread mix before it is placed in the oven. (The yeast cells are active inside the dough mix, producing tiny pockets of carbon dioxide. Once the dough is placed in the oven, the yeast cells are killed and become part of the bread; but the bubbles expand in the heat, helping the bread to rise. So you shouldn't rush to get your dough in the oven – patience can be uplifting.)

OUTCOMES

- Can identify the conditions needed for yeast to grow and reproduce.
- Know the function of yeast in bread-making.

LINKS

Unit 4, Lessons 9, 15, 16: irreversible changes.

LESSON 15

Objective	● To know that micro-organisms are used in food production.
Resources	A broad bean or pea plant, wine, beer, yoghurt, butter, bread, Stilton cheese, vinegar, reference materials (such as books, CD-ROMs, the Internet); old magazines with pictures of different foods, relevant food labels, scissors, adhesive, sheets of A3 paper.
Main activity	Gather the class and place in front of them the resources you have collected. *What do all these things have in common?* Explain that they all depend on microbes. Bean and pea plants (legumes) have bacteria living in their roots (in nodules) as partners with the plant: the plant provides the bacteria with sugars and the bacteria make vital nitrates for the plant (see Unit 2, Lesson 8). Beer and wine rely on the fermentation process carried out by yeast (a fungus). Bacteria turn ethanol (an alcohol) into vinegar. Carbon dioxide produced by yeast helps bread to rise when baked. Bacteria make milk curdle because of the acid they produce. Adding flavouring to this curdled milk produces yoghurt. If the curdled milk is allowed to ripen in the presence of a mould, it turns into cheese. Different cheeses are made using different moulds; 'blue' cheeses have veins of mould running through them. Butter is made by churning cream that has soured under the action of bacteria. Bacteria and fungi have even been used to make protein as a meat substitute for humans.

Type of food	How microbes help
Pea and bean plants	Bacteria provide vital nitrates for their growth.
Wine, beer Vinegar Yoghurt Cheese Butter Bread Protein (meat) substitute	

	Ask the children to draw up a chart like the one shown above and work in pairs to fill in the blanks, using reference materials. They can then design a poster, *Making Meals with Microbes*, illustrating all the different ways that microbes are useful in making food. They can include food labels or pictures from magazines. Ask them to write a line under each picture explaining how microbes have helped.
Differentiation	Less able children may need help to find references for the food types; you may want to photocopy some resources for them. More able children could research the history of the use of microbes to make foods.
Assessment	Check in the Plenary session that the children know at least four different types of food made using microbes. From previous work, they should be able to explain how yeast causes bread to rise.
Plenary	Ask the children to feed back what they have learned about microbes and share examples of the display work produced. Now ask them to imagine that some cheese is left in the open. *What will happen to it?* Remind them that microbes eventually cause things to decay, and that the continual recycling of materials is necessary to provide the nutrients needed for new life.
Outcome	● Can describe how micro-organisms are used in food production.

LESSON 16

OBJECTIVES
● To assess the children's understanding of food chains and of adaptations.
● To assess the children's ability to plan an investigation and apply environmental survey techniques.

RESOURCES
1. Photocopiable page 79, pens. **2.** A4 lined paper, pens, photocopiable page 48 (optional).

INTRODUCTION
You may want to go through the terms covered in this unit that relate to food chains and adaptations. A word wall containing these terms would form a useful focus for the start of the lesson. You could give each group a selection of the vocabulary and ask them to share their understanding of each word.

ASSESSMENT ACTIVITY 1
Give the children a copy each of photocopiable page 79; let them work through it individually.

Answers
1. wheat → greenfly → carnivorous beetle → vole → hawk
2. P = wheat, H = greenfly.
3. The Sun provides energy for the producers to make food.
4. Powerful wings to hover and swoop, sharp eyesight for spotting prey, claws for grasping prey, hooked beak for tearing flesh.

Looking for levels
All the children should set out the organisms into a food chain, identifying the Sun as the source of energy. They should all identify at least two adaptations of the hawk. Most children should orientate the arrows in the food chain correctly to show the flow of energy through the chain, and should identify the producer. Most children should name four adaptations of the hawk. More able children might identify the consumers, top predator, carnivores and herbivore.

ASSESSMENT ACTIVITY 2
Ask the children to plan an investigation to find out whether dandelions grow longer stems when growing in long grass than they do in short grass. Prompt them to think about the equipment they will need, the measurements they will record, the number of samples they will need to take and so on (give general guidance rather than specific tips). They can write out their plan on a sheet of A4 paper, perhaps using the investigation planning sheet (page 48).

Looking for levels
All the children should suggest the use of a quadrat to survey areas of long grass and short grass. They should all refer to the need to make recordings of dandelion stem length and of the length of grass surrounding the dandelions. Most children should say how accurate the readings will need to be – for example, choosing to record in mm. Most children should explain that repeated recordings will be needed. More able children should specify that a large number of repeated measurements are needed, and mention the need to make sure that the results have not been unfairly influenced (for example, by shading from trees or the addition of lawn fertiliser).

PLENARY
Ask the children whether they think there is a link between length of grass and stem length in flowers. *Why do you think this? How might flowers with longer stems have an advantage?* (More obvious to pollinators and providing a better position for seed dispersal.)

Life in a hedgerow

Read the information below, then draw lines on the picture to show how the living things are linked together.

Most British hedgerows are very old and were made from hawthorn, because the spiky stems are useful as a barrier against livestock. The song thrush uses the cover of the hedgerow to build its nest, hidden from predators. It feeds on slugs and snails, which are herbivores that feed on the leaves of plants in the hedgerow. The thrush also eats the blackberries growing on the bramble bushes, carrying away the seeds in its belly. These seeds pass out in the thrush's droppings, giving them the chance to germinate in a new location. The hedgehog nests in hollows and old burrows between the roots of the hedge. It eats slugs, snails, beetles and fruits. Bumble bees feed on the nectar of wild flowers. They pollinate the flowers as they move between them, and so play a vital role in the life of the hedgerow.

Make a pitfall trap

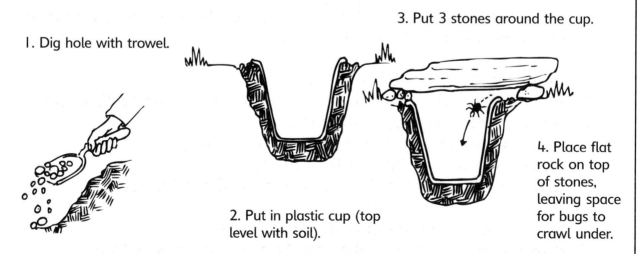

3. Put 3 stones around the cup.

1. Dig hole with trowel.

2. Put in plastic cup (top level with soil).

4. Place flat rock on top of stones, leaving space for bugs to crawl under.

Make sure you check the trap every day. Collect the bugs and try to identify them. Draw three examples. Remember to return the bugs unhurt to where you found them. When you have finished, remove the cup and fill in the pit.

Life in the Arctic

The most northern part of Canada extends into the Arctic Circle. The summers here are brief but beautiful, with the landscape bathed in light for all 24 hours of the day and the melted snow clearing to reveal the Arctic tundra – a special landscape of lichens and small shrubs like heathers that grow slowly, but are tough enough to withstand the fiercest bite of the Arctic cold. For a few short months flowers bloom and are pollinated, then shed their seeds, and Arctic hares and grazing deer feed on the new growth of the plants. The summer melting of the sea ice allows walruses and ringed seals to pull up onto the rocky coastline to have their pups, always looking out for polar bears – the fierce top predators of the Arctic landscape. The seals feed on kelp (a type of seaweed), fish and crustaceans (such as crabs). The fish feed on plankton: tiny plants that float on the currents of the ocean, making food by using the energy from the Sun. Tiny animals in the plankton also feed on it – these are the first consumers in the food chain of the Arctic seas.

Once summer has passed, the chill of winter returns. The light fades and the days rapidly become shorter. Temperatures drop to below –30°C, and the sea ice once more begins to freeze as the tundra is buried beneath a blanket of snow and ice. Polar bears move onto the ice to hunt for food. They wait by the breathing holes made in the ice by seals, ready to ambush them as they surface for air. The polar bear is well adapted to survive in the Arctic landscape with its thick

camouflaged coat, claws for gripping the ice, broad legs (which it uses as paddles when it swims) and tiny ears (to reduce the amount of heat lost from them). As well as these physical adaptations, the polar bear has another survival technique: through the coldest months of the winter it hibernates in a den beneath the snow, and it is here that the mother gives birth to her young in the spring.

With the return of the Sun and the onset of spring, the sea ice melts to reveal a thawing tundra landscape flourishing with life.

Comprehension questions
1. What is the special name given to the land inside the Arctic Circle?
2. Name a producer that grows there.
3. Name a herbivore that feeds on the plants there.
4. What is the top predator in this habitat?
5. Name three ways in which this animal is adapted to survive in the Arctic environment.
6. Name one prey of the top predator.
7. How do the tiny plants called plankton get the energy they need to survive?
8. Write out a food chain for this habitat.

UNIT 3 THE ENVIRONMENT

Surveying techniques: using a quadrat

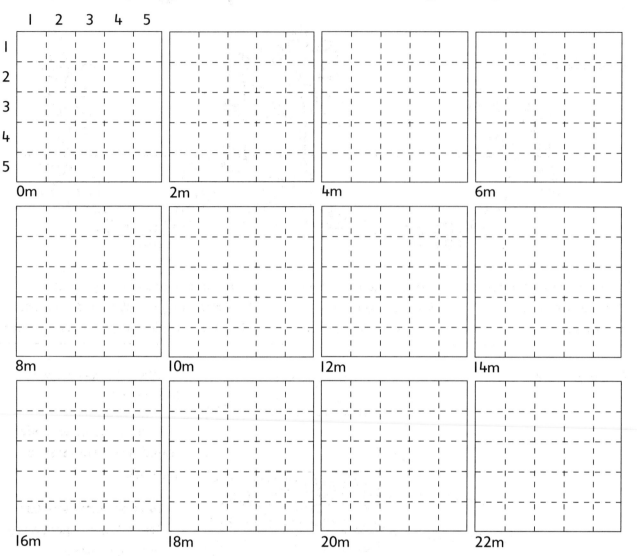

Use a tape measure to make a line transect.

0m   10m   20m

Place your quadrat along the tape every 2m.

Key

☐ = bare ground
☐ = grass
☐ =
☐ =
☐ =
☐ =
☐ =
☐ =

To work out percentages

1. Look at your grid for each quadrat. Count up the number of squares covered by each type of plant. If most of a square is covered, count it as a whole square.

2. There are 25 squares, so each square covers 4% of the total area. Multiply the number of squares covered by each type of plant by 4%. So if 5 squares are grass, area covered = 5 × 4% = 20%.

3. Try to list the plant species found along the transect from the most common to the least common.

Name

Microbes and recycling

Exercise A

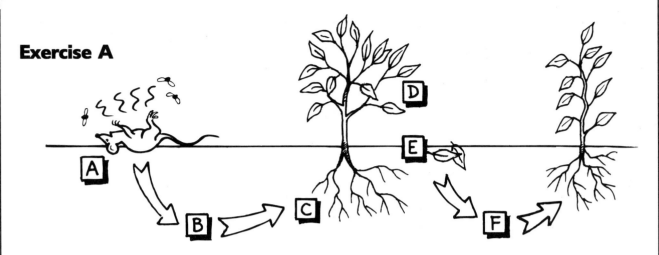

Write the correct letter (A–F) next to each statement.

Microbes release nutrients.
Animal dies and decays.
Microbes decompose leaves.

Soil nutrients absorbed by roots.
Released nutrients absorbed by roots.
Nutrients used in the growth of the plant.

Exercise B

Compost bin

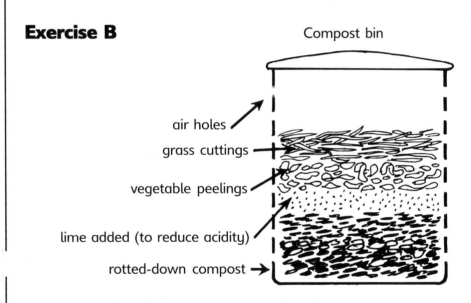

air holes
grass cuttings
vegetable peelings
lime added (to reduce acidity)
rotted-down compost

1. Why are the air holes important?

2. Why do gardeners add rotted-down compost to their soil?

3. Why do gardeners add water to the compost heap from time to time?

4. What materials could your family add to a compost bin?

Exercise C

drink can   crisp wrapper   jam jar   plastic bottle   apple core   chip wrapper

burger box   plastic sweet wrapper   matches

Biodegradable waste

Non-biodegradable waste

1. Add each piece of litter to one of the lists.
2. Put ® next to each item that could be recycled.

UNIT 3 **THE ENVIRONMENT**

FACTFILE: the understanding of diseases

Quarantine: the Black Death (1377) and the Great Plague (1665)

Bubonic plague has caused millions of deaths in its travels around the world, and almost every possible idea was tried out to stop its spread. In 1377, people travelling from plague-struck towns on their journey to Ragusa in Croatia were made to stay outside the town for forty days (if anyone had the plague, they would usually die within five days). The people didn't quite understand how the disease spread, but quarantine (separating germ-carriers from healthy people) worked. Even today, it is used to control outbreaks of dangerous diseases. Unfortunately, the idea of quarantine didn't spread as quickly as the Black Death. In 1665, fleas in cloth taken from London to a village called Eyam carried the plague with them. The village quarantined itself. Of the 350 villagers 266 died, but their bravery stopped the disease spreading.

Smallpox vaccination: Edward Jenner, 1796

Edward Jenner noticed that patients who had suffered from the mild disease cowpox (often caught by milkmaids) never caught the deadly disease smallpox. In 1796, he injected a small boy with pus from a cowpox sufferer. Six weeks later, he injected the boy with the deadly smallpox virus. The boy remained healthy. Jenner had developed the first **vaccine** against a disease. Jenner had no idea that the disease was caused by a virus or how the body fought diseases, but his discovery was a vital step on the road to understanding diseases.

Antiseptics in hospitals: Joseph Lister, 1856

Nobody much likes the idea of being operated on, but today surgery is far safer than it used to be. Joseph Lister found that over half of the people operated on in hospitals died of a deadly infection called gangrene. He read about Louis Pasteur's ideas on germs and started using carbolic acid on surgical instruments, wounds and dressings. Thanks to Lister's work, the number of people dying after operations fell to 15 out of 100 – a huge improvement. Today, infections in hospitals are far less common.

Pasteurisation: Louis Pasteur, 1860

French wine producers had problems with their wine going sour – it was costing France a lot of money. Louis Pasteur found that if the sugar solutions used were heated to a high temperature, it killed any bacteria present and prevented the wine from going sour. Pasteur also showed that if milk was heated to a high temperature and pressure before being bottled, it would last longer. The process called pasteurisation is still used today to treat the milk we drink. Pasteur also demonstrated that microbes (germs) cause food to go bad.

Vaccination: Louis Pasteur, 1881

Having shown that micro-organisms can cause disease, Pasteur grew cultures of harmful bacteria to experiment with. By accident, he let a culture of cholera bacteria die. Instead of throwing away the dead bacteria, he injected them into chickens. Not only did the chickens not fall sick, they stayed healthy when they were injected with living cholera bacteria later. Pasteur realised that the dead microbes gave the chickens a chance to develop their own defences to fight cholera. On 2nd June 1881 in Paris, Pasteur demonstrated his method of vaccination for the deadly disease anthrax. In one pen were cows, sheep and a goat grazing quietly. In the other, the same livestock lay dead or dying. The animals in both pens had been injected with anthrax, but nearly all the ones that survived had been vaccinated before the experiment. Pasteur's demonstration was important for sharing his discovery with other scientists.

Germs: Robert Koch (1843–1910)

Koch discovered some of the deadliest germs of all by taking samples from sick victims, staining them so that the germs showed up better, then looking at them under the microscope. He proved that germs caused diseases by finding the killer germs, growing them on a culture plate (though he first used the liquid inside eyeballs), then injecting them into healthy animals (often rabbits or mice) and observing as they fell sick. He showed that the injected germ was responsible for the disease.

Antibiotics: Alexander Fleming, 1928

Alexander Fleming had been working on some microbes called bacteria that caused influenza. He accidentally left one of his culture plates uncovered. When he checked the plate later, he found that the bacteria had all died and that there was a mould called **penicillin** growing on the plate. Chemicals produced by this mould were used to make the first antibiotics (chemicals that fight bacteria). Since that discovery, many lives have been saved by the use of antibiotics to kill bacteria that cause infections.

A very sore throat

Complete this table to show how the number of bacteria found in your throat could increase during one night.

Remember: the number of bacteria doubles every 20 minutes.

Time in minutes	O'clock time	Number of bacteria
0	10pm	1
20		2
40		4
60	11pm	8
80		
100		
120	12am	
140		
160		
180	1am	
200		
220		
240	2am	
260		
280		
300	3am	
320		
340		
360	4am	
380		
400		
420	5am	
440		
460		
480	6am	
500		
520		
540	7am	

Is it any wonder that we can feel so unwell when we wake up?

Yeast experiment

Find out what conditions are best for the growth of yeast.

1. Label six test tubes A–F.
2. Put a small piece of fresh or dried yeast into each tube.
3. Set up each test tube as follows, shake the tube to mix together the contents, then place a deflated balloon over the top of the tube.

A – just the yeast (one teaspoon).
B – yeast and a pinch of sugar.
C – yeast and 10ml cold (tap) water. Record the temperature.
D – yeast, a pinch of sugar and 10ml warm water (about 35°C).
E – yeast, a pinch of sugar and 10ml boiling water.
F – yeast, a pinch of sugar and 10ml cold water.

SAFETY: take care with boiling water – ask an adult to help you do this!

Record the changes that you see taking place over 30 minutes.

Test tube	Result
A	
B	
C	
D	
E	
F	

What my results show:

The living world

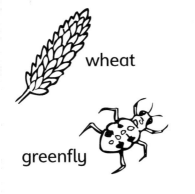

wheat

greenfly

hawk

vole

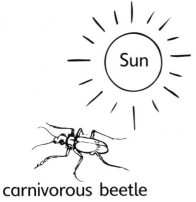

Sun

carnivorous beetle

1. Write out a food chain using the organisms above.

2. Put a P above the producer and an H next to a herbivore.

3. Why is the Sun so important to food chains?

4. Write down the special adaptations that the hawk has for hunting.

Reversible and non-reversible changes

ORGANISATION (23 LESSONS)

	OBJECTIVES	MAIN ACTIVITY	GROUP ACTIVITIES	PLENARY	OUTCOMES
LESSON 1	● To revise the concept of a mixture and ways of separating materials from mixtures. ● To know that some materials dissolve in water. ● To know that solids that do not dissolve in a liquid can be separated from it by filtering. ● To be able to separate an insoluble solid from a liquid by filtering.	A demonstration and a 'question and answer' session to explore dissolving and filtering.	Separate soil from water using filtration. Label a diagram of a model filter bed.	A quick 'question and answer' session based on the Main activity.	● Know that solids that dissolve/do not dissolve in water are soluble/insoluble. ● Know that insoluble solids can be separated from water using sieving or filtration. ● Can describe how to separate a mixture such as soil and water using filtration. ● Know some everyday uses of filtration. ● Know that soluble solids cannot be separated from water by filtration.
LESSON 2	● To know that a dissolved solid can be separated from a liquid by evaporation.	A demonstration to show evaporation of water from a salt solution.	An experiment to separate salt from water using evaporation.	A 'question and answer' session based on the Group activity.	● Can describe how a dissolved solid can be separated from a liquid by evaporation.
LESSON 3	● To know that when a gas is cooled it becomes a liquid, and that this process is called condensing.	A demonstration to show how you can separate salt from water and collect the water.	Label a diagram and complete a cloze text about evaporation and condensation.	Recap on the worksheet and the demonstration, using questions.	● Can describe how a liquid can be separated from a solution.
LESSON 4	● To know how the temperature of water affects the speed of dissolving. ● To make a prediction based on relevant experiences. ● To record results in a table.	A discussion and teacher demonstration of an experiment to find out how temperature affects the speed of dissolving.	Carry out the same experiment.	A review of the lesson's activity.	● Can plan an investigation to find a relationship between two variables. ● Know that increasing the temperature of a liquid results in quicker dissolving.
LESSON 5	● To know how the temperature of water affects the rate of dissolving. ● To be able to plot a line graph accurately. ● To be able to interpret results.	Analyse the class results and take a close look at 'lines of best fit'.	Plot a graph of their results and draw a line of best fit. Draw a conclusion from their results.	The children plot a graph using a set of exemplary results.	● Know the relationship between temperature of water and rate of dissolving. ● Understand why taking several measurements increases the reliability of the data. ● Can decide on a line for their graph that fits the data. ● Can explain why one line fits the data better than others.

ORGANISATION (23 LESSONS)

	OBJECTIVES	MAIN ACTIVITY	GROUP ACTIVITIES	PLENARY	OUTCOMES
LESSON 6	● Carry out an investigation: make a prediction; decide what apparatus to use; plan a fair test; make careful observations and measurements; record results in an appropriate manner; know that repeating measurements improves the reliability of data; use a line graph or bar chart to present results; make comparisons and draw conclusions.	Present the information that the children will need to carry out their investigation.	Carry out an investigation to find out how the temperature of the water affects the speed at which salt dissolves in water.	Review of the lesson.	● Can carry out an investigation: plan a fair test to investigate a question; make a simple prediction, based on knowledge gained from a previous experiment; record results in a table; present results, perhaps with some help, in the form of a bar chart or line graph; decide on a line for their graph that fits the data; explain what the results show. ● Can identify the presence or absence of anomalous results.
LESSON 7	● To know how particle size affects the rate of dissolving.	The children plan an investigation, carry it out and record their results, then draw a conclusion.		Review the lesson.	● Can describe how the rate of dissolving is affected by particle size.
LESSON 8	● To know how stirring affects the speed of dissolving. ● To make a prediction; plan and carry out an experiment; record results; interpret the results to draw a conclusion.	The children plan an investigation, carry it out and record their results, then draw a conclusion.		Review the experiment and relate it to the previous lessons.	● Can describe how the rate of dissolving is affected by stirring.
LESSON 9	● To understand that changes sometimes happen when materials are mixed together, and that these changes cannot be reversed easily. ● To observe an irreversible change.	Discuss the instructions for the Group activities. Demonstration of an irreversible change that happens when materials are mixed.	Carry out experiments that show irreversible changes happening when materials are mixed.	Review the Group activities.	● Recognise that mixing materials can cause them to change. ● Can describe some ways in which mixing materials causes a gas to be produced. ● Know that some changes are not reversible.
LESSON 10	● To know that mixing materials can cause them to change. ● To know that some changes can be reversed easily, and so are called 'reversible' changes. ● To carry out an experiment to reverse the change that occurs when sand, salt and water are mixed together.	Discuss ways of separating components of a mixture. A demonstration of how to separate components of a mixture. The children carry out an experiment to separate a mixture of salt, sand and water.		Review the observed changes and how they could be reversed.	● Can use previous knowledge to solve a problem. ● Can explain what happens in the process of filtering and evaporating. ● Understand what is meant by 'reversible' and 'irreversible' changes.
LESSON 11	● To know that heating and cooling can cause changes. ● To observe how heating can cause non-reversible changes. ● To observe how heating can cause a reversible change. ● To observe how cooling can cause a reversible change.	Demonstrations to show how heating and cooling can cause reversible changes and how heating can cause an irreversible change.	The children record their observations in words and/or diagrams.	Review the examples in the lesson.	● Know that some changes that take place when materials are heated cannot be reversed. ● Know that changes made by cooling materials can be reversed.
LESSON 12	● To know that burning brings about changes that are irreversible. ● To confirm this knowledge by observation.	Discussion in the course of the Group activities to help the children interpret what they have seen.	A circus of observation and recording activities related to burning (the activities do not require the children to burn anything).	The children feed back their observations to the class.	● Can describe what they observe when different materials burn. ● Know that when burning occurs, new materials are made such as ash and gases. ● Know that burning is a non-reversible change.

ORGANISATION (23 LESSONS)

	OBJECTIVES	MAIN ACTIVITY	GROUP ACTIVITIES	PLENARY	OUTCOMES
LESSON 13	● To know that burning materials can be dangerous. ● To know what to do to reduce the hazards of burning. ● To know what to do if a problem arises when something is burning.	A group discussion of how to make burning materials safe. Some children design a poster about the hazards of burning materials. Other children use role-play to highlight the safety procedures needed when burning things.		Review the children's work and draw up a class list of safety precautions.	● Recognise hazards associated with burning materials.
LESSON 14	● To know which household products are hazardous. ● To know the warning symbols used on such products.	Explanation of the most common safety or warning symbols.	Record the safety symbols that appear on various products. Identify the correct safety signs for various situations.	A quick quiz about safety signs.	● Can describe some materials that are flammable, some that are poisonous, and some that are corrosive. ● Know some common safety signs and their meanings.
LESSON 15	● To carry out an experiment to show what causes rusting. ● To carry out an experiment to show that only iron and steel rust.	Discuss the experiment with the children.	The children carry out an experiment to find out which metals rust and what causes rusting.	A 'question and answer' session to test the children's understanding.	● Know that only iron and steel rust. ● Know that oxygen and water are needed for rusting. ● Know that rusting is an irreversible reaction.
LESSON 16	● To carry out an experiment. ● To know how to prevent iron and steel rusting.	Review Lesson 15. Plan an experiment to find out how to prevent iron and steel from rusting. The children carry out the experiment.		Review the children's work.	● Can describe ways of preventing rusting.
LESSON 17	● To know that some materials that we use in everyday life (such as paper) are made by changes that are irreversible.	Watch a video about how paper is made. Demonstrate how to make paper.	A written activity related to making paper.	Build up a concept map about reversible and irreversible changes.	● Know that many manufacturing processes involve permanent changes.
LESSON 18	● To know that there are many energy sources in the home. ● To know what these energy sources are used for.	Discuss what energy is and what it is used for.	Identify uses and sources of energy in the home.	Discuss uses and sources of energy in the school.	● Recognise items in the home that need energy to work. ● Recognise sources of energy in the home.
LESSON 19	● To know how electricity is made from non-renewable fuels.	Discussion and explanation of how electricity is made.	Match pictures to captions on how electricity is made. Use a CD-ROM to research Michael Faraday.	Consolidate the children's learning through a 'question and answer' session.	● Can describe how a non-renewable source of energy is used in power stations.
LESSON 20	● To know that there are non-renewable sources of energy.	Discuss the nature and uses of fossil fuels. The children make posters to show the chain of events from fossil fuels being formed to electricity being used.		'Question and answer' session on fossil fuels.	● Can describe how non-renewable sources of energy are used in power stations.
LESSON 21	● To know that there are renewable sources of energy.	Discussion and explanation of renewable sources of energy and how they are used to make electricity. The children make posters to show how electricity is made from these energy sources.		'Question and answer' session on renewable sources of energy.	● Can describe how renewable energy sources are used to generate electricity.

ORGANISATION (23 LESSONS)

	OBJECTIVES	MAIN ACTIVITY	GROUP ACTIVITIES	PLENARY	OUTCOMES
LESSON 22	● To understand why we need to be economical in our use of fuels. ● To interpret a graph.	Explain why we need to be economical with the use of fossil fuels. The children answer questions about energy consumption.		Build up a concept map on fuels and other energy sources.	● Can explain why there is a need for fuel economy.

	OBJECTIVES	ACTIVITY 1		ACTIVITY 2	
ASSESSMENT 23	● To review work done on the topic of materials. ● To carry out a formative or summative assessment for this unit.	Form a concept map to link the ideas in this topic.		Complete a test on reversible and irreversible reactions.	

LESSON 1

OBJECTIVES
● To revise the concept of a mixture and ways of separating materials from mixtures.
● To know that some materials dissolve in water.
● To know that solids that do not dissolve in a liquid can be separated from it by filtering.
● To be able to separate an insoluble solid from a liquid by filtering.

RESOURCES

Introduction: Mixtures of (a) flour and currants, (b) gravel and sand, (c) sand and water; a fine sieve, a coarser sieve.
Main teaching activity: Sand (3 tsp), water (200ml), two stirring implements (spoons or sticks), filter funnels, filter papers and beakers or jars; salt (3 tsps), a drinking straw (cut up). A microscope would be useful for examining the filter paper; your local secondary school may be able to lend you one.
Group activities: 1. For each group (3 or 4 pupils): soil (3 tsps), water (100ml), beakers or jam jars, spoons or spatulas, glass rods or any stirring implement, filter paper, a filter funnel. **2.** Photocopiable page 115 (one copy per child), a jam jar, a plant pot to fit above it (see diagram on page 84), sand, small stones, large stones, cloth, dirty water.

PREPARATION

If you wish the children to taste the water used in the teacher demonstration, you need to make sure that it, the salt and all the apparatus are very clean. Write the instructions and cloze test for Group activity 1 on the board.
It might be a good idea to organise a trip to a local water treatment plant. Most water authorities have educational services.

BACKGROUND

This lesson allows the children to revisit past work (see *100 Science Lessons: Year 4/Primary 5*), and to learn more about solutions and filtration. They need to remind themselves what a 'mixture' is, and what is meant by the terms 'dissolving', 'insoluble' and 'soluble'. In science, a mixture is two or more materials 'mixed' together *without any chemical reaction between them*, and hence mixtures can be separated. There are several different kinds of mixture: solid bits and smaller solid bits; insoluble solids in a liquid (suspension); soluble solids in a liquid (solution); and combinations of these.

The children must be steered clear of the idea that when something dissolves, it disappears. When sugar or salt dissolves in water, the solid particles are broken down by the water molecules into very small pieces – so small that they cannot be seen with the human eye. When a solid dissolves into a liquid, a solution is formed. A solution is always clear: it may be coloured, but has no bits floating around in it. For example, the solid copper sulphate takes the form of blue crystals. When these crystals are dissolved in water, a clear blue solution is formed. Other examples of water-soluble substances are sugar, salt and instant coffee.

If you put sand in water, the sand does not dissolve because the particles are not broken down by the water molecules. They remain as relatively large pieces. The children should already know that we can strain larger solid particles from a liquid with a sieve. However, the particles of sand are too small for them all to be separated from the water by a sieve.

Filter paper can be used as a very fine sieve to separate very small solid particles that are mixed with a liquid such as water. A piece of filter paper has very tiny holes that can only be seen under a microscope. Water molecules are small enough to pass through these holes, but all the sand particles are too large, so they stay behind in the filter paper. Filtration is thus a good method for separating bits of an insoluble solid (such as chalk, clay or wax) from a liquid. However, when salt or sugar dissolves in water, the solid particles are broken down into very tiny, invisible particles that can pass easily through the holes in the filter paper. Filtration is thus not a good method for separating a soluble solid from a solution.

Filtration has many uses in our everyday life. In a coffee maker, a filter is used to separate the bits of ground bean from the dissolved coffee. Filter beds are used in the water supply to clean dirty water before it is reused. The diagram below shows how a home-made filter bed can be made.

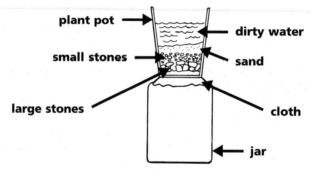

INTRODUCTION

Start by revising previous work on mixtures and ways of separating them. Offer some or all of the following examples to help the children consider their ideas. As visual aids, provide mixtures of flour and currants, sand and gravel, and soil and water, as well as suitable equipment to separate them. Ask the children: *A chef has dropped a packet of currants accidentally into a big bowl of flour. What has he made?* (A mixture of flour and currants.) *How could he separate the currants and the flour?* (Using a sieve.) Demonstrate this. *What if a builder drops some gravel into a pile of sand? What has he made?* (A mixture of sand and gravel.) *If he puts in too much gravel, how could he separate the gravel from the sand?* (Using a sieve.) Demonstrate this if possible. *If you put some sand into water, what will you make?* (A mixture of sand and water.) *What is a 'mixture'?* Make sure the children have grasped that mixtures can be separated.

MAIN TEACHING ACTIVITY

Ask: *How would you separate the sand from the water?* With help, the children should suggest a sieve with very small holes. Show them a piece of filter paper. *Can anyone remember what this is?* Tell them if necessary. Explain that if you looked at the filter paper under a microscope, you would see that it is made up of lots of tiny holes. If you have access to a simple microscope, set this up for the children to take turns looking at the filter paper during the course of the day.

Ask: *Does sand dissolve in water?* (No.) Put some sand in water to demonstrate. *Is sand soluble or insoluble in water?* (Insoluble.) *How do you think we could use the filter paper to separate the mixture of sand and water?* Show the children how to fold a piece of filter paper in four so that it fits in a funnel (see illustration opposite) and how to set up the apparatus necessary for filtering. Demonstrate how to separate sand from water using this apparatus. Tell the children that this process is called 'filtration'.

Now ask: *If you add salt to water, what do you notice?* (The salt dissolves.) Put some salt in water to demonstrate. *Is salt soluble or insoluble in water?* (Soluble.) *Can you see the salt particles when they have dissolved in water?* (No.)

Ask for a volunteer to taste the salt water, using a drop on the end of a piece of drinking straw. Make sure that all the equipment and the salt and water are clean beforehand. Ask: *Can you taste the salt in the water?* (Yes.) *So has the salt disappeared, or is it still in the water?* (Still in the water.) *When salt dissolves in water, the salt particles do not disappear even though we cannot see them. So what do you think happens to the size of the particles of salt?* (They get smaller.)

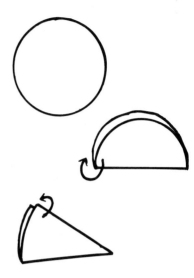

Do you think we can separate the salt from the water using filtration? Carry out filtration with the salt and water solution to demonstrate that the salt passes through the filter paper. If you want a child to taste the solution collected in the container, all the apparatus must be exceptionally clean. Again, the child should use a clean piece of cut-up drinking straw to put a drop on the tongue. *Would anyone like to see what the solution which has passed through the filter paper tastes like?* Hopefully someone will volunteer and tell the rest of the class that it tastes of salt. Then ask: *Do you think the filter paper was able to catch the salt?* (No.) *Why do you think the salt went through the filter paper?* (When the salt dissolves in water, the salt particles become so small that you cannot see them. They are able to pass through the tiny holes in the filter paper.) *So has filtration allowed us to separate salt from water?* (No.)

GROUP ACTIVITIES

1. The children could work in pairs or groups of three. Introduce the task: *Today we have already discussed the fact that sand is insoluble in water and that we can separate sand from water using filtration.* Direct the children to the following instructions, written on the board:
1. Add 6 teaspoonfuls (or 12 spatula measures) of soil to 200ml of water. Stir for 20 seconds.
2. Leave the soil and water mixture for about five minutes. Set up the apparatus that was used for separating sand from water.
3. After five minutes, have a close look at the soil and water mixture. What does it look like now? Draw what you see.
4. Pour the mixture of soil and water into the filter paper.
5. Draw and label the apparatus you have just used. [See illustration below.]
6. Copy the following, filling in the missing words:

When I looked at my mixture of soil and water, I noticed that some of the soil [sank] to the bottom and some bits of soil [floated] around in the water. Soil does not [dissolve] in water. Soil is [insoluble] in water. We can separate soil from water using [filtration]. If you look at filter paper under a microscope, you can see that it is full of [tiny holes]. The soil particles are too [large] to pass through the holes in the filter paper.

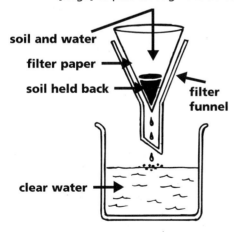

soil and water
filter paper
soil held back
filter funnel
clear water

Salt [dissolves] in water. Salt is [soluble] in water. When salt is dissolved in water, it passes straight through [filter paper] because the salt particles are [smaller] than the holes in the filter paper.

2. When the children have completed the task above, tell them: *We have carried out an activity to separate soil from water using filtration. Now we are going to look at how filtration is used in everyday life.* Give each child a copy of page 115. Explain: *A filter bed is like a giant piece of filter paper. Filter beds are used to clean our water. The dirty water is passed through a filter bed at a water treatment plant before it goes back to be used again. We can make a model like this.* Demonstrate how to put the model together, inviting individuals to add parts in order. Then try it out. *Let's see if it can make this dirty water clean.* Ask the children to label the diagram of the model filter bed on page 115.

DIFFERENTIATION

For less able children, set up a 'word wall' in the classroom so that when you are asking questions, the words will act as a prompt.

1. Less able children may find it useful to have the apparatus they are to set up within their view, and a reminder sketch of how to fold the filter paper. The least able might find it useful to have a worksheet with a diagram of the apparatus and the missing words paragraph, so all they have to do is label the apparatus and fill in the words. More able children could be asked the following questions:

● *If you put some soil and chalk in water, why would filtering be no use for separating the soil from the chalk?* (They are both insoluble.)

● *Why do you use filter papers in a coffee percolator?* (To separate the coffee solution from the ground beans.)

2. Add blank labels and a word list to copies of page 115 for less able children. More able children could also write a description of how the filter bed works.

ASSESSMENT

Note which children can follow the instructions; understand what is meant by the terms 'soluble' and 'insoluble'; can decide when filtration is the best method of separation.

PLENARY

Finish off with a quick-fire question session based on the Main teaching activity: *Does soil dissolve in water?* (No.) *How do you separate soil from water?* (Filtration.) *How do we fold filter paper?* (Ask a child to demonstrate.) *Name some everyday uses of filtering.* (Filter beds for water, coffee filters.) *In a filter bed, are the small stones on top of the sand or below it?* (Below it.)

OUTCOMES

● Know that solids that dissolve/do not dissolve in water are soluble/insoluble.
● Know that insoluble solids can be separated from water using sieving or filtration.
● Can describe how to separate a mixture such as soil and water using filtration.
● Know some everyday uses of filtration.
● Know that soluble solids cannot be separated from water by filtration.

LINKS

English: group discussion and interaction.

LESSON 2

OBJECTIVE

● To know that a dissolved solid can be separated from a liquid by evaporation.

RESOURCES

Main teaching activity: A watering can, bucket or cup of water; chalk; sugar or salt (2 tsp), water (100ml), a stirring implement (spoon or wooden stick), a wide dish.

Group activity: For each group: salt or sugar (about 10 tsp), water, a stirring implement, a spatula or teaspoon, a measuring cylinder or jug (to measure out water), three wide dishes (all exactly the same type).

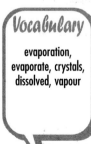

Vocabulary

evaporation, evaporate, crystals, dissolved, vapour

BACKGROUND

In Lesson 1, the children saw that filtration is not a good method for separating a soluble solid from a solution (for example, salt or sugar in water). This lesson looks at how we can do this. It is possible to evaporate the water from a solution by heating it with a flame, or just by putting the water and solid in a wide dish and leaving it in a warm place. The solid that was dissolved in the water is left behind as crystals. When heated, the water particles gain more energy and break free from the weak bonds between them. This results in the evaporation of water (as a gas or vapour) from the water surface. This gas is invisible, and should not be confused with the suspended water droplets that form white clouds above hot water. When liquid water is heated to its boiling point, evaporation takes place not only at the surface but all through the water, resulting in the very rapid release of water vapour.

The rate of evaporation from a water surface depends on temperature, air humidity, air movement and the surface area of the water. Places that are warm and dry and have moving air promote evaporation (for example, a sunny windowsill with a warm breeze). Places that are cold, damp and still (such as a cellar) do not promote evaporation. Washing on a line dries quickest on a warm, dry, breezy day and slowest on a cold, wet, still day.

The ideas covered in this lesson are revisited from a different perspective in Lessons 3 and 10.

INTRODUCTION

Recap on Lesson 1 to focus the children on the vocabulary and concepts that were covered. Ask: *What about salt – does it dissolve in water? So is salt soluble or insoluble in water? Can we separate salt from water by filtration? How do you think we could do it?*

MAIN TEACHING ACTIVITY

At the start of the day, weather permitting, take the children into a part of the playground or school grounds that will not be disturbed. Pour water to make a puddle, and use chalk to draw around the edge of the puddle. If it is a good day for evaporation (warm, dry and breezy), you might want to send out two volunteers every hour to draw around the perimeter of the puddle.

In the afternoon, go out into the playground and observe the perimeter of the puddle again. It should have decreased, due to some of the water having evaporated. Ask: *Has the perimeter of the puddle changed in size? What will eventually happen to the puddle?* (It will disappear.) *When do puddles disappear most quickly?* (When the Sun is out.) *What do you think the Sun does to the water in the puddle that makes the water **seem to** disappear?* (It warms it or heats it up.) *When water is heated up, it **seems to** disappear. Water is a liquid (which we can see), and when a liquid is heated up it turns into a gas (which we cannot see very well). Sometimes you can see the gas turning back into tiny drops of water as it cools down. That's why there are clouds of steam above a kettle. When water turns into a gas as it is heated, we call the process 'evaporation'. The water has 'evaporated off'.*

Teacher demonstration

We can use evaporation to separate salt from water. Add about two teaspoons of salt to about 100ml of water and stir. Pour the solution into a wide dish and leave it in a warm, dry place. Return to it the next day, when you should be able to show the children that all the water has evaporated, leaving behind the salt crystals.

GROUP ACTIVITY

The children could work in pairs or groups of three or four. Tell them: *You are now going to try to separate salt from water by evaporation and find out which is the best place in the classroom for evaporation.* Write on the board: 'To find the best place for evaporation'. *Which places do you think might be good for evaporation?* Draw the children's attention to the fact that when they hang washing out on the line to dry, it dries because the water evaporates from the clothes. *So on what type of day does the washing dry the quickest?* (Warm, sunny, dry, breezy days.) *How many places are you going to test? How will you make sure you are carrying out a fair test? What will you measure?* (How long it takes for the water to evaporate completely.) *How will you decide which is the best place for evaporation?* (The place where evaporation occurred most quickly.) Record the agreed plan on the board.

If the children choose three places, they will need to make up three lots of salt solution. To make the test fair, they need to make up these solutions with the same amount of water (100ml) and salt (2 tsp); the water temperature must be the same in all cases, and the containers must present the same surface area.

The children should set up the test and then leave the dishes for a few days. Ask them to draw and describe what they have done. When all the water has evaporated, ask them to record their results in a table with the headings 'Place' and 'Time taken for all the water to evaporate (days/hours)'. They could also describe or draw what they observed in the container once all the water had evaporated. Finally, they should state which was the best place for evaporation.
NB Don't let the children taste the salt left behind in the dish: you don't know what might have landed in the dish over the days that it has been left exposed.

DIFFERENTIATION

Less able children might find copying from the board difficult, so provide a diagram of the experiment (as well as the results chart) on a worksheet so that they only need to label the diagram and fill in the table. Provide a list of words for the least able children to choose from. More able children might find the following questions challenging:
● *Which of the following could be separated by evaporation: a solution of yellow dye in water; salt and sugar both dissolved in water; orangeade and water?* (The first and third.)
● *How could you separate a mixture of gravel, sand and salt?* (Use a sieve to separate out the gravel. Add water to the sand and salt. The salt will dissolve, but the sand will not. Use filtration to separate the sand from the salt. Then use evaporation to separate the salt from the water.)

ASSESSMENT

Note which children chose suitable places for their dishes, and which children were able to carry out a fair test.

PLENARY

If time does not allow the more able children to attempt the question from Differentiation, they could do so as a Plenary activity. The following questions could also be used to find out what the children have learned: *Does salt dissolve in water? Do you think sugar dissolves in water? How do you know? (It dissolves in tea.) Are sugar and salt soluble or insoluble in water? Why can we not separate salt or sugar from water by filtration? Can anyone tell me what they have done this lesson that will help them to separate salt from water?*

OUTCOME

● Can describe how a dissolved solid can be separated from a liquid by evaporation.

LINKS

English: group discussion and interaction.

LESSON 3

OBJECTIVE

● To know that when a gas is cooled it becomes a liquid, and that this process is called condensing.

RESOURCES

Main teaching activity: A spirit burner or candle burner, a tablespoon, a cold surface (such as a ceramic tile), a salt solution (4 tsp salt dissolved in 100ml water).
Group activity: Photocopiable page 116.

Vocabulary

evaporation, condensation, gas, liquid

BACKGROUND

When water vapour cools, it turns into liquid water:

$$\text{Solid} \; \begin{array}{c} \rightarrow \\ \leftarrow \end{array} \; \begin{array}{c} \text{melting} \\ \text{freezing} \end{array} \; \begin{array}{c} \rightarrow \\ \leftarrow \end{array} \; \text{Liquid} \; \begin{array}{c} \rightarrow \\ \leftarrow \end{array} \; \begin{array}{c} \text{evaporating} \\ \text{condensing} \end{array} \; \begin{array}{c} \rightarrow \\ \leftarrow \end{array} \; \text{Gas}$$

For example:

$$\text{Ice} \; \begin{array}{c} \rightarrow \\ \leftarrow \end{array} \; \begin{array}{c} \text{melting} \\ \text{freezing} \end{array} \; \begin{array}{c} \rightarrow \\ \leftarrow \end{array} \; \text{Water} \; \begin{array}{c} \rightarrow \\ \leftarrow \end{array} \; \begin{array}{c} \text{evaporating} \\ \text{condensing} \end{array} \; \begin{array}{c} \rightarrow \\ \leftarrow \end{array} \; \text{Steam}$$

If the children are unsure about melting and freezing, demonstrate these processes in the lesson. More information is available in *100 Science Lessons: Year 4/Primary 5*.

INTRODUCTION

Tell the children: *In Year 4/Primary 5* [check with the relevant staff or school scheme of work], *you looked at how a solid could be changed into a liquid and a liquid back into a solid.* Write the following on the board:

    Solid → Liquid

After each answer, fill in the relevant part of the flow chart. *Does anyone know what we have to do to a solid to turn it into a liquid? (Heat it up.) What is the name of the process by which a solid turns into a liquid? (Melting.) Does anyone know how to turn a liquid back into a solid? (Cool it down.) What is the name of this process? (Freezing.)*
By now, your diagram should look as follows:

$$\text{Solid} \; \overset{heat}{\rightarrow} \; \text{Liquid}$$

In the previous lesson, we separated a soluble solid from a liquid by evaporation. *By the end of today's lesson you will know a new term, 'condensation', and how to obtain the **liquid** from a solution.*

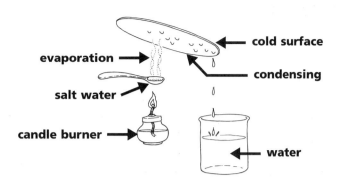

MAIN TEACHING ACTIVITY

Teacher demonstration

Have the apparatus set up as shown above. As with all experiments, it is probably a good idea to practise this demonstration first. It is an established fact that more accidents occur during science lessons when the teacher is demonstrating a practical than when the children are doing the activity themselves.

Start to heat up the salt solution. Ask the following questions while you are waiting for the water to evaporate (or before you start to heat up the solution): *In the spoon, I have got some salt solution. How do you think I made the salt solution?* (Dissolved some salt in water.) *How do you think I could get the salt back on its own again?* (By evaporation.) *If I heat up this salt solution, what do you think will happen?* (We will be left with salt [crystals] in the spoon.) *What about the water – where do you think that will have gone?* Let the children offer their ideas. From Lesson 2, they may know that the water has become a vapour or gas.

Explain that you are going to get the salt on its own again *and* collect the water. Once condensation starts to form on the tile, ask the children to tell you what they can see. *Where else have you seen water collect like this?* (Perhaps condensation on a cold window or on things from the refrigerator.) Once all of the water has evaporated and you have collected some condensed water, draw the children's attention to the fact that the salt is left in the spoon. *Do you think the liquid we have collected is just water, or do you think it is a salt solution? How can we find out?*

The children may suggest tasting it – but for health and safety reasons, this is not advisable. Remind them of the previous investigation, and lead them to suggest leaving the liquid to stand in a sunny place or heating it as before. If it is a salt solution, the water can be evaporated off to leave salt behind. If it is only water, no salt will be left behind. Check this by heating up the liquid or leaving it for a few days on the windowsill. The result should demonstrate that the water collected contained no salt.

Go back to the flow chart on the board. *When we heat up a liquid, it turns into a gas. This is called evaporation.* Extend the flow chart:

$$\text{Solid} \quad \begin{array}{c} \rightarrow \text{ heat (melting) } \rightarrow \\ \leftarrow \text{ cool (freezing) } \leftarrow \end{array} \quad \text{Liquid} \quad \rightarrow \text{ heat (evaporating) } \rightarrow \quad \text{Gas}$$

If we cool the gas down, it turns back into the liquid. This is called condensation. Write 'cool (condensing)' under 'heat (evaporating)' on the flow chart. *In today's experiment, the liquid water that we evaporated turned into a gas called steam. When the gas hit the cold surface, it cooled down and turned back into a liquid. This is condensation.* Redraw the flow chart:

$$\text{Ice} \quad \begin{array}{c} \rightarrow \text{ heat (melting) } \rightarrow \\ \leftarrow \text{ cool (freezing) } \leftarrow \end{array} \quad \text{Water} \quad \begin{array}{c} \rightarrow \text{ heat (evaporating) } \rightarrow \\ \leftarrow \text{ cool (condensing) } \leftarrow \end{array} \quad \text{Steam}$$

GROUP ACTIVITY

Give the children a copy each of page 116. The children need to label the diagram (as above) and complete the cloze text with the words: evaporated, salt crystals, liquid, gas, water, condensation.

DIFFERENTIATION

Provide a word list to help less able children fill in the blanks on the photocopiable sheet. Challenge more able children to answer these questions:
● *Why does condensation often happen in kitchens?* (The water in the pans begins to heat up and evaporate. The liquid water has turned into a gas, steam. When the steam hits the window, which has a cold surface, it turns back into water. This is condensation.)
● *When you breathe onto a mirror, why does it 'steam up'?* (The air you breathe out is a mixture of gases, including water vapour. When the water vapour hits a cold mirror, it turns back into liquid water.)

ASSESSMENT

Note which children were able to fill in the answers correctly on the sheet.

PLENARY

Review the lesson and refer back to these points on the board: *When a liquid is heated up, what does it turn into?* (A gas.) *What is this process called?* (Evaporation.) *When a gas is cooled, what does it turn into?* (A liquid.) *What is this process called?* (Condensation.) *How could I get both the water and the salt crystals from a salt solution?* (The children should be able to describe the method to you.)

For homework, ask the children to complete the photocopiable sheet and/or set questions based on the Plenary sessions for Lessons 1–3.

OUTCOME

● Can describe how a liquid can be separated from a solution.

LINKS

English: group discussion and interaction.
Geography: weather studies.

LESSON 4

OBJECTIVES

● To know how the temperature of water affects the speed of dissolving.
● To make a prediction based on relevant experiences.
● To record results in a table.

RESOURCES

Main teaching activity: Four ordinary white sugar cubes, four beakers, four spoons, a balance (if available), four thermometers, a stopwatch; four 100ml samples of water at different temperatures (see Preparation).
Group activity: Each group needs the same set of apparatus as for the Main teaching activity.

Safety: It is not advisable to use a kettle to heat up water, as this could lead to accidental scalding. Mercury thermometers are not suitable for use in primary schools, because the mercury released when one is broken is both toxic and difficult to clear up.

PREPARATION

Prepare 100ml samples of water in beakers at about 4°C (fridge temperature), 20°C (room temperature), 30°C and 40°C (both from the hot tap, with some cold water in one sample). It will be useful to have an adult classroom assistant for this lesson (see Differentiation).

Vocabulary

temperature, dissolve, prediction, thermometer, stir, stirring

BACKGROUND

(This information will also be useful for lessons 5–7.) When sugar (for example) dissolves in water, the water molecules break down the sugar particles into very tiny pieces. A number of factors can affect how quickly this happens:
1. If the water is heated, the water molecules will have more energy. This means that they will move about much more quickly and so collide with the sugar particles more times per second, breaking them down more quickly; so the sugar dissolves in the water more quickly.
2. Stirring the sugar into the water increases the frequency of collisions between the sugar particles and the water molecules. This means that the water molecules will break down the sugar particles more quickly. So sugar dissolves more quickly in water when it is stirred.
3. The bigger each initial sugar particle is, the longer it will take the water molecules to break it down. So it takes longer to dissolve sugar in water if it is made up of large granules as opposed to small granules (for example, brown sugar takes longer to dissolve in coffee than castor sugar, which in turn takes longer than icing sugar).

The children do not need to know all of the above information. They only need to understand that increasing the temperature, reducing the particle size and stirring will all speed up the rate of dissolving. Offer the idea of particles and energy if it will assist their understanding.

INTRODUCTION

Revise the meanings of 'dissolve', 'soluble' and 'insoluble'. Discuss some examples of each process.

MAIN TEACHING ACTIVITY

In this lesson, you will discuss the experiment with the children, demonstrate it and then let them carry it out for themselves. The following results might give you an idea of what to expect. The amounts of sugar and water used were constant: 1 cube and 100ml respectively.

Temperature (°C)	Time taken for sugar to dissolve (s)
4	135
20	77
30	55
40	23

The above temperatures are just a guideline. When you do the experiment, the water that has just come out of the fridge may be anywhere from 4°C to 10°C. The water from the cold tap should be about 20°C, but this can also vary. It is good practice to take the actual temperature of the water samples, and not to assume that they will have particular temperatures.

Teacher demonstration

Ask: *If I put some sugar in cold water and some in hot water, which will dissolve faster? Why?* The children might say that because sugar dissolves quicker in hot tea than in cold milk, it will dissolve quicker in hot water than in cold water. Develop a prediction based on this idea.

What experiment could we do to show that sugar dissolves faster in hot water than in cold water? With careful questioning, get the children to think about the experiment and tell you what they could do. Agree on a plan. Elicit the idea of using four temperatures of water: from the fridge, at room temperature and from the hot tap (using cold water to cool one sample a little). Decide how to make the test fair: by using the same amount of water (100ml), the same amount and type of sugar (1 cube), the same number of stirs (such as 20) and the same-sized container. The same child should do the stirring for each sample. Make sure the children understand that they must put the sugar cube in the water, then immediately start the stopwatch. As soon as all the sugar has dissolved, they should stop the stopwatch.

Once you have gone over the experiment with the children, you may wish to demonstrate it and show the children how to record their results. Then ask the children to carry out the experiment for themselves. When they have completed the Group activity and recorded their results, collect in the tables and keep them for the next lesson.

GROUP ACTIVITY

Divide the children into groups of three or four to carry out the experiment. Encourage them to use a thermometer to measure the temperature of the water for themselves. Write the investigation title and the class prediction on the board or flip chart. The children can copy this and then describe the experiment in writing and drawings.

DIFFERENTIATION

Less able children will need more individual help during the practical work. An adult classroom assistant could use a picture or diagram to show the experiment, or describe it on audiotape. Some children find it very difficult to write out tables of results; it might be a good idea to have the table drawn up and photocopied for them, so that all they have to do is write in the results. They may need assistance in doing this. They could also describe their experiment orally.

ASSESSMENT

Note which children were able to plan and carry out a fair test; use a thermometer accurately; record their results in the form of a table.

PLENARY

Review the lesson: *Can anyone describe our experiment to find out how temperature affects the rate at which sugar dissolves in water?*

OUTCOMES

● Can plan an investigation to find a relationship between two variables.
● Know that increasing the temperature of a liquid results in quicker dissolving.

LINKS

Maths: understanding measures.

LESSON 5

OBJECTIVES
● To know how the temperature of water affects the rate of dissolving.
● To be able to plot a line graph accurately.
● To be able to interpret results.

RESOURCES

Main teaching activity: The children's group results tables from Lesson 4; copies of a table of the class results (see Preparation); an OHP and two OHTs with graph axes already drawn on them (see Graphs 1 and 2 opposite), OHP pens.
Group activities: Graph paper (or a computer and data-handling software), paper, pens and pencils.

PREPARATION

On an OHT or on the board, have ready a blank 'class results' table. Below is an example, with some typical results. Prepare a sheet of the completed table (using the group results from the previous lesson, but without the averages) and make a copy of this for each child.

Group	Temperature (°C)	Time for sugar to dissolve (s)	Average time taken (s)
1	4	134	
2	4	140	144.6 (including 180)
3	4	180 *	135.8 (excluding 180)
4	4	138	
5	4	131	
1	20	55	
2	20	84	77.2
3	20	60	
4	20	99	
5	20	88	
1	30	54	
2	30	59	55.4
3	30	52	
4	30	57	
5	30	55	
1	40	24	
2	40	26	23
3	40	20	
4	40	24	
5	40	21	

The result marked * can be judged an error or anomalous result.

BACKGROUND

See Background for Lesson 4.

INTRODUCTION

Remind the children of their experiment in Lesson 4. *Can anyone tell me how they did the experiment? How did you record your results? This lesson, we are going to look at your results and find out what they tell us.*

MAIN TEACHING ACTIVITY

Give the children their results tables back. Ask them: *Look at **your** results table. How long did it take the sugar to dissolve at 4°C?* Take a result from each group. Record the results in the table on the board. Repeat the same procedure for all the temperatures. Now plot each group's result on a graph, using prepared axes on an OHT (see Graph 1).

Identify a temperature where the results are spread out (for example, 20°C in Graph 1). *At __°C, you can see that one group found it took __ seconds for the sugar to dissolve in the water, but another group found that it took __ seconds. So it is difficult to say which is the* *correct result. Would you be able to trust that set of results?* (No.) *At __°C, the results are quite close together. Do you think you could trust these results?* (Yes.) Consider a result such as the one marked * (if appropriate). Explain that this is an **anomalous result**: one that does not fit the trend or pattern. This result is probably due to experimental error. On the graph, where the other results are bunched together, this one is separate.

Explain that you now have to join up the points on the graph. *We call this 'drawing a line of best fit'*. Draw a line through the highest points (see line A on Graph 1). *If I draw the line through these points, do you think that would be the line of best fit?* (No.) *Can anyone suggest where I could draw a better line?* Working out the line of best fit for a scatter of results is very subjective. However, in general, a good rule when drawing a line of best fit is to ensure that there are a similar number of points above and below the line. Agree on a line of best fit with the children (see line B on Graph 1).

Hand out copies of the completed results table (this should be the same as the results table on the OHT). *For each temperature, work out the **average** time it takes for the sugar to dissolve. Then write your answer on the results table I have just given you.*

At this point, have the second OHT ready with the graph axes drawn on it. Ask, for example: *Sarah, can you tell me what the average time was for 4°C? Does everyone else agree with Sarah's answer? Does anyone disagree with it?* When you have been given the correct answer and you are sure the children know how to work out an average, plot the answer onto the graph on the OHT. Repeat the same procedure for all temperatures. Draw a line of best fit through the points you have just plotted (see Graph 2).

Once the two graphs are complete, overlay Graph 2 on top of Graph 1. Point out how the line of best fit on the first graph is in a similar position to the line of best fit for the average values – but the latter was much easier to draw. Emphasise that finding average values in this way improves the reliability of your results.

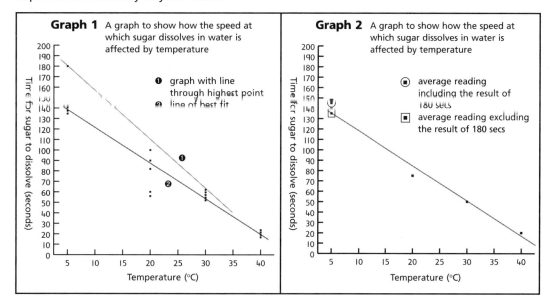

GROUP ACTIVITY

The children should plot a line graph and draw a line of best fit for the average results. This is a good opportunity to use a computer with data-handling software. Use questions to help the children reach and write up a conclusion: *Which temperature made the sugar dissolve the quickest? Which temperature made the sugar dissolve the slowest? Do your results match your prediction? Use your graph to find out how long it would take for one sugar cube to dissolve in 100ml of water at 35°C. What could you have done to make sure that your results were reliable? What else dissolves in water? Do you think salt will dissolve faster or slower in hot water?*

DIFFERENTIATION

The amount of help that individual children need to draw a line graph of their results and write a conclusion will vary with ability. If some children find it difficult to draw a line graph, let them attempt a bar chart instead. To help less able children consider the evidence and write a conclusion, you could copy the questions (see above) onto the sheet with the results table; the children need then only add the answers.

ASSESSMENT

Note which children can work out average results; plot the results (on a line graph or bar chart); draw a line of best fit (on a line graph); and draw a conclusion from their graph.

PLENARY

Give the children the set of results used as an example in Lesson 4 (see page 91). Ask them to plot a graph of the results and draw a line of best fit.

OUTCOMES

● Know the relationship between temperature of water and rate of dissolving.
● Understand why taking several measurements increases the reliability of data.
● Can decide on a line for their graph that fits the data.
● Can explain why one line fits the data better than others.

LINKS

Maths: processing, representing and understanding data.

LESSON 6

OBJECTIVE

● Carry out an investigation: make a prediction; decide what apparatus to use; plan a fair test; make careful observations and measurements; record results in an appropriate manner; know that repeating measurements improves the reliability of data; use a line graph or bar chart to present results; make comparisons and draw conclusions.

RESOURCES

Group activity: For each group: four lots of 1 tsp of salt; beakers, spoons, thermometers, a stopwatch; three 100ml samples of water at about 4°C (fridge temperature), about 20°C (room temperature), and about 30–40°C (from the hot tap, but not so hot that it would scald a child). See the safety note on kettles and mercury thermometers in Lesson 4 (page 90).

BACKGROUND

In Lesson 5, the children reached the conclusion that salt is soluble in water and so can be expected to dissolve faster in hot water than in cold water. This lesson gives the children an opportunity to test that idea. The lesson also allows you to assess the children on all three skill areas of 'Experimental and Investigative Science'. The children will need to make a prediction, plan a fair test, carry out the experiment (repeating the test twice for each temperature), draw a table of results, plot a line graph, draw a line of best fit and make a concluding statement.

INTRODUCTION

What did you find out from your last experiment? (That sugar dissolves faster in hot water than it does in cold water.) *How could you have made the results more reliable?* (By repeating the test at each temperature.) *This lesson, you are going to plan and carry out your own experiment.*

MAIN TEACHING ACTIVITY

Write the following on the board:

To find out whether salt dissolves faster in hot water or cold water

Plan
Think about the last experiment. Read what you wrote.
What apparatus will you use?
How much salt and water will you use?
What will you measure?
What will you keep the same?
What temperatures will you use?
How can you make your results more reliable?

Prediction
At which temperature do you expect the salt to dissolve fastest?
At which temperature do you expect the salt to dissolve slowest?
Why?

Results
Draw a table of results. Use the results table from the last experiment to help you. Don't forget to add an extra column for the average time.

GROUP ACTIVITY

The children should work in groups of three or four to carry out the experiment and record their results. Before they do so, talk it through with them. The procedure is the same as that in Lesson 4, but using salt instead of sugar. The children should repeat the test for each temperature twice, then find the average time for the salt to dissolve in the water at each temperature. They should draw a line graph of their average results (perhaps using a computer), deciding on a line for their graph that fits the data. Finally, they should make some kind of concluding statement about their results. To help them do this, write the following questions on the board:

● *At which temperature did salt dissolve fastest?*
● *At which temperature did salt dissolve slowest?*
● *Are these results what you expected?*
● *Why did you expect/not expect to get these results?*
● *How could you make your results even more reliable?*
● *How long would it take for salt to dissolve in water that was at 35°C?*

A typical conclusion that might be expected from the children is as follows:

My results showed that salt dissolved faster in water at 40°C than it did in water at 4°C. These results match my prediction, where I said that salt would dissolve faster in hot water than it would in cold water. I thought this because, in another experiment, I saw that sugar dissolved faster in water at 40°C than it did in water at 4°C.

In the last experiment, I did not repeat my results. To make my results more reliable this time, I have done the experiment twice at each temperature. If I had the time to repeat the experiment three or four times at each temperature, that would make my results even more reliable.

From my graph, I can see that 1 teaspoon of salt would dissolve in 100ml of water at 35°C in ___ seconds.

DIFFERENTIATION

For some children, a worksheet with the prediction and plan written out would be useful. They could then answer the questions. Less able children could also be given a blank results table to record on. Some children will also need help with their general organisation, and with practical tasks such as using a stopwatch. For the practical activity, you could pair a less able child with a sensitive more able child. Less able children may have difficulty in working out averages, and may prefer to focus on taking just one reading for each temperature. They may also prefer to draw a bar chart instead of a line graph. A cloze text based on the 'model conclusion' above could be added to the worksheet, so that the children only need to fill in the missing words.

With more able children, you could discuss their results with them, focusing on any that do not fit the general trend. Explain that such results are called 'anomalous'. You might ask: *Do you think that result is right?* (No.) *Why do you think that result is wrong?* (Because the salt took longer to dissolve in the water at 40°C than it did at 20°C. I thought that it would dissolve faster at 40°C.) *So what could you do?* (Do that test again.) If time permits, the child could repeat a test that gave an anomalous result. Encourage the child to write down the new result in his or her results table and then make a comment about it in his or her conclusion.

If there are no anomalous results, you could encourage more able children to comment on this fact in their conclusion. The following questions might be useful: *Do you think all of your results are right?* (Yes.) *Why?* (Because the salt dissolved faster in water at 40°C than at 20°C, and it dissolved faster in water at 20°C than at 4°C.)

ASSESSMENT

This activity gives you an opportunity to assess all three areas of Sc1: Experimental and Investigative Science using the Statements of Attainment. The three areas to be assessed are 'Planning experimental work', 'Obtaining evidence' and 'Considering evidence'.

PLENARY

Review the lesson. Highlight the fact that the higher the temperature of water, the higher the rate at which salt will dissolve in it. Also highlight aspects of the experimental procedure such as fair testing and drawing the line of best fit. (Children who have drawn a bar graph should be encouraged to identify the trend in their results without drawing a line.)

OUTCOMES

● Can carry out an investigation: plan a fair test to investigate a question; make a simple prediction, based on knowledge gained from a previous experiment; record results in a table; present results, perhaps with some help, in the form of a bar chart or line graph; decide on a line for their graph that fits the data; explain what the results show.
● Can identify the presence or absence of anomalous results.

LESSON 7

OBJECTIVE
● To know how particle size affects the rate of dissolving.

RESOURCES

Group activity: For each group: 2g or 1 tsp samples of icing sugar, caster sugar and brown sugar; a stirring implement, 3 × 100ml water in beakers, a stopwatch, a thermometer.

PREPARATION

Have amounts of each type of sugar and the water already measured out. Write the following questions on the board to help the children plan their experiment and consider their results:

Plan
What are the three types of sugar that you are going to use?
What apparatus will you need?
What will you do?
What things will you keep the same? What will you measure?

Prediction
What do you think will happen? Why?

Results
Which type of sugar dissolved the fastest?
Which type of sugar dissolved the slowest?
Why do you think one type of sugar dissolved faster than another?
Which type of sugar did you say would dissolve the fastest?
Does this prediction match with your results?

BACKGROUND

This activity will allow you to assess the children on the following skills for Scientific Enquiry: 'Planning experimental work', 'Obtaining evidence' and 'Considering evidence'. You should expect the children's prediction, plan and recording to contain the following information:

Prediction
I think the icing sugar will dissolve in water faster than caster sugar and brown sugar. This is because icing sugar is made up of very, very small pieces. The pieces in caster sugar are larger than in icing sugar, and the pieces in brown sugar are larger than those in caster sugar. When sugar dissolves in water, the water breaks down the pieces of sugar into pieces that are too small to be seen. So if the pieces of sugar are big, as in brown sugar, it will take longer to break them down. With icing sugar, the pieces are tiny to begin with, so it will not take as long for the water to break them down into pieces that are too small to see.

Plan
I will put 2g/1 tsp of icing sugar in 100ml of water. I will stir it until it has all dissolved and time how long it takes. I will repeat the test using caster sugar and brown sugar.

Fair test
Same amount of water (100ml) for each experiment.
Same amount of sugar (2g/1tsp).
Same temperature of water.
Same person stirring (to keep rate of stirring the same).

Results	Type of sugar	Time to dissolve (s)
	Icing	
	Caster	
	Brown	

INTRODUCTION

Remind the children what happens to salt when it is put in water: it dissolves. *Can anyone remember what happens when salt dissolves in water?* (The water breaks down the salt into pieces that are too small to be seen.)

Present the three types of sugar for today's experiment. *Which of these types of sugar is made* of the smallest pieces? (Icing sugar.) *Which is made of the largest pieces?* (Brown sugar.) *Which do you think will take the longest to dissolve in water?* (Brown sugar.) *Why?* (Brown sugar is made up of big pieces of sugar. It will take the water longer to break down these big bits into pieces that are too small to see, compared to the smaller bits of caster or icing sugar.)

Tell the children that they are going to plan and carry out an experiment. Write the title on the board: *To find out whether particle size affects the speed at which sugar dissolves.*

MAIN TEACHING ACTIVITY and GROUP ACTIVITY

Let the children devise an experiment, using the questions written on the board to help them with their planning, and then carry it out. They should draw a bar chart of their results (perhaps using a computer). Finally, they should use the second set of questions on the board to help them decide what their results show and write a conclusion.

DIFFERENTIATION

Less able children could use pictures or diagrams to describe the experiment and/or describe it orally onto audio tape. Provide a blank results table and a cloze text for the conclusion, such as: *The results showed that the [icing] sugar dissolved the fastest and the [brown] sugar dissolved the slowest. This shows that the [smaller] the particle size, the [faster] it dissolves.* More able children can write up the experiment in their own words, evaluate the results and write their own conclusion.

ASSESSMENT

This activity gives you an opportunity to assess all three areas of Sc1: Experimental and Investigative Science using the Statements of Attainment. The three areas to be assessed are 'Planning experimental work', 'Obtaining evidence' and 'Considering evidence'.

PLENARY

Review the lesson. Highlight the conclusion that larger particles take longer to dissolve. Discuss why this is: smaller particles present a greater surface area to the liquid.

OUTCOME

● Can describe how the rate of dissolving is affected by particle size.

LESSON 8

Objectives	● To know how stirring affects the speed of dissolving. ● To make a prediction; plan and carry out an experiment; record results; and interpret the results to draw a conclusion.
Resources	Two white sugar cubes, a stirring implement, two 100ml samples of water in beakers (both at room temperature), a stopwatch.
Main activity	Ask some questions about the work covered in Lessons 4–7. Tell the children that today, they are going to look at how stirring affects the rate at which sugar dissolves in water. Write the title of the investigation on the board: 'Do you think stirring will make sugar dissolve in water faster or slower? Why?' Discuss the children's answers and their reasons (for example, the experience of stirring a cup of tea). Ask them to write down their own prediction. Discuss and plan the investigation as a class or in groups, depending on their ability. The children will need to add sugar to water, stir and time how long it takes for the sugar to dissolve; then repeat the test, but without stirring. Discuss how the test can be made fair. The children should work in groups of three or four to carry out the experiment and record their results. Individually or as a class, they should analyse the results and decide whether the results match their prediction, then write a conclusion.
Differentiation	Less able children could be given an outline of the investigation for them to complete by adding a title, filling in missing words in the prediction, labelling a diagram of the apparatus, writing results in a prepared table and filling in missing words in the conclusion. The least able children could describe their experiment orally onto audio tape. More able children could write up their own prediction, plan, results and conclusion. The amount of individual help needed will vary with ability.
Assessment	As for Lesson 7.
Plenary	Review the experiment and relate it to the two previous lessons: *Did the sugar dissolve faster when stirred or not stirred? What other things affect the rate at which sugar dissolves in water?*
Outcome	● Can describe how the rate of dissolving is affected by stirring.

LESSON 9

OBJECTIVES
● To understand that changes sometimes happen when materials are mixed together, and that these changes cannot be reversed easily.
● To observe an irreversible change.

RESOURCES

Main teaching activity: Baking powder, vinegar, a beaker, a spoon.
Group activities: 1. Plaster of Paris, water, spoons, beakers, modelling moulds. **2.** Andrew's Liver Salts, water, spoons, beakers.

PREPARATION

Obtain the necessary materials. DAP (Bandex) plaster of Paris should be mixed two parts plaster to one part cold water and mixed until smooth. It sets in 20–30 minutes.

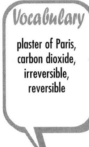

Vocabulary

plaster of Paris, carbon dioxide, irreversible, reversible

BACKGROUND

When different materials are mixed together, they may change by reacting with each other. Sometimes these changes can be reversed. For example, if you dissolve salt in water, you can get the salt back by evaporating, and get the pure water back by condensing. Dissolving salt in water is an example of a reversible change.

Lesson 10 looks at the use of reversible changes to separate sand and salt: the salt can be dissolved in water; the sand can be removed from the salt solution by filtration; and the salt can be separated from the water by evaporation.

However, when some materials are mixed together, a change occurs that cannot be reversed. This lesson looks at two examples of irreversible changes:
1. Adding water to plaster of Paris. Plaster of Paris is a white powder; but when water is added to it, it dries into a hard solid mass. It is used to make plaster casts to protect injured limbs. We cannot get back to plaster of Paris and water. Adding water to cement (powder) has a similar effect.
2. When you add Andrew's Liver Salts to water, you will see bubbles. Carbon dioxide gas is being given off. The gas escapes; once gone, it cannot be put back. You cannot get back to the original powder and water. Adding baking soda to vinegar has a similar effect.

INTRODUCTION

Briefly review the children's work on mixtures and separating mixtures. Explain that when you mix certain materials together, they change – for example, salt dissolves in water. Because you can get the salt back by evaporation, this change, or 'reaction', is called a 'reversible reaction'. Make sure the children understand the term 'reversible': relate it to their experience of vehicles reversing (going backwards). Continue: *However, if you mix certain materials together you cannot separate them again. A change takes place in the materials that cannot be reversed. Reactions of this kind are called 'irreversible' reactions. Today, we are going to look at some irreversible reactions. You may remember some of these reactions from Year 5/Primary 6.*

MAIN TEACHING ACTIVITY – PART 1

You may wish to write a set of instructions on the board for the children to follow. Go through these instructions before the children start the Group activities.

GROUP ACTIVITIES

1. The children should work in groups of three or four. Ask them to mix some plaster of Paris with water (see Preparation), pour the mixture into a mould and leave until set. The moulded shapes can then be painted in art lessons, or used to create a science display that represents irreversible changes. Ask the children to describe what they did and what they observed.
2. Ask the children to add a teaspoon of Andrew's Liver Salts to 100ml water, then observe and record what happens.

MAIN TEACHING ACTIVITY – PART 2

Demonstrate the effect of adding baking powder to vinegar. *What did you notice? What did you notice when you added Andrew's Liver Salts to water? The bubbles you saw mean that a gas is being produced. The gas is called carbon dioxide. The carbon dioxide escapes, and once it has gone it cannot be put back. That is why these two changes are said to be irreversible. When the plaster of Paris dries, you cannot get back the original powder and water. So this is another example of an irreversible change.*

DIFFERENTIATION

Less able children will need help with carrying out the Group activities. Provide a worksheet with titles and diagrams of the activities. The children have to label the diagrams and write their observations underneath. Let them copy the following and fill in the missing words (or provide this as a cloze text on the worksheet):

When plaster of Paris is added to water and left to dry, it cannot be changed back into [plaster of Paris] and water. The change is said to be [irreversible]. When Andrew's Liver Salts are added to water, the result is [fizzing or bubbles]. This shows that a [gas] is being given off. This gas is called [carbon dioxide]. Once the gas has escaped, it cannot be put back. So we cannot get back the Liver Salts and water. This is another example of an [irreversible] change. When vinegar is added to baking powder, [carbon dioxide] gas is given off. Once the gas has escaped, it cannot be put back. So we cannot get back the vinegar and baking powder. This is another example of an [irreversible] change.

More able children should be able to write their own account, but may find a word bank useful for spelling the names of the chemicals and so on.

ASSESSMENT

Note which children are able to write their own account, or to complete the worksheet.

PLENARY

Review what has been discovered. *Why do we say these changes are irreversible?* For homework, the children can complete the worksheet or finish writing their own account.

OUTCOMES

- Recognise that mixing materials can cause them to change.
- Can describe some ways in which mixing materials can cause a gas to be produced.
- Know that some changes are not reversible.

LESSON 10

Objectives	• To know that mixing materials can cause them to change. • To know that some changes can be reversed easily, and so are called 'reversible'. • To carry out an experiment to reverse the change that occurs when sand, salt and water are mixed together.
Resources	Sand, salt, water, filter papers, filter funnels, beakers, wide dishes, paper, pens.
Main activity	Review the previous lesson, emphasising how and why the mixtures were different from the original starting materials. Introduce the term 'reversible changes', reminding them how salt and water could be separated. Explain that because we can get salt and water back from the solution, we say that the dissolving of salt in water is reversible. Discuss the methods used to separate salt from water in detail. Ask the children, working in groups of three or four, to work out how they could separate a mixture of salt, sand and water. Provide each group with a large sheet of paper and a felt-tipped pen to jot down their ideas. Give them 10–15 minutes to do this, then ask each group to feed back their ideas to the class. You could demonstrate the experiment according to an agreed method or, if time and resources permit, the children could carry out the experiment themselves. You may prefer to separate the sand and the salt by dissolving and filtration, then discuss how the salt and the water could be separated (by evaporation). Encourage the children to write up the experiment using diagrams and their own words. You may wish to display their written work as a summary of this topic.
Differentiation	Less able children may prefer to describe the experiment orally into a cassette recorder. You may prefer to provide a cloze text as a worksheet, describing the experiment and drawing conclusions, for these children to complete. More able children may have tackled the extension questions in Lesson 2, which means that they will be more familiar with this experiment. It might be useful to put them into groups where they can assist less able friends. Give this placing careful thought, so that no less able children are made to feel inadequate, and no more able children are left feeling that they are not achieving anything, or are allowed to take over and not give others in the group a chance, or let the others have an easy time. More able children should describe the experiment in their own words.
Assessment	Note which children come up with an idea for separating the components of the mixture. Note which of the less able children complete the worksheet.
Plenary	Review how the materials changed when they were mixed together, and how they could be changed back. *Why do we call this a reversible change?*
Outcomes	• Can use previous knowledge to solve a problem. • Can explain what happens in the process of filtering and evaporating. • Understand what is meant by 'reversible' and 'irreversible' changes.

LESSON 11

OBJECTIVES
● To know that heating and cooling can cause changes.
● To observe how heating can cause irreversible changes.
● To observe how heating can cause a reversible change.
● To observe how cooling can cause a reversible change.

RESOURCES

Introduction: An egg box with one raw egg and one, two or three hard-boiled eggs in it; a glass bowl or jug, a raw potato, a baked potato (cut in half), a plate.
Main teaching activity: The ingredients and equipment necessary to make bread, pancakes, Christmas cake or Simnel cake; ice cubes, a glass.

Vocabulary

heating, cooling, reversible, irreversible

BACKGROUND

This lesson looks at how, when some mixtures are heated, changes take place that cannot be reversed. If a mixture of flour, eggs, sugar and butter is heated, the cake made is very different from the raw mixture. This change cannot be reversed: it is impossible to get the ingredients back. When an egg is boiled, it is changed irreversibly. To make bread, you mix together flour and yeast to make a dough, then put the dough in a tin and bake it. The baked bread is very different from the dough; it is impossible to get the flour back.

The above are all examples of irreversible changes. These tend to be 'chemical' changes. In chemical reactions, the materials break down completely into their constituent atoms. The atoms rearrange themselves and recombine, forming a new substance. It can often be seen that the original materials have undergone a change. This change is permanent: it cannot be reversed. Irreversible changes often produce new materials. Those chemical changes that are irreversible are often triggered by heat.

During this lesson, the children will also observe some changes that can be reversed. Reversible changes can be brought about by cooling and heating. For example, ice cubes (solid) melt when warmed above 0°C to form liquid water, which can then be cooled below 0°C to re-form the ice cubes. Chocolate behaves in a similar way. Reversible changes tend to be 'physical' changes or changes of state: the materials do not break down, but change in appearance and form. No new materials are made.

INTRODUCTION

Gather the class around you. Crack an egg into a glass bowl or jug. Ask the children to make observations. *What does the egg look like?* Now take a hard-boiled egg out of the egg box (do not say that it is hard-boiled). Pretend to drop the egg (or take a couple of hard-boiled eggs, juggle with them and then drop them). *Why didn't it smash?* (Because it has been hard-boiled.)

Give a child a potato and ask: *Would you eat this?* (Don't ask the class jester, because they might just have a go at eating it for a laugh!) When the child says 'No', show him or her a baked potato cut in half and say: *Well, would you eat this?* When the child says 'Yes', ask: *Well, if you would eat this, why would you not eat that?* (Because one is cooked and the other is not.)

When you boil or cook something, what do you need? (Heat.) *Could you turn the boiled egg back into the raw egg?* (No.) *Could you turn the baked potato back into a raw potato?* (No.) *Do you think that by heating the egg and the potato, you have caused them to change for ever?* (Yes. Unless someone eats them!) *So would you say that when you cook an egg or a potato, the change is reversible or irreversible?* (Irreversible.)

Introduce a cooking activity suitable for Shrove Tuesday, Harvest Festival and so on.

MAIN TEACHING ACTIVITY

Show the children some ice cubes in a glass. Leave these to melt while you carry out the following demonstration. Show the children the ingredients for bread, pancakes or a cake. Mix these together (or ask a couple of children to help you do so). Ask: *Would you eat this now?* Most of the children will say 'No'. Be prepared for those who like eating cake mixture and so say 'Yes'. In that case, you might say: *Is this the best way to eat cake?* Do **not** allow the children to eat the cake mixture, as there is a risk of catching Salmonella from the uncooked eggs.

What do we have to do to turn this mixture into a cake? Pour the cake mixture into a tin and place in an oven. If an oven is not available, you might have to have a cake already baked and 'waiting in the wings': *Here's one I made earlier!* This procedure should be followed if you are making pancakes.

Ask: *Does the cake look anything like the original materials?* (No.) *What do you think has caused the change?* (Heating or cooking.) *Could I get back to the original ingredients?* (No.) *Do you think the heating has made something new?* (Yes.) *Do you think the heating has caused a reversible change or an irreversible change?* (Irreversible.)

   Look at the ice cubes now. *Do the ice cubes we started with look the same as the water we have got now? What did we do to the ice cubes to turn them into water?* (Melted them or warmed them up.) *To melt something, what do we need?* (Heat or warmth.) *Can we turn the water back into ice?* (Yes.) *What do we have to do to turn the water back into ice?* (Freeze it or make it cold.) *If you can turn ice into water and then back into ice, do you think these changes are reversible or irreversible?* (Reversible.)

   Discuss how heating can cause both reversible and irreversible changes by comparing how ice melts with how food is cooked. Say that changes caused by cooling can generally be reversed.

GROUP ACTIVITY

Encourage the children to write up or draw one or more of the irreversible changes that have been demonstrated and/or discussed, then the reversible change of ice melting and water freezing. They can work individually or in groups. For example:

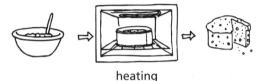

heating

Heating some materials causes irreversible changes. It is not possible to get the flour, eggs, sugar and butter back after the cake has been baked. Something new has been made.

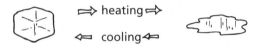

Heating some materials causes a reversible reaction. The liquid water made when ice melts can be frozen again by cooling. No new materials have been made.

DIFFERENTIATION

Less able children will need a prepared worksheet on which they only have to fill in the missing words. Offer more able children the following extension questions (✓ marks the correct answers):
1. Which of the following are irreversible changes?
a) Dissolving sugar in water.
b) Mixing sand in water.
c) Making a model from clay. ✓
d) Freezing water.
e) Frying an egg. ✓
2. Which of the following are reversible changes?
a) Candle wax melting. ✓
b) Wood burning.
c) Mixing flour and currants. ✓
d) Dissolving sugar in water. ✓
e) Frying an egg.

ASSESSMENT

Note which children are able to complete the Group activity with confidence.

PLENARY

Review the examples in the lesson to make sure the children understand which changes are reversible and which are irreversible. For homework, ask the children to do (or finish off) the tasks outlined in Differentiation.

OUTCOMES

● Know that some changes that take place when materials are heated cannot be reversed.
● Know that changes made by cooling materials can be reversed.

LINKS

English: group discussion and interpretation.

LESSON 12

OBJECTIVES

● To know that burning brings about changes that are irreversible.
● To confirm this knowledge by observation.

RESOURCES

Introduction: A wooden splint, matches, a heat-resistant mat.
Main teaching activity: A prepared worksheet (see Preparation), candles in secure holders, matches, tongs, materials for burning (see Background), heat-resistant mats.
Group activities: A TV and video player, a video showing a short clip of something burning; a candle in a secure holder; pictures of objects burning.

PREPARATION

Prepare a worksheet with the following table for the children to record their observations:

What material is burning?	What do you notice when it burns?	Are any new materials made?	Is the reaction reversible or irreversible?

Vocabulary

irreversible, burning, materials, smoke, ash, hazards, fire blanket, heat-resistant, fuel

BACKGROUND

Burning is an irreversible change. It is often called 'combustion'. Materials that burn react with oxygen in the air to produce a new material, usually called an oxide. Carbon-based fuels such as wood, coal and oil produce the gas carbon dioxide when they burn. Because oil and wood are hydrocarbons (they contain hydrogen), burning them also produces water.

A fuel is a material that has energy 'locked up' in it. Most fuels are carbon-based 'fossil fuels' such as coal, crude oil and natural gas, formed from long-dead vegetable matter. By refining crude oil, we obtain purer fuels such as petrol, diesel and propane (Calor gas). During combustion, the energy in a fuel is 'unlocked'. The energy (heat and light) released can be used for heating, cooking, transport and industry.

The oxygen required for burning is usually obtained from the air (oxygen makes up about 20% of air). Where carbon dioxide and water are formed, they are released into the atmosphere. These products of fuel combustion cannot be converted back into fuel and oxygen, so we can say that combustion is an irreversible chemical reaction. During combustion, a flame appears and smoke and ash (carbon) are also produced. Whereas carbon dioxide and water vapour cannot be seen, flame and smoke can – so they provide an indication that combustion is occurring.

Heating and burning are not the same thing, though some heat is needed to start something burning. We burn fuels to create heat energy, which can then be used to heat things. Burning is an irreversible reaction, whereas heating can cause both reversible and irreversible reactions.
IMPORTANT: Only set up experiments and demonstrations for which you feel confident to take responsibility. When demonstrating burning materials, it is essential to consider the risks and necessary health and safety precautions. Never leave children unattended with matches and candles. When a candle is used, keep a heat-resistant mat under it (if possible) so as not to risk burning the table. You and the children should tie back long hair, tuck ties into shirts (or take them off) and fasten any loose clothing in place.

The burning material could cause other things to catch fire. Have a fire blanket and a bucket of sand close by in case clothing or other materials catch fire. Be aware of the immediate first aid measures for the treatment of burns (for example, see CLEAPS' *Model Safety Policy*). Make sure the children know that if they suffer a burn, they must tell you or another adult who will help them. Make it clear to them that if the end product of burning is touched, it could cause serious burns: just because it's not red, that doesn't mean it's not hot. Even if you are outside, make sure the children are not too close to the demonstration in case the breeze catches a spark.

INTRODUCTION

Discuss the previous lesson, drawing out the children's understanding that cooking is an irreversible chemical change whereas the melting of ice is a reversible physical change. *How do you know if something is a chemical reaction?* (New products are made and the reaction cannot be reversed.) *How do you know if something is a physical reaction?* (New materials are not made and the reaction can be reversed.)

Take a splint and burn it in front of the class. Ask the children: *What did you see when the wooden splint burned?* (Flames, smoke.) *Has there been a change?* (Yes.) *What is the change?* (The stick has turned into burnt wood. You may have to explain that the burnt wood is called ash.) *Have any new materials been made?* (Yes, ash. Some children may also say 'smoke' and 'flame'. If necessary, explain that flame is just heat and light.) *Could I turn the ash and smoke* back into the wooden splint? (No.) *So do you think burning is an irreversible or reversible reaction?* (Irreversible.) *Why?* (Because something new has been made that cannot be turned back into the wooden splint.)

MAIN TEACHING ACTIVITY

The children should work in groups to look at examples of burning (see Group activities). They should do different tasks and swap around every five minutes. Distribute copies of the worksheet (see Preparation) to help the children record their observations. When the children have completed the activity, tell them that a material that burns in a useful way is called a 'fuel'. Ask them for examples of fuels and situations where they are used, such as natural gas in cookers, wood in bonfires, lighter fuel in barbecues and petrol in vehicles.

Discuss the children's observations. *What did you notice when the materials burned? Were any new materials made?* They will have noticed flames, smoke and heat when burning was taking place. They will also notice ash as a new material. Discuss whether you could get the original material back. *Was the burning of this material reversible or irreversible?*

Discuss whether the children think a gas was made. The more observant children may comment that you appear to end up with a lot less of the new material than there was of the original material. You could prove this by finding the mass of a wooden splint before burning, then finding out the mass of the ash. *How much mass has been lost?* Explain that the lost mass could have been released as an invisible gas, though some of it could have been released as smoke.

GROUP ACTIVITIES

1. The children look at pictures of things burning and record what they see (answering the same questions as before).
2. Show a brief video clip of something burning (perhaps only a couple of minutes). The children record what they see.
3. The children watch a candle burning and record their observations. Do not leave them unattended while they are carrying out this activity.
4. The children can record their observations of the teacher demonstration of how a wooden splint burns.

DIFFERENTIATION

Less able children could draw a picture or poster to warn people of the dangers of burning things. More able children could answer the following questions (on the board or a worksheet) as an extension task: 1. *When something burns, what do you see and feel?* (Flames, smoke, heat.) 2. *What do we call a material that burns?* (A fuel.) 3. *Does burning create new materials?* (Yes.) 4. *Is burning a reversible or an irreversible reaction?* (Irreversible.) 5. *When something burns, do you think an invisible gas might be formed?* (Yes.) 6. *How could you show that an invisible gas is formed?* (Find the mass of the starting material and the mass of the new material. If the mass of the new material is less than the mass of the starting material, some mass has been lost during burning. This could have been because some gas escaped into the atmosphere.)

ASSESSMENT

Note which children are able to answer questions correctly in the Plenary session.

PLENARY

Ask some children to feed back their observations to the rest of the class. More able children could be given the extension questions as homework; less able children could finish their picture or poster (see Differentiation).

OUTCOMES

● Can describe what they observe when different materials burn.
● Know that when burning occurs, new materials are made such as ash and gases.
● Know that burning is a non-reversible change.

LESSON 13

Objectives	● To know that burning materials can be dangerous. ● To know what to do to reduce the hazards of burning. ● To know what to do if a problem arises when something is burning.
Resources	A bucket of sand, a fire blanket, crayons, A3 paper, pencils.

Main activity	*Why is burning things dangerous?* Discuss the dangers of intense heat, smoke, spreading fire and so on. Consider the risks of barbecues, camping stoves and Bonfire Night. Be aware that some children may have had traumatic experiences with fire.
	     Have a group discussion: *What things could you do to make burning materials safe?* Write down suggestions on the board or flip chart. Show the children the bucket of sand and the fire blanket. Ask the children (working individually or in groups) to research and then make a poster about the hazards of burning materials. Some children could also design a poster to show how to make the burning of materials more safe. They should cover the following: long hair tied back; ties tucked out of the way; safety glasses; standing up, so you can move out of the way if a heat source falls over; keeping desks clear of books and paper.
	     Alternatively, the children could practise and perform a role-play to highlight the safety precautions that they should take when burning something or to show what they would do if they were burning something and it went wrong. When they are acting out their scenes, the children should not actually burn anything.

Differentiation	Less able children may need help with spelling and general organisation when making the poster. They may find the role-play more suitable.
Assessment	Note which children are able to convey the necessary precautions.
Plenary	Review the work. Make a class list of precautions to take when burning materials.
Outcome	● Recognise hazards associated with burning materials.

LESSON 14

OBJECTIVES
● To know which household products are hazardous.
● To know the warning symbols used on such products.

RESOURCES

Main teaching activity: A4-sized photocopies of some of the signs on photocopiable page 117; one copy per child of page 117.
Group activities: 1. Examples of a few containers for household chemicals with warning signs (see Background); a worksheet of safety signs (see Preparation). **2.** Five A4 cards with scenarios (see Preparation); A4 photocopies of the safety signs for 'corrosive', 'highly flammable' and 'harmful/irritant', without a square or triangle; yellow crayons, black crayons, rulers.

PREPARATION

Prepare copies of page 117 and enlarged copies of the logos, as listed above. Prepare a worksheet (not the same as page 117) featuring only the signs that appear on the products you are showing the children. Make sure that if, for example, there are four products with the 'corrosive' sign, there are four 'corrosive' signs on the worksheet.
     Prepare a set of five A4 cards with scenarios, as follows:

---

1. A tanker is carrying a substance that is extremely or highly flammable.
Colour in the safety sign and decide what shape should go around it.
2. Paintbrush cleaner is harmful and also an irritant. It is normally kept in a bottle.
Colour in the safety sign and decide what shape should go around it.
3. Oven cleaner is corrosive. It is normally kept in a spray can.
Colour in the safety sign and decide what shape should go around it.
4. You find a bottle of clear liquid in the garden shed. You don't know what the liquid is (it might just be an empty bottle that someone has found and filled up with water), but on the bottle there is a safety sign that means 'toxic'.
Would you taste it to find out whether it was water?
Colour in the safety sign and decide what shape should go around it.
5. On a cupboard door, you see the sign for danger.
Would you open the door?
Colour in the safety sign and decide what shape should go around it.

Vocabulary

corrosive, flammable, radioactive, explosive, toxic, harmful, irritant, electric shock

BACKGROUND

We all come across potentially dangerous substances in our everyday lives – but because we use them in the home, we tend to forget about the hazards they can present. To help us identify potentially hazardous substances, safety signs are used as warning symbols. These signs are essential for our health and safety. They are used to give information: they tell us whether a substance is corrosive, flammable and so on. Page 117 shows all of the safety signs you will come across on containers.

Safety signs should be black on a yellow background. The signs are usually shown in a triangle if displayed on a wall, in a square if on bottles, and in a diamond if on vehicles. Some examples of familiar hazardous substances are: dishwasher tablets (irritant/harmful), antifreeze (irritant/harmful), cleaning spray for suede shoes (extremely or highly flammable), fly spray (extremely or highly flammable), oven cleaner (extremely or highly flammable, corrosive), descaler (irritant/harmful), room spray (extremely or highly flammable), paintbrush cleaner (irritant/harmful), spray adhesive (irritant/harmful), hair mousse (extremely or highly flammable).

IMPORTANT: For health and safety reasons, it is not recommended that the children handle the containers of dangerous substances that you are going to show them. In the home, these products are normally kept out of the reach of children. When you display these items, make sure (for your own safety) that the lids are on tightly and that the containers are well-sealed. When the items are not being used, make sure they are stored in a safe place.

INTRODUCTION

Refer back to the safety factors that were considered when you burned materials. Tell the children that you are going to carry on thinking about safety: *We all come across dangerous and poisonous substances in our everyday lives, but they are not always obvious. To help us identify them, we have safety signs which use particular warning symbols.*

MAIN TEACHING ACTIVITY

Give each child a copy of page 117. Give a brief explanation of the most common symbols. For example, hold up an A4-sized version of the safety sign for 'corrosive', then ask the children to find it on their sheet. *If you see this symbol on a bottle, it means that whatever is in the bottle is **corrosive**. Does anyone know what we mean by this word?* (Like an acid, it can cause burns and damage the eyes.) Repeat the same questions for 'toxic', 'irritant' and 'extremely or highly flammable'. Also tell the children that safety signs should be black on a yellow background. The signs displayed on walls are often in a triangle; on bottles, the picture will be in a square; on vehicles it will be in a diamond.

GROUP ACTIVITIES

1. Have several household products with safety signs available to show a small group of children. Work with this group while the remaining children, in small groups, get on with the other task. Hold up each household product and ask the children what warning signs are on it. Fill in the following chart together on the board or flip chart: Give out copies of the worksheet (see Preparation). Ask the children to copy the chart into their own books, then cut out the signs from the worksheet and stick each one, next to the appropriate item, in the right-hand column.

Item	Safety signs

2. Give each of the other small groups a set of enlarged safety signs and an A4 card with a scenario written on it (see Resources and Preparation). Leave them to follow the instruction(s) on the card.

DIFFERENTIATION

1. Less able children will need help with filling in their chart. More able children could go on to make posters of the warning signs for display in the classroom. **2.** All the children should be able to take part in this activity.

ASSESSMENT

Note which children can answer the questions in the Plenary session.

PLENARY

Have a quick quiz with questions such as: *What is the warning sign for something that is corrosive? Highly flammable? Can you name a household substance that is corrosive? Highly flammable? If you were going to put a warning sign on a tanker, what shape would it be? If you were going to put a warning sign on a bottle, what shape would it be? If you were going to put a warning sign on the wall, what shape would it be?*

OUTCOMES

● Can describe some materials that are flammable, some that are poisonous, and some that are corrosive.
● Know some common safety signs and their meanings.

LINKS

PSHE: dangerous substances in the home.

LESSON 15

OBJECTIVES

● To carry out an experiment to show what causes rusting.
● To carry out an experiment to show that only iron and steel rust.

RESOURCES

Group activity: Iron nails, steel panel pins, pieces of aluminium foil, pieces of copper, pieces of plastic, jam jars with lids (or test tubes with bungs borrowed from your local secondary school), tap water, salt water, cooled boiled water, packets of silica gel, paraffin.

PREPARATION

Write the title of the investigation, 'Finding out what causes things to rust', and draw the diagram shown below on the board or flip chart.

Vocabulary

prevent, rust, rusting, conditions, grease, oxygen

BACKGROUND

Rusting is the corrosion of iron (or steel, which is mostly iron) to iron oxide. Water and oxygen are both needed for rusting to occur. Iron in dry air, or in water that is free of dissolved oxygen, will not rust. Metal salts, such as sodium chloride (table salt), help to speed up the process.

$$\text{Iron} + \text{water} + \text{oxygen} = \text{iron oxide (rust)}$$

Rusting can be prevented by keeping the iron object near to a substance that absorbs water from the air, such as silica gel. Iron can be coated with paint, grease or oil to stop air and water getting to it. Plating iron involves putting a thin coat of a metal that does not rust over the iron. Chromium and zinc plating are common. When iron is coated in zinc, it is said to be 'galvanised'. The zinc will protect the iron even if it is scratched. Stainless steel is made by mixing iron with other metals such as chromium and nickel; it does not rust at all.

This lesson will look at what causes rusting and which types of materials rust. It will also highlight the fact that rusting is an irreversible reaction. Following the experiment in this lesson, the recording of results will take a little time every day for a week. Use a lesson in the following week to review the overall outcome. Lesson 16 looks at things we can do to prevent rusting.

INTRODUCTION

Does anyone here have a bike? Does it tend to rust in bad weather? Can you give me an example of something else that rusts? List suggestions (such as cars and railings) on the board. *What are these objects made from?* You might get answers such as 'metal', 'chrome', 'iron', 'steel'. *Iron and steel are the correct answers. Can anyone describe to me what rust looks like? Where else have you seen rust?*

Rusting causes millions of pounds worth of damage every year. Many companies spend lots of money trying to stop things rusting. To know how to stop rusting, we have to know what causes it. What do you think causes things to rust? 'Rain' and 'water' will be the two most popular answers. *Today, you are going to find out what causes rusting.*

MAIN TEACHING ACTIVITY

Draw the children's attention to the title and diagram on the board. Discuss the experiment so that they know what to do with each jam jar. Explain to the children that by boiling water, you get rid of any oxygen that might be in the water, and that oxygen gets into water from the air. Discuss why they need to put paraffin on top of the boiled water. Also explain that silica gel takes any moisture out of the air in the jar. Discuss how the test can be made fair – for example, using the same amounts of water and salt for each metal. Tell the children that they will need to check their experiments every day and record their observations.

GROUP ACTIVITY

The children can work in groups of three or four. One group should set up four jars as shown in the diagram on the board. Other groups should carry out the same experiment with pieces of steel, copper, aluminium and plastic. By observing over a period of time, they should establish how many days it takes for each sample to become rusty (if it happens at all). The class results can then be shared.

After a week of observations, you should come to the following conclusions together:
1. Iron and steel both rust, but other metals and plastic do not.
2. Both water and air are needed to make iron or steel rust.
3. Salt speeds up rusting.

Explain that scientists call rust 'iron oxide'. It is formed by iron reacting with oxygen in the presence of water. Salt speeds up the reaction because it dissolves in the water and helps to 'break down' the iron. The children can copy out and complete the following conclusion: *[Water] and [oxygen] are needed for iron to rust. [Salt] speeds up the rusting of iron. Boiling water removes any [oxygen] that might be in it. Silica gel is a chemical that takes the [water] out of air. Metals such as [copper] and [zinc] do not rust. [Plastic] does not rust. Scientists call rust [iron oxide].*

DIFFERENTIATION

Provide less able children with support to record their observations and conclusions. More able children could attempt to answer the following question: *Why do you think that if you live by the sea, your car or bike will rust much more quickly?*

ASSESSMENT

Note which children can answer the questions in the Plenary session.

PLENARY

Test the children's understanding of the lesson with a quick 'question and answer' session. *Does iron rust? Does steel rust? Does copper rust? Does zinc rust? What is needed for rusting? What speeds up rusting? Rust is called 'iron oxide'. You have seen what iron oxide looks like. Do you think it is a new material compared to the iron, water and oxygen? Do you think it would be possible to turn the iron oxide back into iron, oxygen and water? So do you think rusting is a reversible or an irreversible reaction?*

OUTCOMES

● Know that only iron and steel rust.
● Know that oxygen and water are needed for rusting.
● Know that rusting is an irreversible reaction.

LINKS

English: group discussion and interaction.

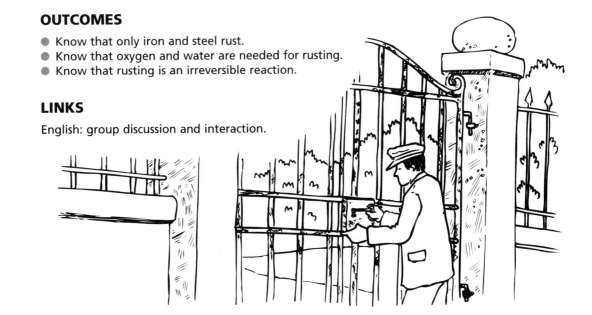

LESSON 16

Objectives	● To carry out an experiment. ● To know how to prevent iron and steel rusting.
Resources	Iron nails, Vaseline, painted iron nails, water, jam jars.
Main activity	Review what causes iron and steel to rust. Emphasise that it is a non-reversible reaction. *How can we stop things rusting?* Discuss why painting an iron bridge might slow down rusting. *How could we investigate this using a fair test?* Plan an experiment to coat iron nails in Vaseline or paint and see how quickly they rust in tap water or in air. The children should check the nails every day and record what they see. They should find that only the uncoated nails rust. Lead them to conclude that to stop things rusting, we have to keep air and water from touching them.
Differentiation	Less able children will need support when recording their observations and conclusions. More able children could be asked: *How would you stop these items getting rusty: a lawnmower in the winter; iron fencing; moving parts on a machine?*
Assessment	Note which children are able to: plan and carry out a fair test; make observations and record them in an appropriate way; say what their results show them.
Plenary	Review the children's work. Ask: *How do we stop iron from rusting?*
Outcome	● Can describe ways of preventing rusting.

LESSON 17

OBJECTIVE
● To know that some materials that we use in everyday life (such as paper) are made by changes that are irreversible.

RESOURCES

Main teaching activity: The video *Materials We Need* (Channel 4, 254255), a TV and video; a wooden picture frame (the size of the paper you wish to make), a bowl (large enough to hold the picture frame), straw, fabric, a kitchen blender, newspaper, two kitchen cloths, a rolling pin, a staple gun. (If the children carry out the activity, more sets of these things will be needed.)
Group activity: Paper, writing materials; photocopiable page 118 (see Differentiation).

BACKGROUND

Paper and plastic are materials that we use every day. They are manufactured materials that have been made from natural raw materials. Paper is made from wood and other fibrous materials such as straw, fabric or leaves. The choice of starting materials depends on what the paper will be used for (for example, banknotes are made from cotton, which is more durable than wood pulp). When wood is changed into paper, the change is irreversible. The wood fibres have been broken down and cannot re-form. When plastic is made from crude oil, the change is also irreversible: the oil molecules have been chemically transformed and cannot be restored.

Vocabulary

plastic, pulp, paper, permanent

INTRODUCTION

Review previous work on reversible and irreversible changes. Hold up a piece of paper and ask the children what it is. *What do we use paper for? Does anyone know how we make paper? This lesson, we are going to look at how paper is made.*

MAIN TEACHING ACTIVITY

Show the children the video about paper. Reinforce the idea that paper is made from wood, which comes from trees. Explain that you are going to make paper, using straw instead of wood.

The following activity could be done as a teacher demonstration. Alternatively, if you wish all the children to make their own sheet of paper, they could carry out Step 1 during a design and technology lesson. Steps 2 to 4 could then be done as a demonstration. Each child could carry out Steps 5 to 10 (to save time, you might want to have a few bowls of pulp already made).
1. Make a paper-making frame by stretching some fabric taut across an old picture frame and stapling it in place. The frame needs to be small enough to fit inside a bowl for Step 5.
2. Take four generous handfuls of straw and cut it into lengths of about 3cm. Boil the straw in a pan of water for about one hour (keep the water topped up so the straw is always covered).
3. Place the boiled straw and water in a blender. Make sure the straw is covered with water – top it up if necessary. You might not get all the straw in the blender at once. Blend until the straw pulp is well mashed-up. Only the teacher should use the blender.
4. Pour the pulp into the bowl. There should be enough pulp to half-fill it.

5. Put the frame into the bowl and swish it around to get a layer of pulp in the frame. You may need to do this a few times to get the pulp evenly spread across the frame.

6. Cover the work surface with newspaper and lay a kitchen cloth over it.

7. Take the frame out of the pulp. Tip the layer of pulp out of the frame and on to the kitchen cloth. You may need to give the frame a knock to get the pulp out. Place another kitchen cloth over the top of the pulp and press down firmly.

8. Use a rolling-pin to press down evenly and firmly on the cloth, removing any excess water.

9. Leave the sheet of paper to dry.

10. It will take practice to get the amount of pulp right and to learn how to spread the pulp evenly across the frame.

GROUP ACTIVITY

Ask the children to copy and complete the following from the board:
In factories, paper is made from [wood]. Today we made paper from [straw]. To help turn the straw into paper, we had to [heat] it up. We started with straw and made a new material, [paper]. We could not turn the paper back into straw. Paper-making is an [irreversible reaction], because a new material is made that cannot be turned back into straw.

DIFFERENTIATION

Less able children could be given the above text on a prepared worksheet, with the missing words listed. They could also be given a copy of page 118 and asked to cut out the pictures, arrange them in the correct order and stick them into their exercise books. More able children could be encouraged to write an account of how paper is made.

ASSESSMENT

A concept map (see Plenary) shows the connections between different ideas in a particular topic, and is a useful source of information about children's understanding. Use the Plenary session to assess which children understand what is meant by the terms 'reversible change' and 'irreversible change', and can give examples.

PLENARY

Use questions to build up a concept map on the board. *What material did we use today to make paper?* (Straw.) *In today's activity, did we make a new material from straw?* (Yes, paper.) *What did we do to the straw that you think might have turned it into a new material?* (Boiled/heated it.) *So the starting material was straw and the new material is paper. Do you think we could turn the paper back into straw?* (No.) *When we make paper from straw or wood, do you think this is a reversible or an irreversible reaction?* (Irreversible.) *Why?* (Because a new material has been made that cannot be turned back into straw or wood.)

OUTCOME

● Know that many manufacturing processes involve permanent changes.

LINKS

Design and technology: working with tools, equipment, materials and components to make quality products.

LESSON 18

OBJECTIVES

● To know that there are many energy sources in the home.
● To know what these energy sources are used for.

RESOURCES

Main teaching activity: A lamp; a battery-operated toy with batteries.
Group activities: 1. Photocopiable page 119, paper, writing materials. **2.** Catalogues containing household items, scissors, adhesive, A3 paper.

BACKGROUND

To make things move, change or do work, you need energy. You cannot see energy (apart from some kinds of light energy), but it takes many different forms. Chemical energy is stored in

batteries. Food is also a source of chemical energy. Other types of energy are heat energy, sound energy, light energy, kinetic (movement) energy and electrical energy.

Fuels are a source of heat energy. The energy stored in them is released during combustion, which generates heat and light energy (see Lesson 12). Carbon-based 'fossil fuels', such as coal, oil and natural gas, are a major natural source of energy. They are burned in power stations to release heat energy, which is used to boil water into steam. The steam builds up, and its pressure drives turbines that generate electricity. The electricity is itself used as a source of energy.

INTRODUCTION

Tell the children that they are going to look at energy, what it does and where it comes from.

MAIN TEACHING ACTIVITY

Display a lamp, not plugged in. Switch it on. *Oh, it's not working!* Hopefully one of the children will spot that it is not plugged in and let you know about it. *Why do I need to plug it in?* (Because the lamp needs electricity to make it work.) Plug the lamp in and switch it on.

Try working a toy that needs batteries, but does not have batteries in. *Oh, I wonder why it's not working!* The children might tell you that the batteries have run out. Some might ask you whether you put batteries in. Check the toy and notice that the batteries are missing. Put the batteries in and show the children that the toy is working.

Do you know, on my way to school this morning my car just stopped. I've got no idea what is wrong with it. Perhaps I should phone up the garage and ask them to help. Hopefully someone will say that it has probably run out of petrol.

Does anyone know what we mean by the word 'energy'? Explain that energy is needed to get jobs done, or to make things work. *So the lamp needs energy to work. The energy comes from electricity. The toy also needs energy to work. Where do you think the energy comes from?* (Batteries.) *What does a car need to work?* (Energy.) *Where does the energy come from?* (Petrol.) *Lots of things that are in our homes need energy to work. Now we are going to look at where these things get their energy from.*

GROUP ACTIVITIES

1. Give each child a copy of page 119. For each room in the house, the children have to list the items that need energy to work and then say where the energy is coming from. For example (see also Differentiation):

Room	Which things need energy?	Where does the energy come from?
Bedroom	Lamp	Electricity
Bedroom	Alarm clock	Batteries
Garage	Car	Petrol
Lounge	Fire	Coal/wood
Kitchen	People	Food
Kitchen	Cooker	Gas/electricity
Garden	Barbeque	Lighter fuel, briquettes

2. The children can look through some old catalogues and find items that need energy, cut them out and stick them onto a large sheet of paper to make a collage. The collages could then be used for a classroom display.

DIFFERENTIATION

For Group activity 1, less able children could be given an outline of a table with some of the words (such as those underlined in the example) already written in. They should cope well with Group activity 2. More able children could attempt to write a story about what it would be like if there were no energy sources available.

ASSESSMENT

Note which children can say which items in the home require energy in order to work, and which children can name some different types of energy that we use in the home.

PLENARY

Can anyone give me an example of something we have in school that needs energy? Can anyone tell me the source of energy this item needs in order to work? Elicit several suggestions and discuss what energy sources they use.

OUTCOMES

● Recognise items in the home that need energy to work.
● Recognise sources of energy in the home.

LINKS

PSHE and citizenship: preparing to play an active role as citizens.

LESSON 19

OBJECTIVE

● To know how electricity is made from non-renewable fuels.

RESOURCES

Main teaching activity: A video about electricity generation, such as *Cat's Eyes: Electricity Light and Sound* (BBC, 37604X); a TV and video.
Group activities: 1. Photocopiable page 120, scissors, glue. **2.** The *Encarta* CD-ROM (Microsoft).

BACKGROUND

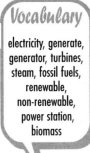

Vocabulary

electricity, generate, generator, turbines, steam, fossil fuels, renewable, non-renewable, power station, biomass

We say that electricity is 'generated' rather than 'made', because it is a form of energy and not a material. Electricity is generated in power stations, which can be identified by their distinctive cooling towers. Fossil fuels (coal, oil and natural gas) are burned in power stations, releasing heat energy which boils water; the steam drives turbines which generate electricity.

Fossil fuels are 'non-renewable' forms of energy. It has taken millions of years to form them; once they have been used up, they cannot be replaced within a human timescale. Thus they will eventually run out. Uranium can also be used in nuclear power stations to generate electricity; but as well as producing dangerous waste, nuclear power uses up the non-renewable supplies of uranium. It is important for everyone to be economical in their use of fossil fuels, because one day these resources will run out. The burning of fossil fuels also releases carbon dioxide into the atmosphere, which causes global warming; and it also releases sulphur dioxide into the atmosphere, causing the formation of acid rain.

Some energy sources are said to be 'renewable', because they are naturally replaced as quickly as they are used up and so will not run out. Examples are solar energy, tidal energy, geothermal energy (heat from naturally hot springs) and energy from wind, rivers and biomass. Biomass is living material such as wood; the energy stored in it is released when the wood is burned. Biomass is renewable through the replanting of forests.

Some of these renewable forms of energy are sources of heat energy (solar or geothermal) that can be used to heat up water, making steam that can be used to generate electricity. Other renewable forms of energy are sources of kinetic (movement) energy that can be used directly to turn the turbines that generate electricity. When renewable forms of energy are used (except biomass), there is no burning to generate heat energy. So these forms of energy are much better for the environment in terms of avoiding pollution.

INTRODUCTION

Last lesson, we saw that many items in our homes need energy to work. Can anyone give me an example? Where does the energy come from? Electricity provides many things with the energy they need to work. This lesson, we are going to find out more about electricity.

MAIN TEACHING ACTIVITY

Does anyone have any idea where electricity comes from or how it is made? Collect the children's ideas and write them on the board or flip chart. Explain how electricity is made, using careful questioning and drawing a flow chart on the board. *When you burn something like coal, what is produced?* (Heat, light, smoke.) *The heat produced when coal burns is used to heat up water. When you heat up water and it starts to boil, what is produced?* (Steam.) *The steam pushes against some turbines. Turbines are like big fans that turn. As they turn, they make electricity.*

Coal burned → Heats up water → Steam → Turns turbines → Electricity

This would be a good point to show the children a video about how electricity is made.

GROUP ACTIVITIES

1. Give each child a copy of page 120. Ask them to cut out the pictures, stick them into their exercise book in the correct sequence, then stick the correct caption beside each picture.

2. Ask some children to log on to *Encarta* and find the answers to the following questions: *Who discovered electricity? When was electricity discovered? How did Michael Faraday become interested in science? What two new materials did Michael Faraday discover?*

DIFFERENTIATION

Help less able children to complete both Group activities. More able children could go on to describe in their own words how electricity is made.

ASSESSMENT

Note which children are able to describe how electricity is made from coal (see Differentiation).

PLENARY

Consolidate the children's learning by asking them about how electricity is made. As homework, you could ask them to continue their research (using textbooks) and write a project on Michael Faraday.

OUTCOME

● Can describe how a non-renewable source of energy is used in power stations.

LINKS

ICT: using ICT to find information.

LESSON 20

Objective	● To know that there are non-renewable sources of energy.
Resources	A video on fossil fuels (such as Channel 4's *Pl@net.com*, 254278), a TV and video, A3 paper, collage materials, adhesive, crayons.
Main activity	Recap on Lessons 18 and 19. Explain why coal, oil and gas are called 'fossil fuels', and why they are non-renewable sources of energy. Show a video that explains how fossil fuels were formed. The children then draw a poster to illustrate the sequence of events from fossil fuels being formed to electricity being generated in power stations, and finally to how the electricity is used in the home.
Differentiation	Less able children might find the poster difficult to produce, and may prefer to explain the sequence orally. They might find using the computer to find out how fossil fuels were made a much more rewarding alternative. More able children could find out about the use of another non-renewable source of energy: uranium.
Assessment	Note which children can answer the questions asked in the Plenary session.
Plenary	Ask the children which fossil fuels are used in the home and where; how fossil fuels were formed; why fossil fuels are called non-renewable sources of energy.
Outcomes	● Can describe how non-renewable sources of energy are used in power stations.

LESSON 21

Objective	● To know that there are renewable sources of energy.
Resources	A video on renewable sources of energy (such as Channel 4's *Pl@net.com, 254278*), a TV and video; poster-making materials (as for Lesson 20).
Main activity	Have a quick 'question and answer' session to recap on Lesson 20. *This lesson, we are going to look at some other energy sources that are used to generate electricity.* *If any of you have been abroad, you may have noticed that the roofs of some houses have what look like shiny sheets of plastic on them. These are 'solar panels', and they collect the energy from the Sun (which is called 'solar energy'). The solar energy is used to heat up water, which creates steam to drive turbines and generate electricity. Do you think we will run out of solar energy?* (No.) *Would it be right to call it a non-renewable energy source?* (No.) *Why not?* (Because it is replaced as fast as we use it, so it will not run out.) *Sometimes wood is burned to create heat energy that can be used to heat up water and make steam and so generate electricity. Do you think wood is a renewable or a non-renewable source of energy?* (Renewable.) *Why?* (Because we can plant and grow trees quite quickly, and so replace the wood as we use it up.) Show an appropriate video at this point. Ask the children to draw a poster showing how renewable sources of energy can be used to generate electricity.
Differentiation	For less able children, see Lesson 20. More able children could design a poster to show how there are two types of renewable energy, and how both types are used to generate electricity: sources of heat energy that are used to heat up water, and sources of kinetic energy that are used to turn turbines directly.
Assessment	Note which children can tell you about some renewable energy sources.
Plenary	Consolidate the lesson by asking the children questions about renewable energy sources and how they are used to make electricity.
Outcome	● Can describe how renewable energy sources are used to generate electricity.

LESSON 22

Objectives	● To understand why we need to be economical in our use of fuels. ● To interpret a graph.
Resources	Photocopiable page 121, writing and poster-making materials (as for Lesson 20).
Main activity	Recap on fossil fuels: how they are used and why they are non-renewable. Explain that there is a need for everyone to be economical with the use of fossil fuels, because we are using them up and cannot remake them, so they will eventually run out. Another reason why we need to reduce the burning of fossil fuels is because burning them releases massive amounts of carbon dioxide (which causes global warming) and sulphur dioxide (which is thought to cause the formation of acid rain) into the atmosphere. Give the children a copy each of page 121. They should use the time chart to answer the questions on the sheet. You might find it useful to discuss the data and the questions with the children before they complete the sheet.
Differentiation	Less able children may wish to give their answers orally into a tape recorder. More able children could design a poster to say why we need to be more economical with fossil fuels and how we could achieve this.
Assessment	The concept map activity (see Plenary) will be a useful source of information about the children's understanding of the topic. If they have not previously made a concept map, they will need to be taught how to do so.
Plenary	*Can you name a fuel that we use to make electricity? Is this a renewable or a non-renewable source?* Repeat for several examples. *Why do we have to be economical in our use of fossil fuels?* Use this discussion to build up a concept map on the board.
Outcome	● Can explain why there is a need for fuel economy.

ASSESSMENT

LESSON 23

OBJECTIVES
● To review work done on the topic of materials.
● To carry out a formative or summative assessment for this unit.

RESOURCES

1. Samples of materials (such as sugar, salt, sand, filter paper, a lump of coal, a piece of wood), safety symbols, paper, pens. **2.** Photocopiable page 122, pens.

INTRODUCTION

You may wish to begin the Assessment activities straight away, or you may like to begin by helping the children prepare for the test. Devise (or ask the children to devise as a homework task) ten questions from the work you have covered. Ask these quickly round the class, or let the children pose questions to each other and evaluate the answers with your help. This could be done as a quiz where the class is split up into teams, or children can just answer their questions individually. If the children have prepared questions at home, watch out for questions that cannot be answered without recourse to reference materials!

ASSESSMENT ACTIVITY 1

This activity will also be useful preparation for the photocopiable test. Ask the children to form a concept map to show the connections between the different ideas in this topic. This can be done as a whole-class activity; if you wish it to be done as a group activity, the children will need to be taught how to do so. The concept map should cover as much of this unit as the children can incorporate or recall.

Very briefly, go over the work covered in this unit by showing the children various objects and samples of materials (see Resources). Ask the children which materials dissolve and which do not dissolve. Build this into a concept map, linking dissolving to reversible and irreversible reactions and then to burning, health and safety and fuels.

ASSESSMENT ACTIVITY 2

Give out copies of photocopiable page 122 for the children to complete individually. You may wish to mark the sheets yourself, or exchange them around the class and let the children mark each other's sheets to encourage discussion of the questions and answers.

Answers

1. Soluble: salt, instant coffee, artificial sweetener, Insoluble: sand, soil, chalk (3 marks for all 6 correct, 2 marks for 4 or 5 correct, 1 mark for 2 or 3 correct). 2a. Filtration (1 mark); 2b. Evaporation (1 mark). 3. Below the sand (1 mark). 4. Catch it on a cold surface (1 mark). The water vapour condenses back to a liquid (1 mark).
5. Increase the temperature of the water (1 mark), stir the water (1 mark), make the size of the particles smaller (1 mark). 6a. Carbon dioxide (1 mark). 6b. Irreversible (1 mark). 6c. We cannot get Andrew's Liver Salts and water back (1 mark), a new material has been made (1 mark). 7. Reversible change (1 mark). 8. See table, right (2 marks for 4 correct, 1 mark for 2 or 3 correct). 9. Water and oxygen (1 mark – accept 'air' instead of 'oxygen'). 10. Non-renewable sources of energy (1 mark). Total possible marks = 20.

Safety sign	Meaning
☠	Toxic
🔥	Flammable
✗	Harmful
🧪	Corrosive

Looking for levels

All the children should be able to identify which common substances are soluble and which are insoluble (question 1). Most children should be able to describe how to separate certain mixtures; understand how a filter bed works to clean water; be able to identify the conditions that help to speed up dissolving and the conditions needed for rusting; and be able to identify the common safety symbols (questions 2, 3, 4, 5, 8 and 9). More able children should be able to identify reversible and irreversible changes, and understand what is meant by a renewable or non-renewable form of energy (questions 6, 7 and 10).

PLENARY

You may wish to go through the answers to the tests with the children after you have collected in the work for marking.

There may be a question that many of the children got wrong (for example, question 2b). If this is the case, it is advisable that you go over the concepts that relate to this question with the children and then give them a question that is different from the one in the test but covers the same concepts (for example: *How would you separate sugar from water?*)

On the other hand, there may be a question that the majority of children got right. In this case, it would be a good idea to give them an extension question or task that covers the same concepts. For example, if most children get question 9 right, you could ask them to describe how they would prevent their bike from rusting and why these methods would work.

Name

Filter beds

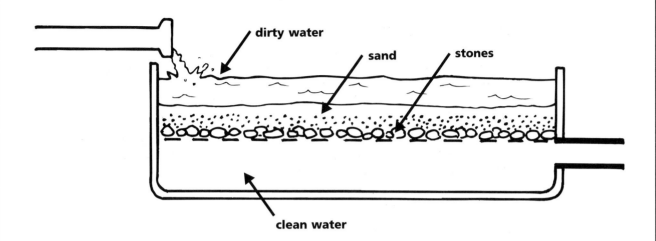

dirty water · sand · stones · clean water

Filter beds are used to clean water. The dirty water is passed through a filter bed before it goes back to the river.

Home-made filter bed

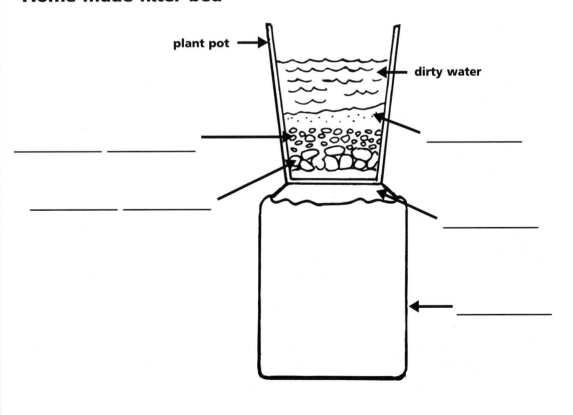

plant pot · dirty water

Changes of state

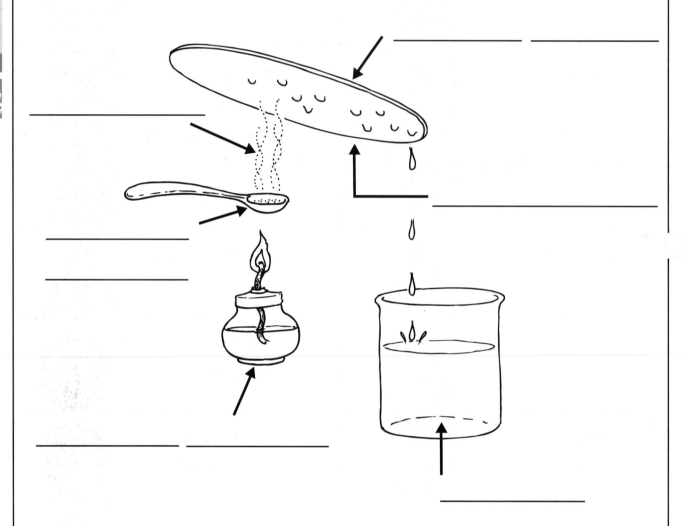

When the salt solution was heated up the water _____, leaving

_____ behind in the spoon. Water is a _____, and

so when it is heated it turns into steam, which is a _____.

When the steam hit the cold surface it cooled down and turned back into

_____, which is a liquid. When a gas turns back into a liquid,

this is called _____.

Name

Safety signs

Explosive		Corrosive	
Oxidising		Irritant	
Extremely or highly flammable		Biohazard	
Radioactive		Risk of electric shock	
Laser radiation		You MUST wear eye protection	
Harmful to the environment		You MUST wear protective gloves	
Danger		You MUST NOT have naked flames	
Toxic		You MUST NOT drink this water	
Harmful		You MUST NOT use water to put out fires	

Notes: Symbols inside squares are used only on bottles and other containers. Safety signs that are circular are required by law: you MUST or MUST NOT. For further information, consult the latest edition of the CLEAPSS *Hazcards* or *Laboratory Handbook*.

How to make paper from straw

old picture frame

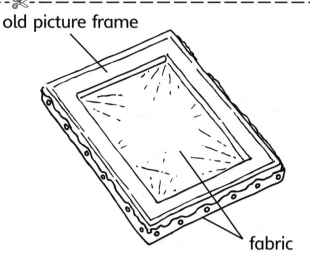

fabric

boil up straw
with water

blend into pulp

scoop up pulp and spread
evenly on surface of fabric
inside frame

place another kitchen
cloth over the top of the
pulp and press down

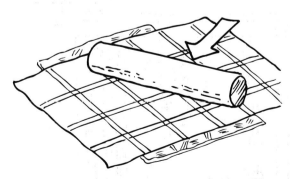

remove excess water by rolling

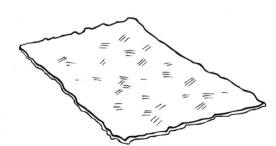

leave the sheet of
paper to dry

Things that need energy

Power generation

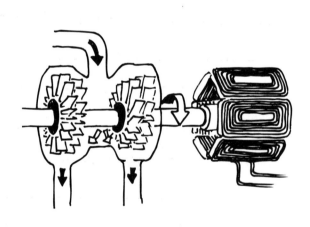

Electricity is generated in power stations. Coal is burned to boil water into steam.

The steam is forced through large fans called turbines. As these turn they generate electricity.

When coal is burned, heat and light are produced.

Electricity is used in the home for many things, such as heating up water in a kettle and making the lights work.

Energy consumption

Fossil fuels are non-renewable sources of energy. Once we have used them up, they are gone for ever.

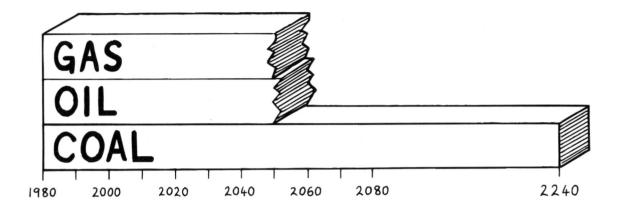

1. Use the time chart to answer the following questions.

● What year were you born? Find this on the time chart.

_____

● What year is it now? Find this on the time chart.

_____

● When you are 30, what year will it be? Find this on the time chart.

_____

● When you are 60, what year will it be? Find this on the time chart.

_____

● From the chart, what do you notice about the fuels?

_____

_____

● What can you predict about your life when you are 60?

_____

_____

_____

2. Make a poster showing how people could save fossil fuels.

Reversible and non-reversible changes

1. Put the following substances into the correct list:
sand, salt, soil, chalk, instant coffee, artificial sweeteners.

Soluble:

Insoluble:

2. (a) To separate sand from water, I would use _____

(b) To separate salt from water, I would use _____

3. In a filter bed, are the small stones on top of the sand or below the sand?

_____

4. When water evaporates into the air, how can you catch the water and turn it back into liquid?

_____

5. What three things can you do to increase the speed at which sugar dissolves in water?

_____

_____

6. When you add Andrew's liver salts to water, you see fizzing and bubbles.

(a) What is the name of the gas that is given off? _____

(b) Is this a reversible or an irreversible change? _____

(c) Give reasons for your answer to question 6b. _____

_____

7. When an ice cube melts and forms liquid water, is this a reversible or an irreversible change?

_____

8. On the back of this sheet, draw the safety signs that mean: toxic, flammable, harmful, corrosive.

9. What conditions are needed for rusting of iron to take place?

_____

10. Are fossil fuels renewable or non-renewable sources of energy? _____

Changing circuits

ORGANISATION (11 LESSONS)

	OBJECTIVES	MAIN ACTIVITY	GROUP ACTIVITIES	PLENARY	OUTCOMES
LESSON 1	● To find out how the number of batteries affects the brightness of a bulb.	Demonstrate how the brightness of a bulb depends on the energy in the batteries in the circuit.	Build circuits with varying numbers of batteries and bulbs or motors to observe how the circuit is affected.	Review group work. Discuss power requirements for stronger light sources.	● Can interpret diagrams to set up electrical circuits. ● Can make and record observations and analyse results. ● Know that more batteries make a bulb brighter or a motor faster.
LESSON 2	● To know that having more bulbs in a circuit makes the light dimmer.	The children build circuits with the same number of batteries but different numbers of bulbs, and compare the brightness.		Discuss resistance and its effect on a circuit: the more bulbs, the greater the resistance.	● Know that including more bulbs in a circuit makes all the bulbs dimmer, because they reduce the flow of electricity around the circuit.
LESSON 3	● To learn that electrical circuits and components can be represented by conventional symbols.	Introduce circuit symbols and how they are used to build up a circuit diagram.	Convert circuit drawings into circuit diagrams. Build real circuits based on circuit diagrams provided.	Consider how specifications for components can be represented in circuit diagrams.	● Know the conventional symbols for circuit components and understand why they are used. ● Can draw circuits using symbols. ● Can build circuits from diagrams.
LESSON 4	● To know that switches can be placed between parts of a circuit to provide alternative routes for the current to pass along.	Construct circuits and investigate how the switches are arranged to operate the components in each circuit.		Discuss real-life applications of these circuits for the safe or easy use of an appliance.	● Know that different switches can be used to operate a circuit in different ways.
LESSON 5	● To look at types of switch that could operate a burglar alarm.	Look at diagrams of different types of switch and discuss how they operate.	Build a switch, then write about how it works and where it could be used.	Look at how the switches made could be used in a burglar alarm.	● Can make a simple switch. ● Can consider real-life applications of different switches.
LESSON 6	● To consider the technological applications of switches.	Children design and build a switch for use in a burglar alarm.		Use the switches in a buzzer circuit. Discuss their operation.	● Can apply knowledge of electric circuits in a practical context.
LESSON 7	● To recognise dangers associated with electricity. ● To know what a 'short circuit' is and why it can be dangerous.	Demonstrate a short circuit. Explain the dangers of short circuits and how fuses are used to prevent them.	Look at a picture of some unsafe uses of electricity. Explain the cause of each danger and its likely effects.	Discuss basic procedures for electrical safety.	● Know how a short circuit occurs. ● Know about the dangers associated with a short circuit. ● Can produce a list of safe electrical practices.
LESSON 8	● To know that the amount of electricity flowing in a circuit is related to the total resistance in the circuit.	Demonstrate that the brightness of a bulb changes when different lengths or types of wire are used.	Observe the effect of using different lengths of wire with the speed of rotation of a motor. Record results in a table, draw a graph and analyse the results. Answer questions on a similar experiment.	Reinforce the link between resistance and current (and hence the brightness of a bulb).	● Know how the length of a wire affects the electricity flowing in a circuit. ● Can carry out an investigation and analyse the results.

ORGANISATION (11 LESSONS)

	OBJECTIVES	MAIN ACTIVITY	GROUP ACTIVITIES	PLENARY	OUTCOMES
LESSON 9	● To know that the current in a circuit depends on the resistance. ● To know that a variable resistor can be used to control the amount of electricity flowing in a circuit.	The children use secondary sources on dimmer switches, volume controls and speed controllers to make a display of pictures and descriptions.		Review the children's work.	● Can describe how a variable resistor affects the flow of electricity through a circuit.
LESSON 10	● To revise the knowledge of electricity needed for the construction of electrical circuits in real life.	Use diagrams of real-life circuits to revise aspects of electrical circuits. The children use secondary sources to prepare a presentation on electrical safety or energy saving.		The children present their ideas. Discuss points raised.	● Understand how circuits can be used for a range of purposes. ● Can explain the uses of different circuit components. ● Can describe the dangers associated with electricity. ● Can describe how the waste of electrical energy can be reduced.

	OBJECTIVES	ACTIVITY 1		ACTIVITY 2	
ASSESSMENT 11	● To assess the children's knowledge of ways that a circuit can be changed and the effect the changes have on components. ● To assess the children's ability to recognise circuit symbols and interpret circuit diagrams in order to build circuits. ● To assess the children's knowledge that the relative brightness of a bulb is related to the amount of current in the circuit.	Complete a short written test to examine their knowledge of how electrical current can be varied and how that affects the components in a circuit.		Build four simple circuits and compare the relative brightness of the bulbs. Give reasons for the differences in brightness.	

LESSON 1

OBJECTIVE
● To find out how the number of batteries affects the brightness of a bulb.

RESOURCES

Main teaching activity: A two-cell torch with batteries, one flat battery, two good batteries, a bulb in a holder, two connecting wires.
Group activity: Photocopiable page 134, 15 batteries, six switches, three bulbs (2.5V), three motors (3–4V).

BACKGROUND

For an electric current to flow around a circuit, an electrical supply must be connected within it. Batteries can be used to supply the energy to make an electric current flow. A battery has a **potential difference**: a difference in electrical energy between the two ends, due to the chemicals inside. These chemicals have different properties that create the potential difference.

Vocabulary

battery, flat (battery), bulb, motor, current, circuit, potential difference.

Different chemicals result in higher or lower potential differences, and so to the different voltages labelled on the batteries. Layers of these chemicals can also be placed within a single battery to build up a higher potential difference. If the battery is placed in a circuit, free charged particles in the wire (known as 'electrons') will move around the circuit because of the potential difference. This is the electric current. If a greater number of batteries are used, there is a greater potential difference across them all together, and so a greater current is produced. The potential difference is like a water pump for a fountain: the greater the power of the pump, the faster the water moves around the pipes, and so the greater the height of the fountain.

An electric current can cause different effects, one of which is heating as the current passes through a wire or other conducting material. In a narrow wire that the electrons have more difficulty passing through, as in a light bulb, this heating effect is greatly increased. Rather in the way that a narrow pipe restricts the flow of water, the narrow wire in a bulb resists the electric current. The wire will glow when a sufficiently high current goes through it. The higher the current, the greater the heating effect and hence the more intense the glow. For a low current, a bulb may be seen to glow red hot, while for a greater current it will glow white hot. Thus more batteries means a greater current and a brighter bulb.

Too great a current will 'blow' the bulb, as the amount of electricity flowing through the filament causes a heating effect greater than the filament can take. In effect, you are overloading the filament with passing electrons. This is similar to the effect of putting too much water through a hosepipe that has a narrow connector: the pipe 'blows up'. The effect of a current that causes a motor to turn (the electromagnetic effect) is also increased when more batteries are added. More batteries on a single motor will cause it to spin at a higher rate.

Conversely, having more components (such as bulbs) in a circuit that uses the electric current from a fixed number of batteries causes a reduction in the rate of flow of electricity (the current). This is due to the wire in each bulb resisting the flow of electricity. If the current is reduced by the increased resistance of additional bulbs, the brightness of each bulb is reduced. If there are several identical bulbs, they are all dimmed by the same amount.

INTRODUCTION

Ask the children how they would get a bulb to light and what equipment they would need. They should be able to list all the appropriate parts and to tell you that a complete circuit is needed. Ask them what each part of the circuit is for.

MAIN TEACHING ACTIVITY

Show the children the torch and, if possible, the connections inside. Put in the batteries, making sure that one is the flat one. Shine the torch towards the pupils: it should have a dim light. The children should notice this, but prompt them if necessary. *How could the light be improved?* (By changing the batteries to two good batteries.) Demonstrate this, then remove the batteries and use them to light the bulb in a simple circuit. *What does it mean if a battery is 'flat'?* (It has insufficient energy to make the electricity flow around the circuit.) Explain that with only one good battery in the torch, a small electric current passes through the bulb; two good batteries provide a greater amount of energy to give a higher current, and hence a brighter bulb.

GROUP ACTIVITY

Divide the class into six groups. Give each group a tray containing the apparatus shown on page 134. Give each child or group a copy of page 134. Each group should set up the circuits described on the sheet. Ask the children to write a comment under each diagram on the sheet to describe what happens in the circuit. At the end of their experiments, they should make a general comment about what their experiments showed.

DIFFERENTIATION

Less able children could be grouped together and given the easiest circuits to build. These circuits should not be taken apart once they have been put together. Children with writing difficulties could have a comment started on the sheet for them to complete. The start of a sentence for the concluding paragraph could be particularly useful, for example: *In our experiments, we have found out that having _____ batteries makes the bulbs _____.* More able children could be encouraged to think about the possible effects of having an even greater number of batteries for a single bulb, and what might happen to the wires and the bulb. (Trying this will create enough heat in the filament of the bulb to cause it to melt, 'blowing' the bulb. Can the children think of any further dangers?)

ASSESSMENT

Have all the children built their circuits in the same way? Are the components placed in the same order? Does this make a difference? (No.) This point can be used in the Plenary to illustrate the idea that the electricity must flow through all parts of the completed circuit. Can the children observe how the changes they make in the circuit affect the components?

PLENARY

Check the groups' answers on the sheet. They should have found that the higher the battery-to-bulb ratio, the brighter the bulb is. Discuss the battery requirements for bigger torches (as used by security guards) and car headlamps. *What power do table lamps need?* (Mains, so 230V.) *How about the lights in concert halls, or the floodlights in football grounds?*

OUTCOMES

- ● Can interpret diagrams to set up electrical circuits.
- ● Can make and record observations and analyse results.
- ● Know that more batteries make a bulb brighter or a motor faster.

LESSON 2

Objective	● To know that having more bulbs in a circuit makes the light dimmer.
Resources	Batteries, bulbs, connecting wires.
Main activity (Assessment)	Ask the children to set up circuits with the same number of batteries but different numbers of bulbs, and to look at whether they become brighter or dimmer. Each child should make and draw two circuits, recording the difference between them and the effect on the bulb(s). Use this work to assess which children have observed the change in brightness as more bulbs are added to the circuit.
Differentiation	Less able children could compare the simplest circuits. More able pupils could comment on how the energy from the batteries is being used, and compare circuits with matching battery-to-bulb ratios (such as 2:1 and 4:2). They should note that the bulbs are equally bright, as there is the same amount of energy per bulb.
Plenary	Discuss how the bulbs restrict the flow of electricity through the circuit: the more bulbs there are, the more the flow is restricted and so the less bright each bulb is. Particular circuits to comment on are: one bulb and two batteries; two bulbs and two batteries; two bulbs and four batteries. Where the ratio of bulbs to batteries is relatively low, the bulbs are brighter. Where the ratios can be simplified to the same value, the bulbs will be equally bright
Outcome	● Know that including more bulbs in a circuit makes all the bulbs dimmer, because they reduce the flow of electricity around the circuit.

LESSON 3

OBJECTIVE
● To learn that electrical circuits and components can be represented by conventional symbols.

RESOURCES

Main teaching activity: A flip chart and marker pen.
Group activities: 1. Photocopiable page 135 (one copy per child), plain paper, pencils, rulers, rubbers. **2.** A tray containing bulbs, motors, batteries, wires and switches for each group, photocopiable page 135.

PREPARATION

Copy the following circuit symbols (or draw easier or more complex ones, according to the children's ability) onto the flip chart.

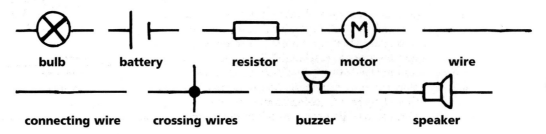

bulb   battery   resistor   motor   wire

connecting wire   crossing wires   buzzer   speaker

Vocabulary

symbol, circuit diagram, component.

BACKGROUND

Scientists want quick methods of recording that leave them time to focus on their experiments. They also want other scientists to understand the work they have done, and technicians to build circuits that they have designed. To do this, they use a system of internationally recognised symbols for components in diagrams of circuits. Each component has a simple symbol that (in most cases!) is difficult to mistake for any other. The commonly occurring symbols that children at KS2/P4–7 will need to know are shown opposite.

Another convention is that all wires are drawn as straight lines and, where possible, circuits are drawn as rectangular (with all corners at 90°). Where wires cross over, to avoid confusing crossing points with joins, the crossing points are drawn as bridges or 'hops' of one wire over another (see example on previous page).

INTRODUCTION

Select a child and show him or her the name of a component used in an electrical circuit, such as 'battery'. Ask the child to represent that component by drawing it on the flip chart so that the rest of the class can guess what it is. When a child guesses the component correctly, he or she can be given the name of another component to draw. Carry on for all the components shown opposite. If they are so quick that you soon run out, offer the name of a component that has already been drawn, but whisper that the child should draw a different type of it (for example, an upright square battery rather than a cylinder on its side). Alternatively, do the drawing yourself. Explain that it is difficult for a scientist to draw components in a way that everybody understands, particularly as there are so many types of motor, bulb, switch and so on. So instead, scientists have come up with a system of symbols.

MAIN TEACHING ACTIVITY

Using the pictures that the children have drawn, write the name of each component and draw its symbol next to the children's sketches. Now ask a child to come out and draw a circuit containing a battery and a bulb. It is likely that the child will draw the symbols for these components, but will draw the wires as curves; if so, explain that both for neatness and for scientific convention, circuits should be drawn as rectangles.

GROUP ACTIVITIES

1. Give each child a copy of page 135. Ask the children to convert the drawings into circuit diagrams, using the correct symbols.
2. Ask the children to convert the circuit drawings on page 135 into real circuits, using the components provided.

DIFFERENTIATION

1. Give less able children copies of page 135 with the first circuit drawn. This will save them having to remember the main symbols or check them with the drawings on the flip chart. **2.** The complexity of the circuits can be extended to challenge more able pupils; or you could make some circuits and ask children to draw the corresponding circuit diagrams.

ASSESSMENT

Note whether the children have completed the sheet correctly. (The answers are shown above right.)

PLENARY

Show the children a 9V square battery and a more common 1.5V cylindrical battery. *How could scientists show the difference between these on a circuit diagram?* The simple solution is to write the voltage number just above the battery symbol. Specifications for other components (see examples on the right) can also be noted on circuit diagrams.

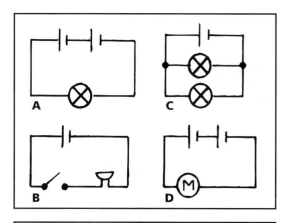

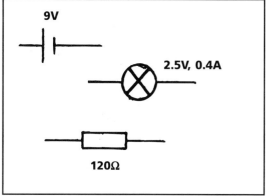

OUTCOMES
● Know the conventional symbols for circuit components and understand why they are used.
● Can draw circuits using symbols.
● Can build circuits from diagrams.

LESSON 4

Objective	● To know that switches can be placed between parts of a circuit to provide alternative routes for the current to pass along.
Resources	Batteries, bulbs, motors, push switches, two-way switches, rocker switches, wires.
Main activity	Draw the four circuits shown below on a board or flip chart. Ask the children to construct two of them (see Differentiation) and investigate how the switches are arranged to make the components in the circuit operate. Circuit A operates with the rocker switch when it is not pressed, but operates with the push switch only when it is pressed. In circuit B, either switch can be pressed. Circuit C requires both switches to be pressed. Circuit D allows the circuit to be operated from either switch.
Differentiation	Less able children could make circuits A and B, more able children circuits C and D.
Assessment	Can the children explain how the switches make the circuits work?
Plenary	Discuss real-life applications of these circuits for the safe or easy use of an appliance. (A. Push switch – keyboards, remote controls, ignitors for gas cookers. Rocker switch – TV on/off, light switches, torch switches. B. For an alarm that can be set off from different places. C. For a machine where the 'On' switch turns on the machine only if another switch is activated by a safety device, such as a guard being in place. D. Used on stairs and in bedrooms where there is a light switch by the door and by the bed.)
Outcome	● Know that different switches can be used to operate a circuit in different ways.

A. Rocker vs push

B. OR circuit

C. AND circuit

D. Stairs circuit

LESSON 5

OBJECTIVE
● To look at types of switch that could operate a burglar alarm.

RESOURCES
Group activities: Photocopiable page 136, batteries, bulbs, connecting wires, materials for making switches (see page 136).

Vocabulary

push switch, circuit

BACKGROUND
This lesson and Lesson 6 are designed to fulfil in some part the suggestions in QCA Unit 5/6H for teachers in England looking to address this topic through a technological project. However, the science aspect must not be lost in the fun of designing, developing and making the switches.
   A switch has a very important role in a circuit. It provides an easy way of breaking and completing a circuit. Depending on its construction, the switch may only operate for the time that it is pressed or may lock into position until reset.

INTRODUCTION
Discuss the difference between the switches the children usually find in circuits and a switch that is used for turning on a computer. The computer switch locks into position, whereas the standard 'push switch' in a circuit only completes the circuit while it is being pressed. Tell the children that they are going to make some switches that work in different ways.

MAIN TEACHING ACTIVITY
Distribute copies of the factfile sheet (page 136) among the children so that they can all see a copy. Go through each switch illustrated and discuss how it might operate. Remind the children

that there must be a place where the switch is connected to the circuit, and a gap that can be opened and closed in order to complete and break the circuit.

GROUP ACTIVITY (DIFFERENTIATION)

The children should work in mixed-ability groups to make one switch from the factfile, then write about how it operates and where they could put it in an alarm or another situation.

ASSESSMENT

Can the children build the switch and make it operate within the circuit? Can they give a satisfactory explanation of how the switch completes and breaks the circuit?

PLENARY

Prepare for Lesson 6 by discussing how the switch the children have built could be applied in a burglar alarm (for example, trip wires or alarms on window or door catches).

OUTCOMES

- Can make a simple switch.
- Can consider real-life applications of different switches.

LINKS

PSHE: security at home and school.
Technology: technological projects.

LESSON 6

Objective	● To consider the technological applications of switches.
Resources	Batteries, bulbs, buzzers, wires, the children's choice of materials for switches.
Main activity	The children should discuss, design and build their own switch for use in a burglar alarm circuit (for example, a 'pressure pad' design where two pieces of aluminium foil become connected when weight is applied). This may take a number of lessons, and the children may wish to build additional items to help with the operation of the circuit (such as model doors or windows). Remind the children that a switch must complete and break a circuit. When the switches have been built, insert them into a simple buzzer circuit to check their operation.
Differentiation	More able children may wish to use magnets or more inventive ideas. They could also draw their circuit and describe its operation in writing.
Assessment	Can the children build a switch that works in the way described?
Plenary	Operate the children's switches in the circuit. Discuss their mode of operation, and where they should be placed to be effective in a burglar alarm system.
Outcome	● Can apply knowledge of electric circuits in a practical context.

LESSON 7

OBJECTIVE
- To recognise dangers associated with electricity.
- To know what a 'short circuit' is and why it can be dangerous.

RESOURCES

Bulbs, batteries, switches, photocopiable page 137, plain paper, pencils.

PREPARATION

Build the circuit shown on the right.

BACKGROUND

Electricity flows around a complete circuit, usually to do a useful job such as lighting a bulb or running a

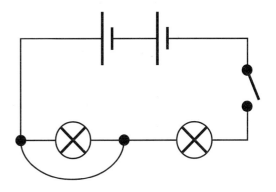

motor. However, electricity tends to take the easiest path through a circuit. In order to flow through the components of a circuit, the current encounters resistance due to the construction of these components. For example, it is more difficult for current to pass through the narrow wire in a bulb than through the thick wires that make up the rest of the circuit. If an alternative path is provided (either deliberately or by accident) for the electricity to flow along that has a lower resistance, that is the path the current will take: it will thus make a 'short circuit' that bypasses the bulb. The great problem with a short circuit is that often the resistance is so low that a very high current will pass along the wires, causing the wire to heat up to such an extent that it may cause a fire. Short circuits can be extremely dangerous.

Mains electricity plugs have a replaceable fuse inside. A fuse contains a thin piece of wire encased in a ceramic holder that is designed to melt if the current flowing through it is too great. This means that a mains short circuit will 'blow' the fuse and not damage the appliance. It is important, therefore, that the right type of fuse is fitted, so that it does not allow an unsafe level of current to flow (but also, does not blow at a normal level of current).

INTRODUCTION

Discuss the children's ideas about the safe use of electricity. They should include not overloading sockets, not mixing water and electricity, not using frayed cables and not poking items into electrical sockets. This discussion should draw on their experiences of electricity at KS2/P4–7.

MAIN TEACHING ACTIVITY

Display the circuit you have made. The two bulbs should be lit normally. Connect the two ends of a wire to either side of one of the bulbs. Ask the children to describe what happens. The 'short-circuited' bulb, with the new wire, will be off and the other bulb will be much brighter. Ask the children to describe what has happened to the amount of electricity flowing through the two bulbs. There is no electricity flowing through the short-circuited bulb, whereas the bulb that has become brighter has more electricity flowing through it.

Can the children identify a potential problem with this increase in current? *What has happened to the wire in the brighter bulb? Why is it brighter?* If necessary, explain that the higher current causes a greater heating effect. *Why is this dangerous?* (It could start a fire.) Tell the children that the extra wire that has been attached has caused a short circuit, and that short circuits are dangerous in real life because they can cause fires in the home or the workplace.

GROUP ACTIVITY

Give each child a copy of photocopiable page 137. Ask the children to identify the dangers of electricity on the sheet, and what the risk is to the people in the picture.

DIFFERENTIATION

You may like to group less able children into pairs or threes to support each other and share ideas. Ask more able children to consider possible remedies to the problems and to write down their chosen solutions on another sheet of paper.

ASSESSMENT

Ask individuals to identify the dangers and, where appropriate, to describe their solutions.

PLENARY

Go through the children's responses to page 137, and discuss their ideas for remedies to the problems. In many cases, this is basic electrical safety procedure; however, some solutions may involve repair work or consulting an electrician – for example, adding extra sockets so that overloading does not occur. Adding extra sockets within the ring main of the house wiring circuit means that less current has to flow through individual wall sockets – instead, the high currents are placed on the ring main, which is designed to cope with them.

OUTCOMES

- Know how a short circuit occurs.
- Know about the dangers associated with a short circuit.
- Can produce a list of safe electrical practices.

LINKS

PSHE: safety in the home, personal responsibility.

LESSON 8

OBJECTIVE

● To know that the amount of electricity flowing in a circuit is related to the total resistance in the circuit.

RESOURCES

Main teaching activity: Batteries, bulbs, 1m nichrome wire, crocodile clips, connecting wires.
Group activities: 1. Batteries, motors, 1m nichrome wire, crocodile clips, connecting wires, hoists (from construction kits), string, small hanging masses. **2.** Photocopiable page 138.

PREPARATION

Set up the circuit shown on the right. Use nichrome wire initially, not copper. Some initial experimentation may be required to find out how much wire and how many batteries give the best results for a given thickness of wire.

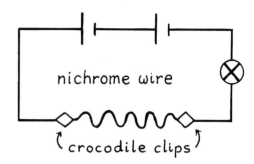

BACKGROUND

As was stated in Lesson 4, the amount of current in a circuit depends on how easily the electricity can flow through the wires and other components in the circuit. The factor that determines how much current flows in the circuit for a given voltage supply is called resistance. The greater the resistance, the lower the current. Resistance depends on the type of material the current is flowing through, and the length and thickness of that material in the circuit. A variable resistor allows the length of a high-resistance material in the circuit to be varied.

Vocabulary

resistance, resistor, current

INTRODUCTION

Gather the children around you and ask them to imagine the corridor outside the classroom just as lunch starts. The corridor is full of people trying to get to one part of the school. *What do you think it would be like trying to get to lunch if the corridor were narrower? Or wider? How does being at the far end of the corridor compare with being halfway down the corridor in terms of the time it takes to get to the dining room?* Tell the children that this is similar to the situation when electricity is trying to pass along a wire. The different widths and lengths of wire are similar to the different sizes of corridor. The ease with which you can get down the corridor is like the ease with which electricity can travel through the wire. The factors that would cause a crush in the school corridor are like the factors that cause resistance in an electrical circuit.

MAIN TEACHING ACTIVITY

Show the children the prepared circuit and demonstrate that moving the connections up and down the wire at random changes how bright the bulb is. Can they suggest a more systematic method for finding out the effect of changing the amount of wire in the circuit? They should suggest comparing the brightness of the bulb for every extra 5cm or 10cm along the wire. In this way, it should be possible to prove that the more wire is used, the dimmer the bulb is. Ask the children to explain what is happening to the current in the circuit, based on their observations of the bulb. They should be able to say that when the bulb is dimmer, the current is reduced – and therefore deduce that the greater the length of wire used, the lower the current.

Repeat the experiment with copper wire. This time, no obvious change in brightness should be observed. *What is different about this wire?* Copper wire is normally used for domestic wiring, because it allows electricity through easily and so saves energy and avoids unnecessary heating. Tell the children that different materials that conduct electricity have a different 'resistance', and that copper has a lower resistance (and so lets electricity flow through more easily) than the first wire. With a more able group, this idea could be extended to say that materials that are considered to be insulators (non-conductors) have a very high resistance.

GROUP ACTIVITIES

1. Ask the children to investigate the effect of using different lengths of wire on the speed of rotation of a motor operating a hoist to lift a small mass on a string. They need to set up a circuit using a piece of resistance wire, connected so that results can be taken for five or six different lengths of wire (using the full length of the wire in equal steps). The time taken for the motor to lift the mass a short distance (say 10cm) should be measured each time. Encourage the children to repeat their tests in order to improve the reliability of their results. They should record the results in a table, convert them into a line graph and analyse the data to draw a conclusion.

Name

Comparing circuits

Set up each circuit as shown below. Write a sentence under each picture to describe what happens in the circuit. Try to compare it with other circuits.

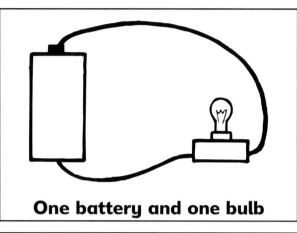

One battery and one bulb

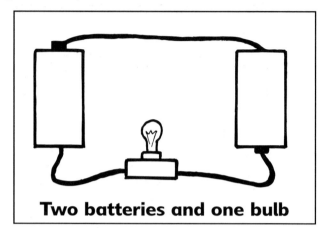

Two batteries and one bulb

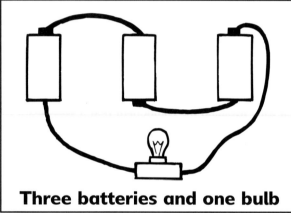

Three batteries and one bulb

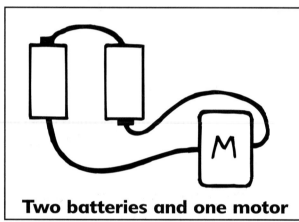

Two batteries and one motor

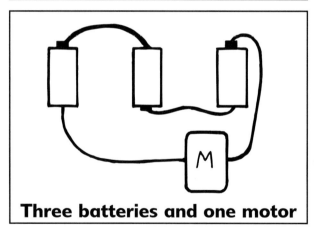

Three batteries and one motor

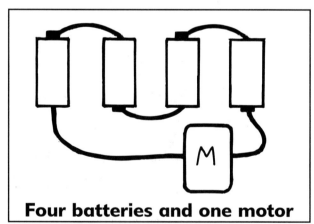

Four batteries and one motor

Can you see any pattern in the results? Can you explain this pattern?

Circuit diagrams

Use your knowledge of circuit symbols to redraw these circuit pictures as proper circuit diagrams on the right-hand side of the page. Use a pencil, ruler and rubber to make your diagram neat and to correct any mistakes you might make.

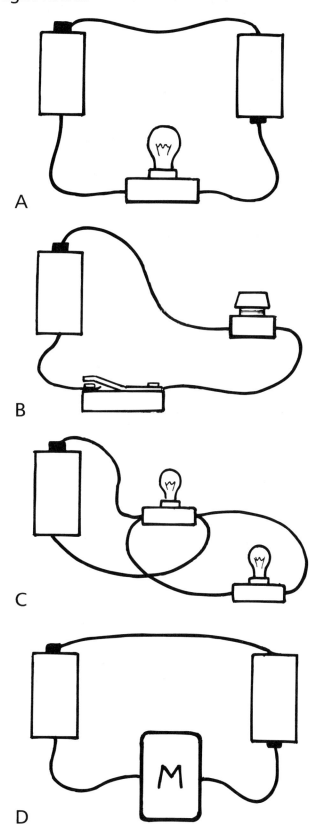

A

B

C

D

FACTFILE: switches

How do these switches work?

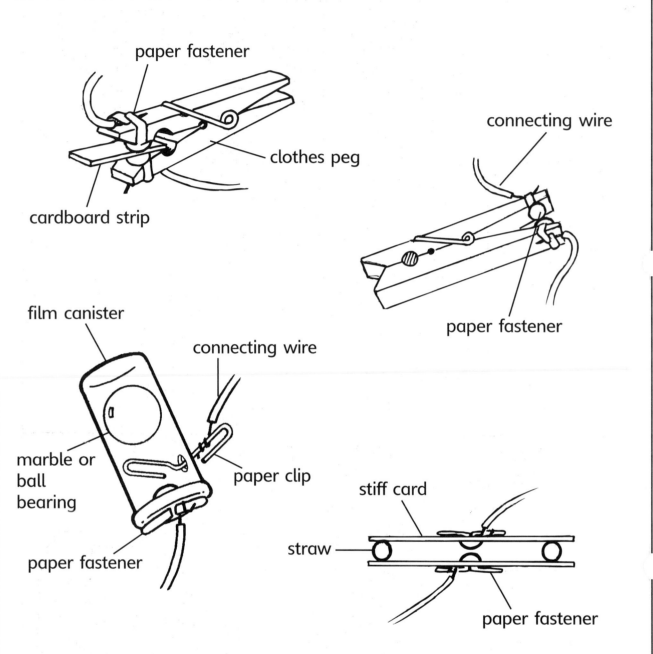

paper fastener

clothes peg

cardboard strip

connecting wire

paper fastener

film canister

connecting wire

marble or ball bearing

paper clip

paper fastener

stiff card

straw

paper fastener

Build this circuit to test the switches.

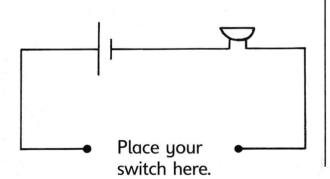

Place your switch here.

Name

Electrical dangers

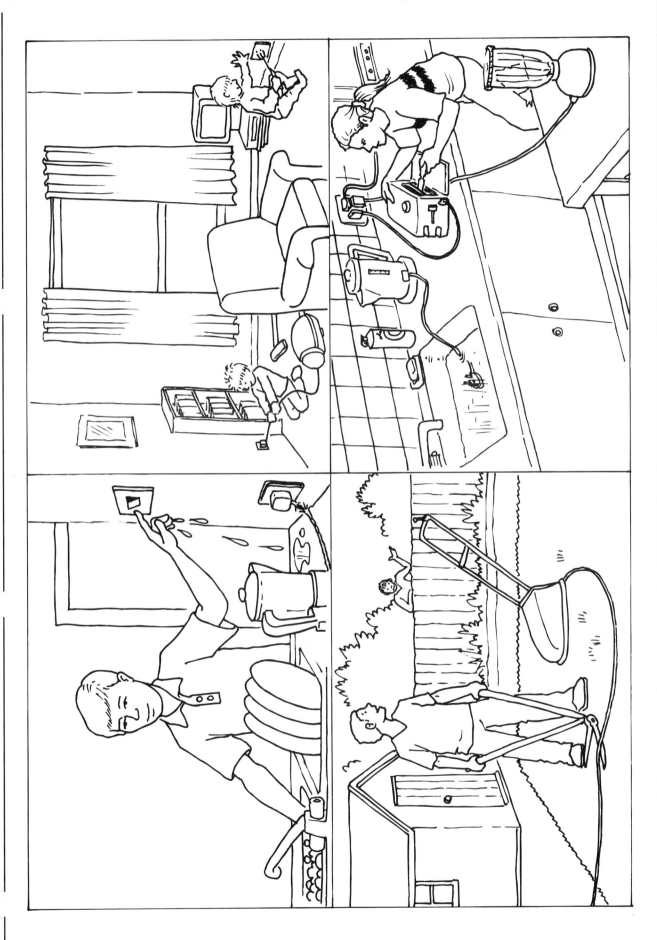

Name

Testing wires

Six groups in a class like yours used the circuit shown below to test different wires by measuring the amount of electricity going around the circuit with each wire in place. Their results are shown in the table.

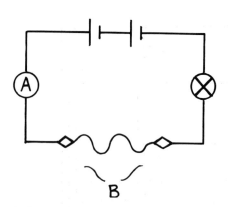

Circuit	Length of wire	Metal	Reading at A
1	10cm	copper	5
2	10cm	nichrome	4
3	20cm	copper	4.5
4	20cm	nichrome	2
5	30cm	nichrome	1.5
6	40cm	nichrome	1

1. Which pair of results could you compare to find out which metal lets the electricity through more easily?

_____

2. Which circuits would have
(a) the brightest bulb?   (b) the dimmest bulb?

_____   _____

3. Which circuits would you compare to find out how the length of wire affects the amount of electricity that passes through?

_____

4. Complete the graph below.

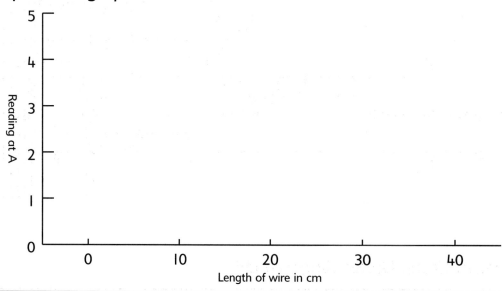

Name

Look at these circuit diagrams for a car.

Can you find any symbols in these diagrams for components you have used in your electricity work?

Real-life circuits

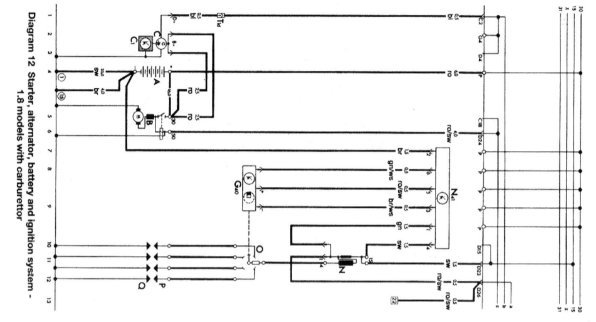

Diagram 12   Starter, alternator, battery and ignition system – 1.8 models with carburettor

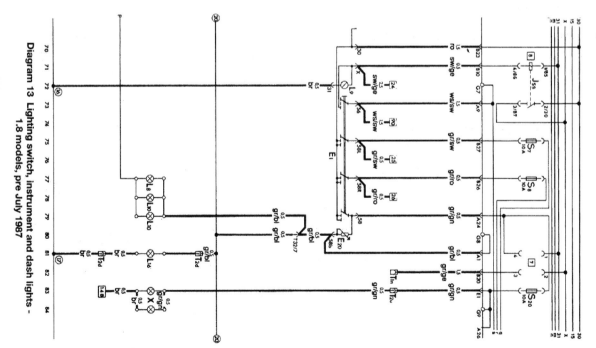

Diagram 13   Lighting switch, instrument and dash lights – 1.8 models, pre July 1987

© Volkswagen Group United Kingdom Ltd

Changing circuits

1. Draw a circuit diagram (with symbols) to show a bulb, a battery and a switch connected so that the bulb will light up when the switch is pressed.

4. Which of the following circuits will have the brightest bulb? Explain why you think this.

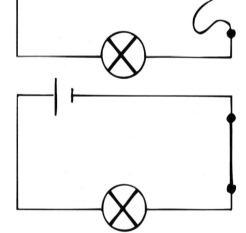

2. Explain why a bulb is brighter if it is powered by two batteries rather than one. Use what you know about electricity flowing through a wire to help you explain.

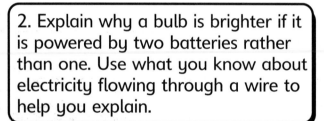

_____

_____

_____

_____

3. What is a 'short circuit'? Why is it dangerous?

_____

_____

_____

_____

_____

_____

Forces and action

ORGANISATION (11 LESSONS)

	OBJECTIVES	MAIN ACTIVITY	GROUP ACTIVITIES	PLENARY	OUTCOMES
LESSON 1	● To know that forces can be measured. ● To know that a force exists between two magnets, and between magnets and magnetic materials.	Demonstrate that a magnet can be used to pick up a steel paper clip. Demonstrate that a newton meter can be used to measure a force.	Measure the force between a magnet and a paper clip when different thicknesses of card are placed between them. Use secondary sources to find out about uses of magnets and electromagnets.	Discuss how the strength of a magnetic field is reduced as the distance from the magnet increases.	● Understand that a force has a value that can be measured. ● Can measure a force with a force meter. ● Can describe the forces between two magnets, and between magnets and magnetic materials.
LESSON 2	● To know that only a limited number of metals are magnetic. ● To know that the magnetic property of some metals allows them to be separated from other metals.	The children test various metals with a magnet to see whether they are attracted.		Discuss how few metals are magnetic, and how this is used in the recycling industry to separate metals.	● Know that only a limited number of metals are magnetic. ● Can use a magnet to separate metals.
LESSON 3	● To know that the force of gravity is responsible for the weight of an object.	Use a newton meter to measure the weight of an object. Compare this with its mass found by placing it on a balance.	Find out the weight and mass of various objects. Use secondary sources to find out what their own weight would be on other planets.	Find the value of the strength of gravity and compare it with values on other planets.	● Can find the mass of an object. ● Know that 'mass' and 'weight' are not the same. ● Understand that the weight of an object will be different on different planets.
LESSON 4	● To know that when a force on an elastic band is increased, its length increases in proportion. ● To make and record observations, draw a graph, analyse results and draw conclusions.	Demonstrate the relationship between load and extension using a spring.	Determine the relationship between load and extension for a hanging band. Answer questions about elastic breaking points.	Consider Hooke's Law in relation to the construction of newton meters.	● Know that the extent to which an elastic material stretches is proportional to the force applied. ● Can make and record observations, select results from a table and draw a conclusion.
LESSON 5	● To know that water exerts an upward force on a solid object suspended in it.	Compare the weight of objects in air and when suspended in water.		Use this experiment to introduce the concept of upthrust.	● Recognise the change in the weight of an object when suspended in water due to the upthrust. ● Can explain the forces acting on an object in water. ● Can make and record observations.
LESSON 6	● To know that when an object floats, the upthrust acting on it is equal to the force of gravity and acting in the opposite direction.	The children repeat the above experiment using objects that float and ones that sink in water.		Discuss the forces of gravity and upthrust when an object is floating.	● Can explain why an object floats.
LESSON 7	● To know that air resistance can slow down a moving object. ● To conduct an investigation.	Demonstrate how parachutes of different sizes affect how objects fall.	Test how different-sized parachutes fall. Answer questions about drag in liquids.	Discuss drag and streamlining.	● Can describe how air resistance affects a falling object. ● Can carry out an investigation.

ORGANISATION (11 LESSONS)

	OBJECTIVES	MAIN ACTIVITY	GROUP ACTIVITIES	PLENARY	OUTCOMES
LESSON 8	● To investigate factors that affect how fast a 'spinner' falls to the ground.	The children investigate how rotor size affects the speed at which 'spinners' fall.		Draw a graph of the results. Discuss the findings and review the experimental method.	● Can investigate how the size of a spinner affects the time it takes to fall. ● Can explain this result in terms of the effects of drag.
LESSON 9	● To look at how objects that move through fluids are streamlined.	The children use secondary sources to put together a display of streamlined objects and explain their uses.		Discuss the items selected, and the importance of streamlining in sports.	● Can identify streamlined shapes in the natural and manufactured world.
LESSON 10	● To be able to explain how objects stay at rest or move by considering the forces acting on them.	Demonstrate the forces acting on a hanging object, a held object, and a moving toy car.	Exert forces in various ways on different objects and draw force diagrams. Label force diagrams provided.	Discuss how forces affect the movement or shape of an object.	● Can explain how forces make things stay at rest or move.

	OBJECTIVES	ACTIVITY 1	ACTIVITY 2
ASSESSMENT 11	● To assess the children's knowledge and understanding of forces: their nature, relative size and direction. ● To assess the children's ability to plan an investigation and predict the results.	Answer questions about forces, including magnets, gravity, springs and balanced forces.	Look at some data from an experiment and analyse it to draw a conclusion.

LESSON 1

OBJECTIVES
● To know that forces can be measured.
● To know that a force exists between two magnets, and between magnets and magnetic materials.

RESOURCES

Main teaching activity: A magnet, a paper clip, *Dead Famous: Isaac Newton and his Apple* by Kjartan Poskitt (Scholastic, 1999) (optional).
Group activities: 1. A copy of photocopiable page 153, a magnet, a paper clip, a newton meter, string and card for each group. **2.** Secondary sources such as library books and CD-ROMs.

BACKGROUND

The children will already have experienced the pushing and pulling effects of the poles of a magnet, and will know that magnets can pick up certain metallic objects. Magnets are magnetic due to the alignment of the particles (atoms) inside the material. This alignment causes one end of the material to be attracted to the Earth's magnetic north pole, while the other is attracted to the magnetic south pole. (These do not exactly coincide with the geographical North and South Poles.) The north and south poles of the magnet will both attract a magnetic material such as steel, and will attract each other. However, if two north poles or two south poles are put close together, their magnetic properties will cause them to repel each other.

The children may have used newton meters to measure force. The newton meter (see illustration) is a simple device, using a spring that gets longer the more force is used to stretch it (by pulling with it or hanging something from it); the stretch is measured on a calibrated scale to show the value of the force being applied.

> **Vocabulary**
>
> magnetic field, magnetism, poles, newton, attract, repel

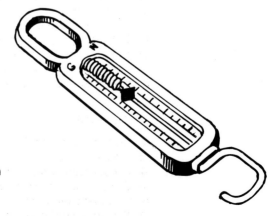

INTRODUCTION

Gather the children around you. Tell them that they are going to explore the force of a magnet. Ask them what a magnet can do. *Does it matter which part of the magnet is used to attract the object? Will all materials be picked up by a magnet?* Emphasise that if magnets can pull/attract or push/repel, they are exerting a force.

Show the children a newton meter. *What is this called? What does it do? How does it do that?* If necessary, demonstrate how to use the meter and read the scale. Tell the children that the unit of force is the newton (symbol N), which is named after the scientist Sir Isaac Newton. You may like to use page 150 of *Dead Famous: Isaac Newton and his Apple* by Kjartan Poskitt as a source for more information on the newton.

MAIN TEACHING ACTIVITY

Use a magnet to pick up a paper clip. Show the children that the paper clip will move towards the magnet and be attracted to it without initially being in contact with it. Say that this shows that the force or pull of a magnet exists beyond the magnet: there is a 'magnetic field' around the magnet that is strongest at each pole. Demonstrate how to use a newton meter to measure the force needed to pull the paper clip off the end of the magnet. Discuss with the children how they could use this equipment to measure how strong the force of the magnet is at different distances from it. Encourage them to think of a way of keeping the magnet and the paper clip a set distance apart; remind them that magnetic forces can travel through card and paper.

GROUP ACTIVITIES

1. Using page 153 as a guide and record sheet, the children can carry out an experiment to measure the force between a magnet and a paper clip when different thicknesses of card are placed between them.
2. The children can use secondary sources to find out about uses of magnets and electromagnets.

DIFFERENTIATION

1. More able children could go on to look at the effect of materials other than card. Less able children could concentrate on repeating their measurement of the effect of two sheets of card to look at how the accuracy of their experimental readings can be improved.
2. All the children should be able to participate in this activity, which revises work from Year 5.

ASSESSMENT

Can the children make accurate measurements of the strength of the magnetic force acting on an object at different distances from the magnet? Did they conclude that a magnetic field becomes weaker as you move away from the magnet?

PLENARY

Discuss the results of the experiment to establish the idea that a magnetic field becomes weaker as distance from the magnet increases. Ask the children how they think the extent of the magnetic field is affected by the strength of the magnet. Show the children a compass and remind them that it always points north. *Do you know why that is? If you were using a compass to find your way around, do you think it would matter if there were lots of magnets close by? What about magnetic materials such as iron and steel?* Show the children that the compass is affected by iron and steel objects around it by passing it over a steel box. *Why is the compass needle deflected, but the box does not move?* (The attraction between them is relatively weak, and the needle can move because it is lighter than the box.)

Time could also be taken to discuss how easy or difficult the newton meters are to read, and to find average measurements by comparing results from different groups. Explain why average measurements should be more accurate than individual measurements. The closer the children's results are, the more reliable they are likely to be.

OUTCOMES

● Understand that a force has a value that can be measured.
● Can measure a force with a force meter.
● Can describe the force of attraction between magnets and magnetic materials.
● Can describe the forces of attraction and repulsion between two magnets.

LESSON 2

Objectives	● To know that only a limited number of metals are magnetic. ● To know that the magnetic property of some metals allows them to be separated from other metals.
Resources	Labelled samples of magnetic metals (iron, steel, cobalt, nickel) and of some other metals; magnets, paper, writing materials. Metal samples are available from commercial sources.
Main activity	Ask the children to test a selection of metal samples with a magnet to see whether they are attracted. To do this, they should place the magnet on the sample and record whether it is possible to lift the sample off the desk with the magnet.
Differentiation	For children who have difficulties with writing, produce a worksheet with the metals listed in a table alongside an 'Is it magnetic?' column to be filled in. This will allow them to complete the experiment without being slowed down by the writing task.
Assessment	Do the children correctly separate the magnetic and non-magnetic materials?
Plenary	Discuss how few metals are magnetic, and how this fact is used in the recycling industry to separate steel and iron (eg steel cans) from other metals.
Outcomes	● Know that only a limited number of metals are magnetic. ● Can use a magnet to separate metals.

LESSON 3

OBJECTIVE
● To know that the force of gravity is responsible for the weight of an object.

RESOURCES

Main teaching activity: A newton meter, Plasticine.
Group activities: 1. A newton meter, weighing scales, small objects for weighing, a bag for hanging objects from the newton meter, graph paper (or a computer and spreadsheet/graphing software). **2.** A secondary source of information about the planets; calculators, bathroom scales (measuring in kilograms).

Vocabulary

gravity, mass, weight, gravitational field

BACKGROUND

Every day, we pick things up and put them down without much thought. Only when an object is particularly heavy do we make a comment. So what makes things 'heavy'? All objects on or near the Earth are attracted to the centre of the Earth. Even the Moon is attracted to the Earth by a force that keeps it in orbit (like a ball on a string). The force that does this is known as gravity. A gravitational attraction exists between all objects due to their mass (the amount of material from which they are made). Only when objects are very massive does this force become noticeable. The Earth is very massive, and so attracts objects to it. That is why everything falls: 'falling down' is being attracted to the Earth by gravity.

An object's weight is a measure of the force of gravity acting on it. The weight of an object is its mass (in kilograms) multiplied by the strength of gravity (in newtons per kilogram). The strength of the Earth's gravitational field is approximately 10 newtons for every kilogram of mass. The Moon is smaller than the Earth and consists of a different material, so it has a different strength of gravity: about one-sixth that of the Earth. So a 1kg bag of sugar has a weight of 10N on Earth, but only 1.6N on the Moon. Other planets in the Solar System also have their own gravitational forces. We can measure the force of gravity acting on an object in the classroom by hanging it from a newton meter.

INTRODUCTION

Gather the children in a group around you and ask a volunteer to stand in a space on one foot. Ask the child how he or she is feeling (besides tired). After a while, the child may start to topple. Ask the child: *Why do you keep falling over? What is making you fall?* (The invisible force of gravity.)

Throw a ball into the air. Ask the children to describe its path. It goes up, then stops for a brief moment, then falls. *What made it stop and then fall?* (The force of gravity.) The children should already know that forces change the speed and direction of moving objects. Tell them that they are going to measure the force of gravity in the classroom.

MAIN TEACHING ACTIVITY

Show the children the newton meter and hang a lump of Plasticine on it. Say that the newton meter measures the weight of the object. Compare this with the value for its mass found by placing the Plasticine on a balance. Tell the children that they will repeat this with several objects to see whether there is a link between the weight in newtons and the mass in grams.

GROUP ACTIVITIES (ASSESSMENT)

1. Each group should use a newton meter to measure the weight of an object, then find the object's mass by placing it on a balance. They should repeat this for at least six objects, record the results in a table, then plot a line graph of weight against mass on graph paper (or using a computer). Thios work can be used to assess their understanding of weight as a force.
2. The children can use secondary sources to find out what the strength of gravity is on the Moon and on different planets in the Solar System. Using bathroom scales, they can find their mass and then work out what their weight would be on different planets (by multiplying their mass by the strength of gravity on each planet). Use this work to assess their understanding.

DIFFERENTIATION

1. Less able children could use labelled masses and concentrate solely on measuring the weight. More able children could discuss how the graph produced would allow them to find the mass of an object given its weight, and vice versa. **2.** Less able children may need help with finding the gravitational field strength data for each planet. It may be appropriate to provide a simplified table for use in their calculations. More able children could be asked: *Would these scales still be accurate on the Moon? Why/why not?*

PLENARY

Discuss Group activity 1, and try to encourage the children to look for a 'magic number' that links the mass and the weight. The number is 10, which is an approximate value for the gravitational field strength on Earth (actually 9.81N/kg). Once this number has been established, random values for greater masses and weights can be chosen for the children to calculate the corresponding weight or mass by multiplying or dividing as appropriate. Explain that the Earth has a **gravitational field** that affects objects around it; like the magnetic field around a magnet, this field gets weaker further away from the Earth.

Discuss Group activity 2, encouraging the children to think about how the differences in gravity between the Earth and other planets in our Solar System would affect astronauts. *Are people heavier or lighter on Mars than on Earth? How would that affect how fast they could run and how high they could jump?*

OUTCOMES

- Can find the mass of an object.
- Know that 'mass' and 'weight' are not the same.
- Understand that the weight of an object will be different on different planets.

LINKS

Unit 8, Lessons 4 and 5: the composition of the Solar System.
Maths: developing mental strategies for multiplying and dividing by 10.

LESSON 4

OBJECTIVES

● To know that when the force stretching an elastic band is increased, its length increases in proportion.
● To make and record observations, present information in the form of graphs or charts, analyse results and draw conclusions.

RESOURCES

Main teaching activity: A light spring, a strong hook or laboratory stand, hanging masses, a strong elastic band, a ruler.
Group activities: 1. Strong elastic bands, newton meters, rulers, calculators, paper, writing materials. **2.** Photocopiable page 154, writing materials.

Vocabulary

elastic, extension, deform, stretch, proportional

BACKGROUND

Consider the effect of lifting a bag of shopping: the handles stretch a little. The greater the weight of the shopping in the bag, the greater the stretch on the handles. Sometimes the stretch is too great for the material the bag is made from and it snaps, with disastrous results! The same rules apply to all elastic materials. An elastic material, in the scientific sense, is one that can be stretched and will then return to its original shape (provided the force used is not too great). Sometimes the force is great enough to cause permanent deformation, and the material will either remain in its 'stretched' shape or break apart. The extent to which a material stretches (its extension) is, up to the point of permanent deformation, directly proportional to the amount of force applied. This law is known as Hooke's Law, after Robert Hooke (1635–1703). We can use this relationship to measure forces: a newton meter is a spring in a plastic case. Conversely, the force required to stretch an object by a certain amount increases as the extension increases.

INTRODUCTION

Gather the children around you and show them a spring. Demonstrate that it can be pushed (compressed) or pulled (extended), but it returns to its original shape. Ask the children what they think will happen if the spring is pulled with a small force. (It will stretch.) *What would happen if the force were greater?* (The spring would get even longer.) *Will the spring go back to the same shape? What if a very strong force were used?* (The spring would straighten out and not go back to its coiled shape.) Say that they are going to look at the effects of forces on stretchy materials.

MAIN TEACHING ACTIVITY

Hang a light spring on a strong hook or laboratory stand. Select a couple of volunteers to carry out the demonstration. One child should measure the length of the spring while the other adds hanging masses to it and then records each length (as reported by the first child) on the board or flip chart. Tell them to measure the unloaded spring first and write this result down. To work out the extension produced by the hanging masses that will be added, this first value must be subtracted from the new length value each time. Ask the volunteers to hang a mass on the spring, record the mass and length and calculate the extension. Repeat for four or five results. Can the children see a relationship between the mass and the extension? *If the mass is doubled or tripled, what happens to the extension?*

GROUP ACTIVITIES

1. Ask the children to carry out an experiment (similar to the demonstration) to see whether the effect is the same for an elastic band. They must record the length of an unstretched band, then measure the length of the band as the amount of force is increased. By pulling the band with a newton meter, the force applied can easily be observed and recorded. The children must then make calculations to find out whether the extension is proportional to the force applied.
2. Give each child or group a copy of page 154. The data on the sheet shows how different types of plastic bag perform when stretched to breaking point. The children can use this information to infer the answers to the questions on the sheet: 1. Savamarket; 2. Shopsafe; 3. Pricemate, Shopsafe, Worthmore; 4. Shopsafe – it is the strongest (can take the most weight); 5. Savamarket – since it is the weakest, it will stretch the most when the weight is not enough to break it.

DIFFERENTIATION

1. Less able children may find it easier to mark out the extension if the experiment is placed on a sheet of paper and the taut but unstretched length of the elastic band is drawn on the paper. Measurements of extension can be made from that point without the need to subtract the original length from the stretched length. **2.** Differentiate by outcome.

ASSESSMENT

In Group activity 1, note whether the children make the appropriate measurements to a good degree of accuracy. Can they select appropriate information from the chart in order to draw a conclusion? In Group activity 2, note whether the children use the information provided to complete the worksheet correctly.

PLENARY

As Group activity 1 is discussed, hand around a newton meter (of the type where the spring is exposed) in order to reinforce the idea that springs are used to measure pulling forces because the relationship between force and extension is so consistent. Group activity 2 provides an opportunity to discuss the type of interpretation question that may appear on a science SAT paper or other test, and how such questions should be answered.

OUTCOMES

- Know that the extent to which an elastic material stretches is proportional to the force applied.
- Can make observations, record them and select results from a table to draw a conclusion.

LESSON 5

Objective	● To know that water exerts an upward force on a solid object suspended in it.
Resources	A water trough or large beaker, a newton meter, some objects that sink in water.
Main activity	Ask the children to assist you in a demonstration. Use a newton meter to measure the weight of an object hanging in air. Repeat the measurement of the weight with the object immersed in water (not floating). Record the following information in a table on the board: the object, its weight in air (N), its weight in water (N), the difference in weight (N). Repeat for a number of different objects that sink in water. After about six objects have been weighed, ask the children to look for a pattern in the results.
Differentiation	With less able children, make sure that the difference in measured force has been noted.
Assessment	Can the children make the measurements required accurately? Do they notice the difference in the measured force? Can they give a reason for the difference?
Plenary	Discuss the difference between the results for an object hanging in air and in water. *What is the force pulling down on the object?* (Gravity or weight.) Explain that the difference between the results is due to another force from the water. *Which direction is this force acting in?* (Upwards.) Say that this force is given the name 'upthrust'.
Outcomes	● Recognise the apparent change in the weight of an object when suspended in water due to the greater upthrust. ● Can explain the forces acting on an object suspended in water. ● Can make and record observations.

LESSON 6

Objective	● To know that when an object floats, the upthrust acting on it is equal to the force of gravity and acting in the opposite direction.
Resources	A water trough or large beaker, a newton meter, some objects that float in water.
Main activity	Ask the children to carry out an experiment similar to the one in the previous lesson, but this time using a mixture of objects that float and ones that do not. An additional column, 'Floats or sinks?', can be added to those used previously. After the children have collected the results, ask them to calculate the upthrust for each object and to look for a link between the upthrust on floating objects and their weight in air.
Differentiation	Less able children could be given a worksheet with the table already drawn. With these children, it may be more helpful just to look at the fact that the weight of a floating object in water is zero, without using calculations, then use the Plenary to deduce the link with upthrust.
Assessment	Can the children take measurements in a suitable way to allow a conclusion to be drawn from them?
Plenary	Discuss the children's results and calculations of upthrust. Ask them to suggest explanations for why things float in terms of the upthrust and weight forces. Develop the idea that these forces are balanced for floating objects.
Outcome	● Can explain why an object floats.

LESSON 7

OBJECTIVES
● To know that air resistance can slow down a moving object.
● To conduct an investigation.

RESOURCES

Main teaching activity: Three small home-made parachutes of different sizes, three identical small hanging weights, a stopwatch, a metre ruler.
Group activities: 1. Parachutes made by the children (from paper, plastic bags or light fabric), paper clips, stopwatches, paper, writing materials, graph paper (or a computer and data-handling software). **2.** Photocopiable page 155 (one copy per child).

PREPARATION

Prepare three small parachutes of different sizes, using thin cloth and string. Attach identical small hanging weights to the three parachutes (see diagram).

friction, lubrication, drag, air resistance, streamlined

BACKGROUND

The children will previously have studied the effect of friction, and will understand it as the force acting between two surfaces. They may have looked briefly at ways of making objects move with less friction by using lubrication. This activity deals with the friction that occurs between a solid object and a fluid. In order to move through a fluid (that is, a gas or a liquid), a solid object has to part the fluid material so that the fluid can move around it. Some shapes move through fluids more easily than others. For example, the bow of a boat is pointed and the stern is flatter, so a boat moves forward more easily than backward.

This activity also focuses on objects moving through air, and looks at which shapes move through air more easily and less easily. The force that restricts the ease of movement through a fluid is called 'drag'. We experience drag when we go out on a windy day. In this situation, not only are we trying to move through the wind, but the wind is being obstructed in its path by our bodies. When the fluid causing drag is air, we call it 'air resistance'.

INTRODUCTION

Gather the children around you. Ask them to imagine a park with people walking, children playing ball games and frisbee, trees all around. The air is still, but then a strong wind starts to build up. *What happens in the park?* (The trees sway and the balls and frisbees start to go where the wind blows.) Ask a volunteer to show how the people might have to walk. Ask the children to explain why these things are happening. (The force of the wind is causing these effects.) The effects can be observed, but how they are applied cannot be seen: wind is an invisible force, like gravity and magnetism. But unlike these, it is not operating at a distance from the material producing the force: the material producing wind force is the air.

Explain that the reason it is difficult to move through a strong wind is a force called 'drag' that opposes movement in that direction. Drag is a friction type of force. It happens when objects try to move through a liquid or a gas, or when a liquid or gas passes a stationary object. If the gas is air, we also call it 'air resistance'.

MAIN TEACHING ACTIVITY

Tell the children that they are going to look at the effect of drag on different parachutes. Show the children the three parachutes and explain that they are of different sizes, but each is carrying the same mass. *Why is this important?* (It is necessary for a fair test to take place.) *What other factors must be kept the same to make a fair test?* (Same height, same shape of parachute, same length of strings, same material for parachutes.) Drop each of the parachutes in turn, asking a child to time the fall carefully. What do the children notice about how the larger, middle-sized and smaller parachute compare? (The largest parachute takes longest to fall, the smallest takes the least time.) Ask them to explain these results, using their knowledge of forces.

Discuss the explanation: gravity pulls all the different parachutes down with equal force (because they have virtually the same mass), but larger parachutes have a greater drag and therefore experience less overall downward force. Note that some anomalous results may be due to the fact that drag is speed-dependent. Different-sized parachutes will take different times to reach their terminal velocity (the maximum speed of the parachute, when the gravitational and drag forces are balanced).

GROUP ACTIVITIES (ASSESSMENT)

1. Ask the children to carry out a fair test to examine the experiment in more detail. They should make parachutes and load each one with a couple of paper clips, then measure the time taken for it to fall to the ground from a constant height (about 1.5m). The results can then be put into a scatter graph or bar chart. This is a good opportunity to use data-handling software to transfer data from a spreadsheet to a graph. The children should then write a conclusion about what they have found out from the experiment, and what patterns they have observed in their results. They should try to give a scientific explanation of these results, using their knowledge of forces. Finally, they can evaluate the experiment, look for possible problems and errors in it, and suggest how they might improve it (perhaps giving tips to a future group). Use this work to assess their understanding of air resistance and their ability to carry out an investigation.
2. The children should work individually through page 155, analysing data on different-shaped pieces of Plasticine falling through different liquids to decide whether there is high or low drag in each case. (Note that if you are following *100 Science Lessons* or the *QCA Science Scheme of Work* as the basis for your school scheme, this activity is given in full for Year 4/Primary 5.) Use this sheet to assess their understanding of drag. The answers are: 2. Dome in paste. The dome is the least streamlined shape (encounters most resistance) and the paste is more resistant to movement through it. 3. Cone in water. The cone is the most streamlined shape (encounters least resistance) and the water is less resistant to movement through it. 4. Paste. 5. Cone.

DIFFERENTIATION

1. More able children could also examine how other factors, such as the load, affect the time of fall. **2.** Less able children could be given a version of page 155 with the results for the second liquid removed, so that they only need to consider the effect of shape on drag.

PLENARY

Use both Group activities to stimulate discussion of how objects that are designed to move through fluids are shaped. The children may remember work from Year 4/Primary 5 on streamlining and how a streamlined shape has low drag. Group activity 1 should be discussed with an emphasis on how the investigation went and how improvements could be made.

OUTCOMES

- Can describe how air resistance affects the speed of a falling object.
- Can carry out an investigation.

LESSON 8

Objective	● To investigate factors that affect how fast a 'spinner' falls to the ground.
Resources	Card, scissors, paper clips, stopwatches, paper, writing materials, graph paper (or a computer and data-handling software).
Main activity	'Spinners' are a popular way of investigating air resistance at KS2/P4–7 (see *100 Science Lessons: Year 4/Primary 5*, for example). Explain to the children that they are going to look at how spinners with different-sized rotors fall by carrying out a fair test. They need to find out whether the rule that worked for the parachutes is also applicable to a two-armed spinner: the bigger the area, the slower the spinner will fall (due to the increase in air resistance). They should make the spinners and load them with a couple of paper clips (this adds stability and holds the spinner together). They should record the size of the rotors on each spinner and the time taken for it to fall to the ground. Ask different groups each to use a different-sized spinner, with several repeats.
Differentiation	More able children could also look at how spinner size affects how far the spinner travels horizontally after being dropped, and relate this to seed dispersal.
Assessment	Have the children carried out a fair test in order to gather their results? Have they recorded the results in an appropriate manner?
Plenary	Collate the class results and use them to draw a scatter graph or bar chart. Discuss the results obtained and how the experiment could be improved to make the results more reliable. *Why is it useful to repeat the test two or three times with each size of spinner?* (To check and improve the overall reliability of the investigation, and to show more clearly any pattern in the results.)
Outcomes	● Can investigate how the size of a spinner affects the time it takes to fall to the ground. ● Can explain this result in terms of the effects of drag.

LESSON 9

Objective	● To look at how objects that move through fluids are streamlined.
Resources	A selection of secondary sources and pictures showing streamlined shapes, both natural (eg fish) and manufactured (eg racing cars).
Main activity	The children use the secondary sources to put together a display of streamlined objects and add appropriate comments to explain why streamlining is necessary.
Differentiation	This activity can be differentiated by selection of secondary source material.
Assessment	Can the children identify streamlined shapes?
Plenary	Review what shapes are streamlined. *Does the direction of movement affect whether a shape is streamlined?* Discuss the importance of streamlining in sports such as cycling and skiing, and how the athletes change their body shapes to become streamlined.
Outcome	● Can identify streamlined shapes, both in the natural and manufactured world.

LESSON 10

OBJECTIVE
● To be able to explain how objects stay at rest or move by considering the forces acting on them.

RESOURCES

Main teaching activity: A simple plumb-bob, a tennis ball, a model car, a stiff board.
Group activities: 1. A 'stress ball' or ball of Plasticine, a marble, an elastic band, a large mass (such as a brick or a box of books), a lollipop stick, sandpaper, thick card, scissors, paper, writing materials. **2.** Photocopiable page 156.

Vocabulary

balanced forces, opposite forces

BACKGROUND

No force ever acts on its own. As Newton's Third Law states, for every action there is an equal and opposite reaction. For example, when you sit on a soft-cushioned chair, it gives to start with, but then supports your weight. The force of gravity acting downwards on you has a reaction from the chair providing support: the springs and cushioning pushing up. These two forces are in opposition. There are always a couple of forces, and sometimes more, acting on any given object. The direction and magnitude of the forces determines what happens to the object.

Consider a ball resting on a table. There are two forces acting on the ball: its weight and the upthrust from the table. These forces are equal and opposite, and so cancel each other out. They are known as 'balanced' forces. The ball will remain stationary. However, if we apply a sideways force, the ball moves in the direction of that force. The bigger the push, the greater the effect on the motion of the ball. However, this very motion immediately introduces a force that tends to reduce the speed of the motion: friction. Unless the propelling force is continued, the force of friction will eventually stop the ball. In that situation, friction is the larger force and slows the moving object down. These forces are not cancelling each other out (they are not balanced), and so they are changing the motion of the ball. It requires a force to slow the ball down or change its direction, as it does to make the ball start moving or speed it up.

In summary, if the forces acting on it are balanced, the object will either stay at rest or continue to move at the same speed in the same direction. If the forces are unbalanced, then a change in speed or direction (or in the shape of the object) will occur. The terminology of balanced and unbalanced forces is not required for children at primary level, but you may find these ideas valuable in helping the children to understand how forces act.

INTRODUCTION

Ask the children to name a force that is acting on them at this moment. Their answers should include 'weight' or 'gravity'. Ask them which direction this force is acting in. (Downwards.) So what is stopping them falling to the centre of the Earth? (The upthrust from the ground.) Remind them that every force has a direction, and that the forces they have mentioned are acting in opposite directions. (It may also be worth discussing the idea, with more able children, that the forces are of equal magnitude and hence balanced.) Explain that they are going to look at the forces acting on an object to see why it moves or stays still.

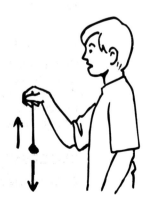

MAIN TEACHING ACTIVITY

Ask a volunteer to hold a small mass (such as a plumb-bob) hanging on a string. Ask the children to identify the forces acting on this mass. It is easy to spot the force of gravity giving the mass its weight – but if this were the only force acting on it, the object would fall. *Where is the other force?* (The tension in the string provides an upward force.) This situation can be represented on a diagram, using arrows to show the directions of the forces. Draw a diagram (see opposite) on the board or flip chart, with equal-sized arrows to represent the tension in the string (pulling upwards) and the weight (pulling downwards).

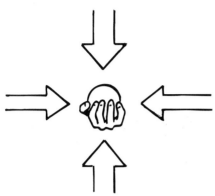

Hold a tennis ball (or similar) between your thumb and finger. Ask the children to describe the forces acting on the ball. Weight is present as always, in a downwards direction, but the opposing force is provided by the finger and thumb grip and the strength of your arm. Ask a volunteer to draw the forces on a diagram on the board. He or she should draw something like the picture on the right.

As a final demonstration, place a small toy car (or similar) on a stiff board. The car does not move, since there are equal forces down and up from the car's weight and the upthrust from the board. Push the car in one direction, so that it moves and then stops. Ask the children to describe the forces acting on the car. As the car is pushed, there is a force from one side. The car slows down because of a friction force in the opposite direction. Two diagrams could be drawn to show this. *How are the forces different if the board is on a slope?* If the board is tilted slowly, initially the car does not move because although the board provides less upthrust when it is at an angle, friction holds the car in place. Eventually the slope is great enough for gravity to overcome the friction and upthrust, so the car moves down the slope.

GROUP ACTIVITIES

1. The children should carry out a number of simple activities in a circus, each time drawing the object and the forces acting on it, naming these forces and describing (in writing) how they affect the object: squashing a stress ball or ball of Plasticine; flicking a marble; pulling an elastic band; lifting a large mass; sliding a lollipop stick along a desk and over sandpaper; cutting thick card with scissors.
2. Give the children a copy each of page 156. Ask them to label the drawings with arrows to show the forces acting in each situation.

DIFFERENTIATION

1. More able pupils could try not only to show the direction of the forces with arrows in their force diagrams, but also to use the relative size of the arrows to give an indication of the relative size of the forces. Less able pupils could be provided with diagrams of the activities on a sheet, leaving them to draw the force arrows; this will prevent them from getting slowed down and distracted by the task of drawing the objects.
2. This task is differentiated by outcome. Drawing correct force arrows on the pictures becomes more difficult as the children work through the sheet.

ASSESSMENT

From their written work, assess whether the children have an idea of the direction of a given force and the relative strength of the forces acting on an object; are able to comment on whether an object will move faster, slow down, stay the same or change shape as a result of the forces acting on it.

PLENARY

Go through the activities in the experiment circus, giving the children opportunities to explain what they have found out. Ask them to confirm the findings or otherwise. Emphasise the names of the forces, the directions in which they act, and whether they are balanced.

OUTCOME

● Can explain how forces make things stay at rest or move.

UNIT 6 FORCES & MOTION

LESSON 11

OBJECTIVES
● To assess the children's knowledge and understanding of forces: their nature, relative size and direction.
● To assess the children's ability to plan an investigation and predict the results.

RESOURCES
Photocopiable pages 157 and 158, pencils, pens.

INTRODUCTION
You may wish to start with the written tasks, or to give the children a short oral test as revision.

ASSESSMENT ACTIVITY 1
Give the children a copy each of photocopiable page 157 and let them complete it individually. When they have finished, you may prefer either to mark the answers yourself or to collect the papers and redistribute them for the children to mark, creating an opportunity to discuss the questions and the relative merits of different answers.

Answers
1. gravity; 2. friction; 3. 4cm; 4. The second and third pairs will attract, the other pairs will repel; 5a. upthrust; 5b. 2 newtons; 6. zero; 7. Answers might include the friction between the tyres and the ground, the push of feet on the pedals, the weight of the rider on the saddle, the upthrust of the saddle on the rider, the weight of the bicycle and rider on the ground, the upthrust of the ground on the wheels, the friction (air resistance) between the air and the rider, the push (in a constant direction) from the wind, and so on.

Looking for levels
Most children will correctly answer questions 1, 2, 3 and 4, and give a little description of how they may feel on a windy day without the qualification through scientific terminology; for example, referring to air resistance. More able children will complete the test giving scientific explanations for their observations in question 7. Less able children may answer questions 1, 2 and 4 correctly, but will find the application of scientific theory difficult in the other questions.

ASSESSMENT ACTIVITY 2
This task focuses on selecting information in order to draw a conclusion from an experiment. Give each child a copy of photocopiable page 158 and ask them to complete the questions.

Answers
Look for a line graph with correctly labelled axes. The explanation should point to a consistent relationship between the weight applied and the degree of stretching up to the point where the bag breaks.

Looking for levels
Most children should be able to draw an appropriate graph of the data. More able children may correctly space out and label the axes. Less able children may space out the markings on the graph incorrectly and not label the axes. When analysing the results, most children will note that as the force (or weight) is increased, the handles on the bag become longer. More able children may comment that doubling the weight in the bag makes the handles twice as long. Less able children may state briefly that the handles are longer when there is more in the bag.

PLENARY
Following Assessment activity 1, it is important to discuss with the children how they need to use the correct scientific vocabulary when answering exam questions. Following Assessment activity 2, use 'anonymous' quotes from the children's graphs and conclusions to reinforce the ideas that: graphs should be completed with labelled axes; when looking for patterns in results and writing a conclusion, the children need to use scientific language and to be as precise as possible.

Name

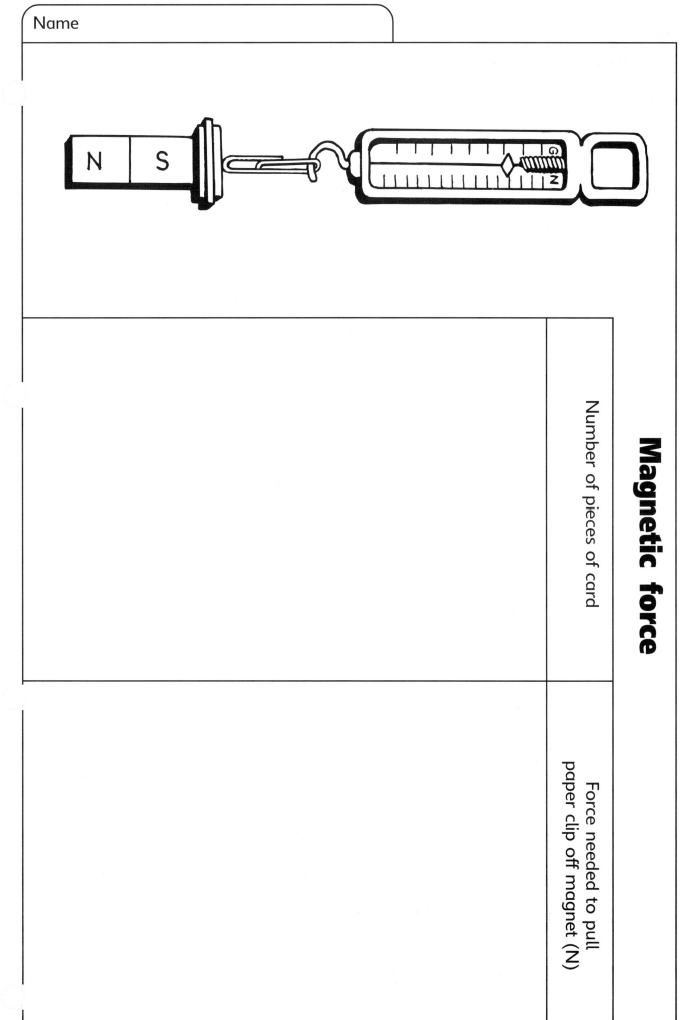

Magnetic force

Number of pieces of card	Force needed to pull paper clip off magnet (N)

Name

Keeping it in the bag

The graph below shows the force needed to break the handles of carrier bags from different grocery stores. Use this information to answer the questions below.

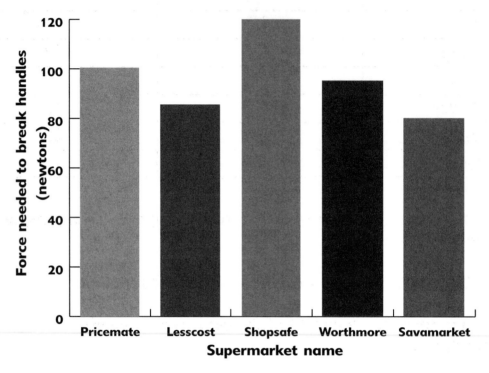

1. Which shop has the weakest bag?

_____

2. Which shop has the strongest bag?

_____

3. A bottle of cola has a weight of 22 newtons. Which bag or bags could carry four bottles without breaking?

_____

4. Which bag is likely to have been made from the thickest plastic? Explain your answer.

_____

_____

5. If a weight of 50 newtons is placed in each carrier bag, which one is likely to have its handles stretched the most? Explain the reason for your prediction.

_____

_____

Sinking slowly

Shape	Time to fall through paste (secs)	Time to fall through water (secs)
ball	2.5	1.0
sausage	3.0	2.0
cone	2.0	0.5
cylinder	3.5	1.5
cube	5.0	2.0
dome	6.0	2.5

This table shows the results for an experiment using several objects, water and wallpaper paste.

1. Plot two bar charts to show the two sets of results.

2. Which shape takes the longest to fall, and in which liquid?
Explain why this is.

_____

_____

_____

3. Which shape falls through the fastest, and in which liquid?
Explain why this is.

_____

_____

_____

4. Which liquid has more drag?

_____

5. Which shape falls faster through paste than the dome falls through water?

_____

UNIT 6 FORCES & MOTION

Force diagrams

Draw arrows to show the forces on each diagram.

Name

Forces and action

1. The force that makes an object fall when you let go is called:

_____

2. The force that helps you to grip is called:

_____

3. A force of 10N pulls on a spring that stretches 2cm. If a force of 20N were used, how far would you expect the spring to stretch?

_____

4. Look at the following pictures of pairs of magnets. Which will attract and which will repel?

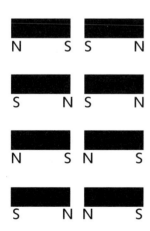

```
■■  ■■
N  S S  N

■■  ■■
S  N S  N

■■  ■■
N  S N  S

■■  ■■
S  N N  S
```

_____

_____

_____

5. A snooker ball has a weight of 7 newtons when in air. In water, the weight of the same ball is 5 newtons.

(a) What force causes the difference?

_____

(b) What is the size of this force?

_____

6. A tennis ball floats on water. In air, it has a weight of 2 newtons. What will its weight be in water?

_____

7. Describe how forces affect you when cycling on a windy day.

_____

_____

_____

_____

_____

_____

_____

Forces and action

Use the following information to draw a graph, then explain any patterns that you see in your results.

Rose and Malik carry out an experiment to find out how much a piece of plastic from a carrier bag would stretch when they hung different masses from it. Here are their results:

Amount of mass used in grams	Amount of stretch in mm
50	2
100	4
150	6
200	8
250	10
300	Plastic snapped

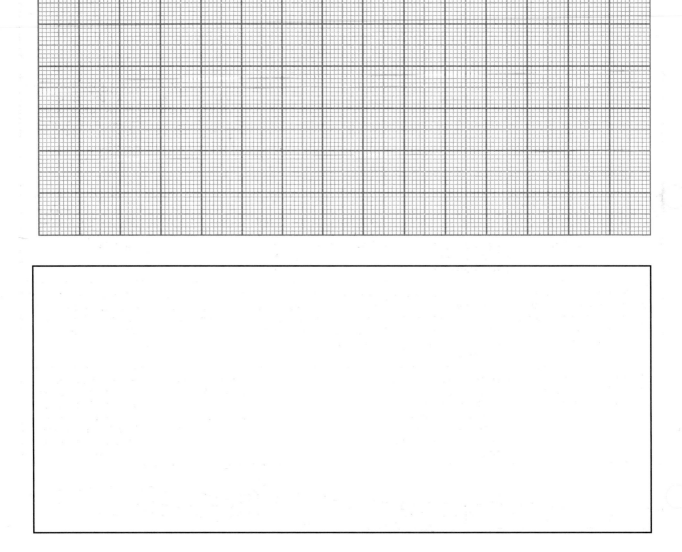

Light and sound around us

ORGANISATION (14 LESSONS)

	OBJECTIVES	MAIN ACTIVITY	GROUP ACTIVITIES	PLENARY	OUTCOMES
LESSON 1	● To know that light travelling from a source can be blocked by an opaque object, making a shadow.	Demonstrate how changing the position of a light source can change the size and shape of a shadow.	Investigate how the position of a light source affects the size and shape of a shadow. Use data about the position of a shadow on a playground to infer where the Sun might be in the sky.	Discuss how the relative positions of a light source, object and screen affect the shadow. Relate to shadow puppets.	● Can use the terms 'light source', 'shadow' and 'opaque' correctly. ● Can make and record observations in an investigation.
LESSON 2	● To know that the size of a shadow depends on several factors.	Demonstrate how a shadow changes in size when the screen is moved. The children investigate how changing the distance of a light source from an object affects the size of the shadow.		Review the children's findings.	● Can describe how the size of a shadow is affected by: the distance from the light source to the object; the distance from the screen to the object.
LESSON 3	● To know that non-luminous objects can be seen because light scattered from them enters the eye.	Use a torch in a darkened room to demonstrate that when we see an object, light travels from a source to the object and then to the eye.	Draw the path of light in a real context, from a source to an object and then to the eye. Draw the paths of light in invented contexts of objects being seen.	Discuss the path that light takes in various examples.	● Can explain how objects are seen in the presence of a light source.
LESSON 4	● To know how our eyes enable us to see. ● To know the names and functions of the parts of the eye.	Use a model or diagram of the eye to explain how we see objects around us. The children draw up a table of the parts of the eye and their functions.		Ask children to identify parts of the eye and explain their functions.	● Can describe how the eye detects light. ● Can name the main parts of the eye and describe their functions.
LESSON 5	● To know that mirrors can be used to change the direction in which light is travelling.	Use a mirror to demonstrate the reflection of a light ray. Distinguish between reflection and scattering.	Use mirrors to look at normally concealed places and to look around corners. Draw diagrams to show how they have done this.	Discuss uses of mirrors in everyday life.	● Know that a mirror changes the direction in which light is travelling.
LESSON 6	● To investigate the relationship between the ray of light striking a mirror and the one reflected from it.	Use a torch and mirror to demonstrate that the angle of incidence of a ray of light is equal to the angle of reflection.	Use a torch, mirror and protractor to measure and compare various angles of incidence and reflection. Use a pair of mirrors to see around corners.	Explain how a periscope works, using mirrors set at 45°.	● Can use the angle of incidence of a light ray to predict the angle of reflection from a mirror.
LESSON 7	● To compare the quality of reflection from different surfaces.	Differentiate between reflections and shadows. The children compare how well different surfaces reflect a beam of light and an image.		Discuss the use of different materials for visibility or concealment.	● Understand that shiny surfaces can be used as mirrors, but dull surfaces cannot. ● Understand the use of reflective materials for safety.

ORGANISATION (14 LESSONS)

	OBJECTIVES	MAIN ACTIVITY	GROUP ACTIVITIES	PLENARY	OUTCOMES
LESSON 8	● To know that differences in reflectivity and shadow formation affect how we see our surroundings.	The children map the classroom in terms of reflections and shadows at different times of the day. From this, they decide which areas are best for working and for resting.		Discuss the children's findings and consolidate the vocabulary.	● Can recognise shadows and reflections in their environment. ● Can tell the difference between a reflection and a shadow. ● Can predict where shadows and reflections will form.
LESSON 9	● To know what parts of a musical instrument vibrate to produce sounds. ● To know that sounds can be described in terms of loudness and pitch.	Demonstrate how to play low and high notes on an instrument, then loud and soft notes. Demonstrate that the latter correspond to greater and lesser degrees of vibration.	Use secondary sources to look at musical instruments from around the world. Find out how different notes are played on them.	Discuss 'families' of musical instruments and how they are used to make different notes.	● Can explain how sound is produced from string, wind and percussion instruments. ● Can describe musical sounds in terms of loudness and pitch.
LESSON 10	● To explore and understand how the pitch and loudness of a sound can be changed.	Examine how a musical instrument has been built, and how it is used to make different sounds. The children build their own simple instruments and describe how the sounds they make can be varied.		Conduct the children as they play their instruments together; focus on how the notes are made.	● Can describe musical sounds in terms of loudness and pitch. ● Can suggest ways to change the sound an instrument makes.
LESSON 11	● To know that sound can pass through solids, liquids and gases.	Use the help of a child to demonstrate that sound can travel through a closed door.	Use secondary sources to prepare a talk (with demonstrations) about situations where sound travels through a particular medium.	The groups present their talks. Follow up with questions to check their understanding of how sound travels through different media.	● Are able to present scientific information. ● Understand how sound travels through solids, liquids and gases.
LESSON 12	● To know how we hear sounds. ● To know the names and functions of the parts of the ear.	Use a model or diagram of the ear to explain how we hear sounds. The children label a diagram with the names and functions of the parts of the ear.		Ask children to identify parts of the ear and explain their functions.	● Can explain how sound travels from a source to our ears. ● Can name parts of the ear and their functions.
LESSON 13	● To know that loud sounds can be an environmental problem.	Ask the children to concentrate on a task in a noisy environment. Discuss the use of soundproofing. The children investigate what materials reduce noise.		Ask the children to try concentrating in silence, then with 'background' music.	● Recognise the need for quietness when working and resting. ● Can identify causes of loud noises in the environment. ● Can test a material for its sound reduction properties.
	OBJECTIVES	**ACTIVITY 1**	**ACTIVITY 2**	**ACTIVITY 3**	**ACTIVITY 4**
ASSESSMENT 14	● To assess the children's knowledge of how shadows are made. ● To assess the children's knowledge of how we see objects. ● To assess the children's knowledge of how light is reflected. ● To assess the children's knowledge of how different sounds are made. ● To assess the children's awareness of noise pollution.	Plan an experiment to make the same-sized shadow with a football and a tennis ball.	Complete a written test covering the work on light in this unit.	Write a description of their journey to school in terms of the sounds they hear.	Complete a written test covering the work on sound in this unit.

LESSON 1

OBJECTIVE

● To know that light travelling from a source can be blocked by an opaque object, making a shadow.

RESOURCES

Main teaching activity: An opaque shape (not a square or triangle), such as a cut-out of a simple snowflake pattern, attached to a piece of string; a lamp, a screen, a metre ruler.
Group activities: 1. A simple card shape, about 5cm²; a lamp, a screen, a metre ruler, paper for recording results, access to a dimly lit area. **2.** Photocopiable page 173.

Vocabulary

opaque, transparent, shadow, light source

BACKGROUND

The children will know that all light comes from a source. It travels in straight lines at high speed. The light is emitted from the source in all directions, not unlike the way that children draw 'sunbeams' coming from the Sun (except that the real rays are not separate). They will also know that light can travel through some materials (transparent materials) and not through others (opaque materials).

In order for a shadow to form, light must fall upon an opaque object that blocks its path, stopping the light from hitting a surface beyond. The size of a shadow is dependent on the area of the object presented to the light source. A sheet of paper placed at a right angle to a beam of light will cast a large shadow; but if you turn the paper around so that it is parallel to the beam of light, the shadow almost disappears.

INTRODUCTION

Ask the class about where light comes from, how we see things and how light travels. *What kind of materials can light travel through? What kind of materials can it not travel through? Can you tell me what appears when light is blocked by an opaque object?* Develop the idea of shadows by discussing how the shadow from an object outdoors changes in size and shape during the day. Explain that the class are going to find out more about this.

MAIN TEACHING ACTIVITY

Reduce the amount of light in the room so that the light from a torch or small lamp can be used to light a small screen such as a flip chart. Ask a child to hold the opaque shape in front of the screen by its string, so that a shadow is cast on the screen. Ask other children in the group to describe the shadow in terms of its shape and size. Now ask the first child to turn the object so that a different shadow is formed. *Why do you think the same object has made a different-shaped shadow?* Move the light source to the left and right, then up and down, to see how the shadow changes shape. It may help the children if one or two of the shadow shapes are drawn in outline on the screen to remind them where these shadows fell and what their shapes were. Discuss when the shadows are longest and when they are shortest, paying attention to the angles between the light, the object and the screen. You should find that larger shadows are produced when the opaque object is closer to the light source.

GROUP ACTIVITIES

1. Let the children work in a dimly lit area of the room, investigating how the size and shape of a shadow changes as they move the light source left and right and up and down. They should draw a diagram of their experiment, describe what they have done and record measurements of the distance of the light source from the centre line, the height of the light source above the object and the length of the shadow (see overleaf).
2. Give the children a copy each of page 173. Ask them to infer from the shadows where the Sun might be in the sky each time. Longer shadows will form when the Sun is lower in the sky (early morning or late evening), shorter shadows when the Sun is high in the sky (around midday).

DIFFERENTIATION

1. Less able children may find it easier to draw the shadow on the paper screen, and to record their measurements directly onto the screen. **2.** Differentiate by outcome.

ASSESSMENT

Can the children make 'fair test' measurements to determine the effect of the angle of the light on the size of a shadow? Can they record the results in an appropriate manner?

PLENARY

Discuss how the relative positions of the light, object and screen affect the shadow. Relate this to the way that we sometimes see scary shadows from simple objects, and the shadow theatre of some Asian cultures.

OUTCOMES

- Can use the terms 'light source', 'shadow' and 'opaque' correctly.
- Can make and record observations in an investigation.

LINKS

Art: making a shadow theatre; researching shadow puppets around the world.
PSHE: cultures around the world.

LESSON 2

Objective	● To know that the size of a shadow depends on several factors.
Resources	As Lesson 1.
Main activity	Demonstrate how a shadow changes size when the screen on which the shadow is falling is moved, but the positions of the light source and object are not changed. Let the children work in a dimly lit area of the room, investigating how the size of a shadow changes as they move the light source towards and away from the object. It is important that neither the object nor the screen is moved, since this would change two variables at once; the children should be able to tell you that this would result in an unfair test being carried out. They should draw a diagram of their experiment (and write a description of it if they can), and record their measurements of the distance from the screen to the object, the distance from the light source to the object and the size of the shadow. Make sure they measure a consistent dimension of the shadow to make fair comparisons.
Differentiation	Less able children will need more assistance with the recording of results. More able children could compare the relative effects of a 10cm movement of the light and a 10cm movement of the screen. (The former has a greater effect.)
Assessment	Are the children making accurate measurements and recording them in a sensible manner?
Plenary	Review the children's results. They should realise that the nearer the object is to the light source, the larger the shadow is.
Outcome	● Can describe how the size of a shadow is affected by: the distance from the light source to the object; the distance from the screen to the object.

LESSON 3

OBJECTIVE

- To know that non-luminous objects can be seen because light scattered from them enters the eye.

RESOURCES

Main teaching activity: A Christmas tree with shiny baubles, tinsel and a string of fairy lights.
Group activities: 1. Plain paper, coloured pencils, rulers. **2.** Photocopiable page 174.

PREPARATION

Before the lesson, check that the Christmas lights are still in working order. Set up the tree and string the lights around it.

BACKGROUND

It is relatively simple to explain how we see luminous objects (which make their own light). Some of the light coming from the object enters the eye, where the light-sensitive cells (grouped into an area called the 'retina') detect the light and send a message to the brain. (See Lesson 4.)

However, the vast majority of the objects we see are not luminous: they do not give off their own light. So how are they seen? We still need light to see them. Light from a source strikes the object, which 'scatters' it (reflects it in all directions). Some of the scattered light enters the eye. Without the light source, the object would have no light 'incident', or falling on it, and so could not be seen. For example, a spotlight may be used to highlight one performer on stage while, unseen by the audience, the scenery is being changed on the rest of the stage. If the incident light is well-scattered by a shiny object, the object will appear bright or shiny; conversely, a dull or dark-coloured object will absorb most of the light and so have a vague, unclear appearance.

Whether the object is bright or dark, the light path is always the same: from the source to the object to the eye. Light does not burst forth from our eyes to allow us to see in the dark.

INTRODUCTION

Ask the children to explain how we see the lights on a Christmas tree. *Where does the light come from, and where does it go to? Are the lights the only things you can see? If you can see other parts of the tree, are some brighter than others?* The children may see the lights reflected in the baubles. Some of the tree's branches can also be seen, but some branches are brighter than others because they are closer to the light and not in the shadow of other branches.

MAIN TEACHING ACTIVITY

With the room dimly lit, ask the children to comment on which objects are easy to see and which objects they know are there but cannot see. Ask: *How might we see these objects more easily?* (We need more light.) Switch on a torch and shine the beam at the children, taking care not to shine it directly into their eyes. *Does this help you to see the object better?* (No.) The children should be able to suggest that the torch should be pointed at the object. Using this example, develop the idea that the light goes from the torch to the object, where it is scattered (reflected) from the object and into our eyes. Are there parts of the room that the children cannot see from their current positions, even with the torch? (For example, the far sides of chairs or cupboards.) Why can't these be seen? (Either the light cannot reach the object or the light will not be scattered in the direction of their eyes.)

GROUP ACTIVITIES

1. Ask the children to draw some paths that light can take from light sources – for example, from a ceiling light to objects in the room or from the sun to parts of the school environment and then to their eyes. Good examples could be redrawn for display (see illustration below).
2. Give the children a copy each of page 174 and ask them to draw the path that light takes when the person in each picture sees the object(s). Remind them that light travels in straight lines, so they should use a ruler to draw the rays of light.

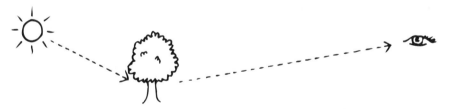

DIFFERENTIATION

1. You may wish to group less able children together and go through the first two examples that they choose with them in order to confirm that they are choosing appropriate objects and marking the paths correctly. **2.** Less able children could be given copies of page 174 with an arrow drawn on a number of the examples.

ASSESSMENT

Can the children correctly identify the path that light takes from the source to the object, where it is scattered to the eye?

PLENARY

Use examples to check that the children understand the path the light takes when we see an object. Include some examples where there is no light or where the object is a light source.

OUTCOME

● Can explain how objects are seen in the presence of a light source.

LINKS

Unit 3, Lesson 4: adapting to life in the dark.

LESSON 4

Objectives	● To know how our eyes enable us to see. ● To know the names and functions of the parts of the eye.
Resources	A model or cross-section diagram of the eye (an example is shown below).
Main activity	Using a model or diagram of the eye, describe how light from the objects around us is detected by the eye. Explain the functions of the cornea, iris, pupil, lens, retina and optic nerve. Ask the children to draw up their own table, listing the parts of the eye and their functions.
Differentiation	Less able children could play a 'match-up' game with the parts of the eye and their functions from prepared paired cards.
Plenary (Assessment)	Choose children to point out parts of the eye on a diagram and explain the function of each. Note which children are able to do this.
Outcomes	● Can describe how the eye detects light. ● Can name the main parts of the eye and describe their functions.

cornea – protects the sensitive parts of the eye

lens – focuses the light to give a sharp image

retina – detects the light

pupil – lets in the correct amount of light

iris – controls the amount of light let in by the pupil

optic nerve – sends messages to the brain

LESSON 5

OBJECTIVE

● To know that mirrors can be used to change the direction in which light is travelling.

RESOURCES

Main teaching activity: A small torch, a mirror.
Group activity: A safety mirror per group; paper, pencils.

Vocabulary

mirror, reflection

BACKGROUND

Light from most non-luminous objects is scattered into our eyes. This means that the light rays that fall, or are 'incident' on an object are reflected in all different directions. The reflective surface of a mirror is so flat and smooth that rays of light that strike it in an almost parallel manner are reflected as a series of almost parallel rays. There is no irregular scattering. This means that light travelling from a source or another object is not 'muddled', and we can see a clear image in the mirror. What we see in the mirror is exactly the same as what we see if we look directly at the object, except that left and right are swapped round (lateral inversion).

INTRODUCTION

Remind the children of the path that a ray of light takes when we see a non-luminous object. Show them a mirror and ask them to describe its surface. The idea that it is 'smooth' or 'shiny' should be developed: *What does 'shiny' mean?* The children may be able to comment that it reflects well. Tell them that they are going to look at how the reflection of light by a mirror and the scattering of light by an ordinary object are different.

MAIN TEACHING ACTIVITY

Ask the children what they would do if they were told to 'scatter'. They should say that they would go off in different directions. Reduce the amount of light in the room, and shine a small torch across the room so that the children can see the spot of light it forms. Now place the torch on the desk and use a mirror to reflect the light to different parts of the room. If the light is not too strong, you could try reflecting it towards the children. **NB** Light should **never** be reflected from the Sun or another strong light source into anyone's eyes.

Ask: *Is the light being scattered?* (It is not.) *How do you know this?* (All the light is travelling in one direction.) Explain that this is called 'reflection'. Mirrors reflect light: they change the direction in which it is travelling. Reflection is different from scattering, because all the rays of light that hit a mirror from a particular direction will travel off in the same direction as each other, whereas scattered rays go off in many different directions.

GROUP ACTIVITY

The children should use mirrors to look at places they do not normally see – for example, inside the waste-paper bin or behind the cupboard. They should try using mirrors to look around corners. They should draw the positions of the mirror, their eyes and the object they are looking at. For example:

DIFFERENTIATION

Differentiate by outcome.

ASSESSMENT

Can the children set the angle of the mirror correctly in order to see around objects?

PLENARY

Discuss some uses of mirrors in our environment: make-up and shaving mirrors; security mirrors in shops; dental mirrors. Focus on how these mirrors help us to see in awkward places, or make things clearer by providing an enlarged reflection.

OUTCOME

● Know that a mirror changes the direction in which light is travelling.

LINKS

Maths: reflective symmetry.
Art: light and perspective.

LESSON 6

OBJECTIVE

● To investigate the relationship between the ray of light striking a mirror and the one reflected from it.

RESOURCES

Main teaching activity: A sheet of A3 paper, a torch, a card with a narrow slit, a mirror, a ruler, a pen, a protractor.
Group activities: 1. Photocopiable page 175, rulers, pens, protractors. **2.** Mirrors on Plasticine bases (two per group).

BACKGROUND

A ray of light is not scattered from a mirror, but reflected so that it travels in a single, predictable direction. How can we predict it? A snooker player knows where a snooker ball will bounce to after it hits a cushion. Similarly, there is a relationship between the angle at which the light hits a mirror (called 'the angle of incidence') and the angle at which it is reflected from the mirror

Vocabulary

reflection, incident

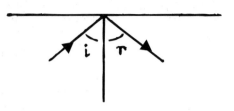

(called 'the angle of reflection'). These two angles are always equal, a fact known as the Law of Reflection (the children do not need to know this name). The two angles are measured from an imaginary line at 90° to the surface of the mirror, called the 'normal'. This law holds for all mirrors, whether plane (flat) or curved.

INTRODUCTION

Ask the children if there was a pattern to the way they had to angle the mirror in order to see into nooks and crannies in the previous lesson. To develop this idea, stand two children at right angles to each other. Hold the mirror at a point where the sight lines of the two children cross. Align the mirror so that it faces one child, then begin to turn it towards the other child. Ask both children to look at the mirror and say when they can see the other child in it. When they can see each other, the mirror is tilted equally towards each child: there is the same angle on each side. (See diagram, left.)

MAIN TEACHING ACTIVITY

Place a sheet of A3 paper on a desk or the floor so that all the children can see it. Reduce the amount of light in the room. Shine a torch through a narrow slit in a piece of card towards the mirror, as shown on the right. Use a metre rule to draw the ray of light going towards the mirror and the ray reflected from the mirror. Use a board protractor to mark a line at 90° to the mirror, then measure the angles from the centre line to the incident ray of light and the reflected ray of light using a protractor. The two angles should be the same (to within 5°).

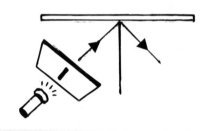

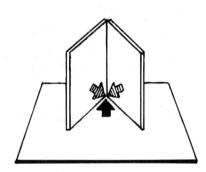

GROUP ACTIVITIES

1. Give each child or pair a copy of page 175 to complete. They should use a protractor to measure the angle of each line, then shine the torch along it, draw the reflected ray and measure that angle also. What do they notice about the two angles?
2. Give each group a pair of mirrors. They should place the mirrors over a range of different shapes (as shown in diagram A), then change the angle between the mirrors and observe the effect on the reflections. Secondly, they should put the mirrors facing each other and then turn each mirror 45° in the same direction – can they use this effect to see around corners? (See diagram B.)

DIFFERENTIATION

1. Less able children may need assistance with angle measurement. **2.** More able children could record their findings in words and pictures.

ASSESSMENT

Can the children draw a reflected line from a mirror and measure its angle to the mirror accurately? Can they see a relationship between the angles of incidence and reflection?

"BOO"

45°   45°

Look here

PLENARY

Discuss the use of a periscope to see over crowds, walls or the surface of water. Explain why the two mirrors must be set at 45° in order to turn the light by 90°.

OUTCOME

● Can use the angle of incidence of a light ray to predict the angle of reflection from a mirror.

Objective	● To compare the quality of reflection from different surfaces.
Resources	A torch; a selection of different surfaces such as mirrors (clean and dirty), aluminium foil paper (flat and crinkled) and painted surfaces (matt and gloss); paper, writing materials.
Main activity	Talk about how different surfaces give different qualities of reflection. Make sure the children do not confuse reflections and shadows. Ask them to look at some different surfaces to determine whether the reflection from a torch is clear or dull, and whether it is correctly shaped or distorted. Can they see their own reflection in the materials? Encourage them to explain their findings in terms of the properties of the materials.
Differentiation	Less able children could focus on a limited number of very different materials and say whether they can see a reflection from a torch and their own reflection. More able children could consider reflective materials (such as bicycle reflectors and Scotchlite tape) and relate them to safety at night.
Assessment	Can the children classify materials in terms of their reflectivity? Can more able children relate the reflectivity of materials to their uses?
Plenary	Discuss the benefits of the different types of material: dull materials for camouflage when hiding, highly reflective materials for visibility on roads and so on.
Outcomes	● Understand that shiny surfaces can be used as mirrors, but dull surfaces cannot. ● Understand the use of reflective materials for safety.

LESSON 8

Objective	● To know that differences in reflectivity and shadow formation affect how we see our surroundings.
Resources	Paper, drawing materials, pencils, a torch.
Main activity	Use natural light or a torch to look at how the apparent shape of a volunteer's face can be changed when the position of the face in relation to the light source is changed. Ask the children to map the classroom, showing where reflections appear and where shadows form at different times of the day. *Is the computer screen difficult to see at certain times of day?* From this, they should be able to say which areas are best for working and resting at different times, and perhaps suggest improvements to the classroom environment or layout. Emphasise the correct vocabulary – for example, distinguish clearly between 'shadows' and 'reflections'.
Differentiation	Differentiate by outcome, according to the sophistication of the children's recording.
Assessment	Do the children use the terms 'reflection' and 'shadow' correctly? Can they identify areas where brighter and dimmer conditions might be more appropriate for the use made of the area?
Plenary	Discuss the children's results, giving some the opportunity to present their findings. Check that all the children are using the appropriate vocabulary. Consider the children's findings regarding the placement of furniture in the room.
Outcomes	● Can recognise shadows and reflections in their environment. ● Can tell the difference between a reflection and a shadow. ● Can predict where shadows and reflections will form.

LESSON 9

OBJECTIVES
● To know what parts of a musical instrument vibrate to produce sounds.
● To know that sounds can be described in terms of loudness and pitch.

RESOURCES

Main teaching activity: A collection of musical instruments in various 'families'; a small drum, rice (optional).
Group activity: Research materials (books and CD-ROMs) on musical instruments; display materials (large sheets of paper, coloured pens and so on).

BACKGROUND

The children will have learned in Year 4/Primary 5 that sounds are made by vibrations. This lesson will develop their understanding of how musical instruments work. The different 'families' of instruments – brass, woodwind, percussion and string – are played in different ways to make vibrations that produce the notes. In brass and woodwind instruments, it is the air inside the instrument that is vibrating. The vibrations in brass instruments are caused by the vibration of

the musician's lips. Those in woodwind instruments are usually caused by the vibration of a reed; however, in the flute, piccolo and recorder, they are caused by the shape of the airhole in the mouthpiece. Percussion instruments are usually struck to make part or all of the instrument vibrate. String instruments are plucked, strummed or bowed to make the strings vibrate. Bowing (drawing a bow across a string), causes the bow to grip and then slip on the string.

The loudness of an instrument depends on the size (amplitude) of the vibration: the greater the amplitude, the louder the sound. The pitch (whether the note is high or low) depends on the frequency of the vibration (the number of vibrations per second). Middle C has a frequency of 256 Hertz (vibrations per second). Higher notes have more vibrations per second, lower notes have fewer. In order to change the pitch of a note, the length of the air or string that is vibrating must be made shorter (for a higher pitch) or longer (for a lower pitch). In stringed instruments, the thickness or tension of the string can also be changed to change the pitch of the note.

INTRODUCTION

Gather the children around you and the collection of instruments. Look at each instrument in turn, asking the children how it is played and what it does when you play it. When all of the instruments have been discussed, ask: *What do all these instruments have in common when they are played?* (They all vibrate.) Ask the children to feel their own instrument, their voice, vibrating by placing their fingers on the front of their throat (the windpipe) and saying 'Aaargh'. Encourage them to feel the difference as they change the sound they are making.

MAIN TEACHING ACTIVITY

Tell the children that they are going to use an instrument to make different sounds. Select an instrument and make a high-pitched note and a low-pitched note. Can the children say which is which? Can they tell you how the instrument was played differently to make the different notes? Now make a loud and soft sound. Again, can the children tell the difference and say how each was made? This can be demonstrated effectively using a small drum sprinkled with dried rice. Hitting the drum softly to make a quiet sound causes the rice grains to move just a little; striking the drum harder to make a loud sound causes the grains to leap clear of the drum. This shows that loud sounds have greater vibrations than soft sounds.

GROUP ACTIVITY

The children can work in groups to look at musical instruments from around the world, using secondary sources such as CD-ROMs and books. They should find out how a range of instruments are played and how the note can be changed. They can build up a display of drawings, photographs and text to convey the information they have found out, then present this to the class. Combining the groups' findings would provide interesting material for an assembly, particularly if you can borrow some world instruments from your local multicultural support service for the children to demonstrate.

DIFFERENTIATION

The children can use methods appropriate to their ability for research and presentation of their information. More able children could use multimedia software, and include recorded sounds.

ASSESSMENT

Can the children explain how a particular musical instrument is played and how its sound can be changed? Can they use different research sources to build a coherent presentation?

PLENARY

Following up the group presentations, emphasise similarities between the instruments in a 'family' (see Background) and the music produced with them. Look at how the note produced can be changed for instruments in that 'family'.

OUTCOMES

● Can explain how sound is produced from string, wind and percussion instruments.
● Can describe musical sounds in terms of loudness and pitch.

LINKS

Music: playing in a group.

LESSON 10

Objective	● To explore and understand how the pitch and loudness of a sound can be changed.
Resources	A selection of musical instruments in different musical 'families'; materials to make simple musical instruments (eg pop bottle flutes, rubber band guitars); paper, writing materials.
Main activity	Show the children a real musical instrument. Together, examine how it was made and how the sound is changed when playing it. Ask the children to make their own simple instruments, and to write a description of how the sound their instrument makes can be varied.
Differentiation	Differentiate by outcome, depending on the complexity of the instrument made and the method of recording. Less able children could make drums and shakers; more able children could make wind or stringed instruments (allowing them to alter the pitch and volume).
Assessment	Can the children make an instrument and record correctly how the pitch is changed and how the volume is changed?
Plenary	Conduct your orchestra! Point out how the notes are being made. Keep the music fairly simple: Vivaldi may be a little too tricky.
Outcomes	● Can describe musical sounds in terms of loudness and pitch. ● Can suggest ways to change the sound an instrument makes.

LESSON 11

OBJECTIVE
● To know that sound can pass through solids, liquids and gases.

RESOURCES
Group activity: Research materials (books and CD-ROMs) on the uses of travelling sound; junk materials; display materials (large sheets of paper, coloured pens and so on).

Vocabulary

speed, particles, vibration, solid, liquid, gas

BACKGROUND
The vibrations made by a sound source travel to our ears, where the sound is detected. Usually, the vibration of the sound source vibrates the nearby air particles in a wave pattern; some of these vibrations enter our ears and vibrate the ear drum, which sets off further vibrations in the small linked bones in our ears until these vibrations reach the auditory nerve. This sends a message to the brain that a sound has been heard. As long as there are particles in between to vibrate, the sound can travel from place to place. In a gas, the particles are far apart and so the sound travels relatively slowly and for a limited distance compared with liquids and solids. In a solid, the particles are arranged in a closely packed structure; when vibrated at one end, this structure passes the vibration through the particles very quickly and for great distances. In a liquid, the particles are closer than in a gas but without the regular structure of a solid; so the speed of sounds and the distances they travel are less than in a solid, but more than in a gas. Typical speeds of sound in different materials are: air 330m/s, water 1400m/s, steel 6000m/s.

INTRODUCTION
Ask the children to come and sit around you. *How did you hear me? Where did the sound start? How did you detect it? How did it get from me to you?* Explain that the vibration made by your voice-box vibrates tiny invisible particles in the air, causing the sound vibration to cross through the air and vibrate their ear drums. Now say that sound doesn't just travel through air, but through other materials too.

ROOM 26

MAIN TEACHING ACTIVITY
Send a pupil out of the classroom. Tell him or her to stand by the door, but not look through any windows. Shut the door, then tell the children in a loud voice that the pupil outside must guess their 'magic word' when he or she comes back. With the class, decide on a 'magic word' and repeat it loudly. Send another pupil to collect the child from outside the room. Ask the child what he or she has missed: *Do you know the magic word?* If he or she does, ask how. The child should be able to say that they heard you through the door and wall. This proves that sound can travel through solids.

GROUP ACTIVITY

In groups, the children should prepare a talk about situations where sound travels through a particular medium. They could include demonstrations stimulated by their research, depending on the resources (such as junk modelling materials) that you have available. For example, they might research: whale and dolphin communication through water; string telephones; sound pipes on old ships (used to speak between the bridge and the engine room); Native Americans listening on the ground for approaching cattle or wagons.

DIFFERENTIATION

This activity will be differentiated by the choice of research and presentation material. More able children could be set the task of finding out what sound does not travel through. (A vacuum, as in outer space, where there are no particles to vibrate.) If the children suggest 'soundproof tiles', explain that these will allow sound vibrations to pass through them, but with a much reduced strength: the resulting sound is reduced to a level below the threshold of human hearing.

ASSESSMENT

Can the children describe how sound travels through different materials?

PLENARY

The groups should present their talks and demonstrations. Follow up with relevant questions to check the level of research and coverage of a range of media (solids, liquids and gases). For example, ask the children about hearing underwater or hearing music from next door at home.

OUTCOMES

- Are able to present scientific information.
- Understand how sound travels through solids, liquids and gases.

LESSON 12

Objectives	• To know how we hear sounds. • To know the names and functions of the parts of the ear.
Resources	A model or cross-section diagram of the ear (see below).
Main activity	Use the model or diagram to explain how sound travels from a source to our ears, and how the different parts of the ear enable us to hear sound. Provide the children with a suitable diagram of the ear and ask them to label each part with its name and function.
Differentiation	Less able children could try to match up parts of the ear and their functions, using pre-cut strips from a prepared worksheet.
Assessment	Can the children identify the main parts of the ear and explain their functions?
Plenary	Choose individual children to point out a named part of the ear on a diagram and explain the job it does.
Outcomes	• Can explain how sound travels from a source to our ears. • Can name parts of the ear and their functions.

auditory nerve – sends messages to the brain

ear canal – sends vibrations to the eardrum

cochlea – a coiled tube containing liquid

pinna – the part of the ear you can see

eardrum – a piece of skin that detects vibrations

hammer, anvil and stirrup – three bones that increase the size of the vibrations

Objective	● To know that loud sounds can be an environmental problem.
Resources	A selection of hard and soft materials, a small battery-operated radio, a shoebox.
Main activity	Demonstrate the difficulty of working in a loud environment when concentration is needed: turn on the radio tuned to a foreign station, turn it up, then do a mental maths test. Discuss which parts of the school might be quiet or noisy. *Do any parts of the local environment have noise problems? Why?* 　　Discuss the use of soundproofing (for example, in a recording studio). Ask the children to investigate what materials reduce noise by packing a radio in a shoebox with material around it to see whether it reduces the loudness of the radio.
Differentiation	More able children could record the distance at which they can no longer hear the radio when different 'soundproofing' materials are used. Ask less able children to make a simple qualitative judgements of which materials make the radio less noisy.
Assessment	Are the children aware that the softer materials damp the sound more effectively?
Plenary	Reinforce the idea that silence can aid concentration by repeating the mental maths test without the distraction of the radio. Now see whether the children perform better with suitable background music. You may also wish to try using a 'moods' tape as a concentration exercise to inspire creative writing.
Outcomes	● Recognise the need for quietness when working and resting. ● Can identify causes of loud noises in the environment. ● Can test a material for its sound reduction properties.

ASSESSMENT

LESSON 14

OBJECTIVES
● To assess the children's knowledge of how shadows are made.
● To assess the children's knowledge of how we see objects.
● To assess the children's knowledge of how light is reflected.
● To assess the children's knowledge of how different sounds are made.
● To assess the children's awareness of the problems of noise pollution.

RESOURCES
Assessment activity 1. Blank A4 paper, pencils, equipment from the experiments with light in this unit. **2.** Paper, pencils, photocopiable page 176. **3.** Blank A4 paper, pencils. **4.** Paper, pencils, photocopiable page 177.

INTRODUCTION
This lesson comprises four Assessment activities: two each for light and sound. You may wish to split the activities over two sessions to allow the children to concentrate on one topic in each session, starting each lesson with a quick-fire quiz for revision of specific vocabulary related to the topic being covered.

ASSESSMENT ACTIVITY 1
Ask the children, in pairs or threes (grouped according to their ability), to plan an experiment to show how they could make the same-sized shadow with a football and a tennis ball. At this stage, do not give them any apparatus, but let them see the kind of equipment that is available. Tell them that later, you will try out some of their ideas together, and will have available all the equipment they have used to experiment with light.

Looking for levels
All the children should be able to describe how to make a shadow. More able children should be able to describe a suitable experiment and explain how they think it will work in terms of the blocking of the light. Less able children may not be able to describe how they can change the size of the shadow.

ASSESSMENT ACTIVITY 2
Give the children a copy each of page 176 and let them complete the test individually. You may prefer to mark the test yourself, or to redistribute the sheets around the class and use the answers to promote discussion of the topic (and why marks have or have not been awarded for particular answers).

Answers
1.

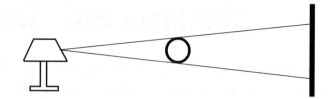

(1 mark for each line.)
2a. Arrow from light to cat to girl's eye (3 marks, –1 for not straight lines, –1 for each arrow with no direction or wrong direction). 2b. Arrow from Sun to car to boy's eye (3 marks, –1 for not straight lines, –1 for each arrow with no direction or wrong direction). 3. Reflection (1 mark). 4. 30° (1 mark). 5. Cooking foil, polished wood, painted wall, freshly cut wood (2 marks, –1 for each error). (Total possible marks = 12.)

Looking for levels
All the children should gain 5 marks. The more able should gain 7 or 8 marks. The most able may gain 10 marks or more.

ASSESSMENT ACTIVITY 3

Ask the children to write a description of their journey to school. Explain that you want them to describe it in terms of the sounds they hear on the way. Remind them that they have learned lots of new words and concepts in this unit that they can use in their descriptions.

Looking for levels
Less able children may only mention familiar noises, using the names of the objects that made each noise (as in 'the dog barked'). More able children may refer to pitch and volume, for example by comparing the loudness of different sounds. Remember that the children's wider vocabulary and literacy skills are important here, as well as their understanding of the science.

ASSESSMENT ACTIVITY 4

Give the children a copy each of page 177 and let them complete the questions individually. You may prefer to mark the test yourself, or to redistribute the sheets around the class and use the answers to promote discussion of the topic (and why marks have or have not been awarded for particular answers).

Answers
1. It becomes louder (1 mark). 2. The smaller one (1 mark). 3. Hit them harder (1 mark) to make a louder sound (1 mark). Put different amounts of water in (1 mark) to change the pitch of the sound (1 mark). 4. Guitar – the strings. Triangle – the metal frame. Trumpet – the player's lips (or the air inside the trumpet). Clarinet – the reed (1 mark each). 5. Deafness, stress, misunderstood speech, poor concentration (1 mark each, maximum 3 marks). (Total possible marks = 13.)

Looking for levels
All the children should gain 4 marks. More able children should gain 7 or 8 marks. The most able children may gain 10 marks or more.

PLENARY

Assessment activities 1 and 2. Try out the children's ideas for experimental set-ups from Assessment activity 1. In order to create similar-sized shadows, the tennis ball will need to be placed nearer the light source than the football. Relate the findings of the experiment to solar and lunar eclipses (see Unit 8, Lesson 2).
Assessment activities 3 and 4. Using the questions from the Assessment activities, promote discussion and ask the children to describe other situations where similar results occur, or where further examples of musical instruments can be vibrated in a similar way.

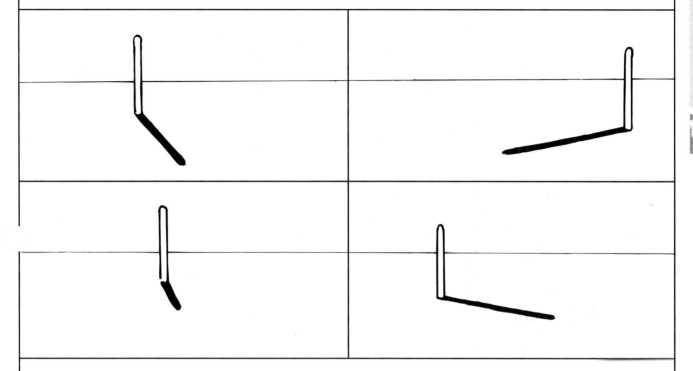

Name

Shadows and times

These four diagrams show the shadow from a stick in the ground at different times. Match each shadow to one of the four times listed underneath.

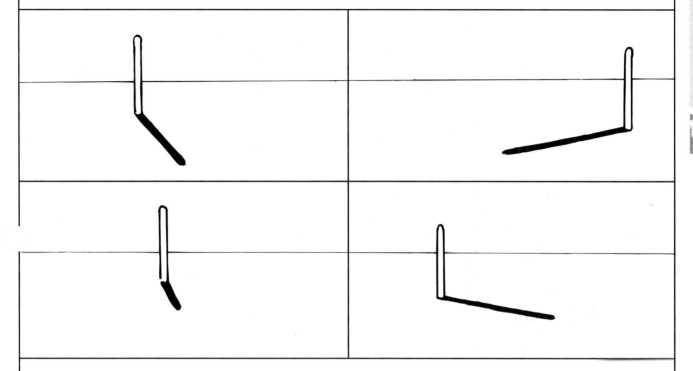

4.00pm   12 noon   7.00am   7.00pm

Where is the sun in the sky to make a long shadow?

_____

Where is the sun in the sky to make a short shadow?

_____

How does the length of your shadow change during the day?

_____

_____

Does the time of year make a difference to your shadow?

_____

_____

Name

How we see things

Draw arrows on each diagram to show how the person marked **X** sees the object(s) in each picture.

Reflected light

Place the mirror here.

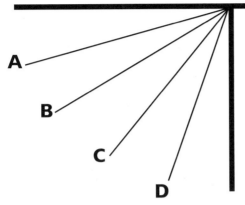

A

B

C

D

Shine a light along each line.

Mark where light reflects from the mirror here.

Measure the angle of each line and each ray of reflected light from the centre line and record the angles in this table.

Line	Angle of line	Angle of reflected light
A		
B		
C		
D		

What can you see from your table of results?

Light around us

1. Draw lines on the diagram to show where the shadow of the ball would be.

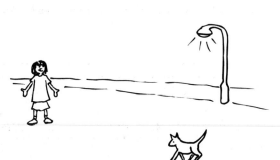

2. Draw arrows to show how the object is seen in each picture.

a.

b.

3. Cross out the word in this sentence that is wrong:

When you look in a mirror, you see your own shadow/reflection.

4.

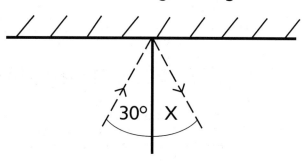

What is the value of X? _____

5. Write the following in order from the most reflective to the dullest:

Polished wood, freshly cut wood, cooking foil, painted wall.

_____

_____

Name

Sounds around us

1. X is playing the recorder and begins to blow harder. What happens to the sound that X makes?

_____

2. Y plays two drums. One drum is smaller than the other. Which drum makes the higher note?

_____

3. Z has a collection of five pop bottles. What could Z do to make different sounds when he hits them with a stick?

_____

4. To make a sound, you need a vibration. What vibrates in the following instruments to make the sound?

Guitar _____

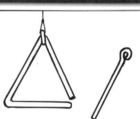

Triangle _____

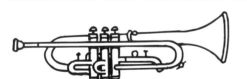

Trumpet _____

Clarinet _____

5. Living and working in a noisy area can cause many problems. Write down three problems that it can cause.

_____

_____

_____

The Solar System

ORGANISATION (8 LESSONS)

	OBJECTIVES	MAIN ACTIVITY	GROUP ACTIVITIES	PLENARY	OUTCOMES
LESSON 1	• To know that the Earth spins as it goes around the Sun, and that the Moon travels with the Earth and in orbit around it. • To reinforce the relative sizes of the Sun, Moon and Earth.	Discuss the relative sizes of the Sun, Moon and Earth, and how these could be modelled.	Make a scale to represent the distances between the Earth, Sun and Moon.	A quick-fire 'question and answer' session.	• Know that the Earth moves around the Sun. • Know that the Sun is larger than the Earth and the Earth is larger than the Moon. • Appreciate the scale of the distances between the Earth, Sun and Moon.
LESSON 2	• To know how a solar eclipse occurs.	Use a model to demonstrate what happens during a solar eclipse, pointing out the umbra and penumbra.	Label a diagram and complete a cloze text. Use a search engine to find out about the solar eclipse in Cornwall in 1999.	A quick-fire 'question and answer' session. Reinforce the ideas with the model.	• Can explain how an eclipse of the Sun occurs.
LESSON 3	• To be able to describe the surface of the Moon. • To know how the craters on the Moon were formed.	Use a photograph to discuss what the surface of the Moon looks like. Use a model to demonstrate how the craters on the Moon's surface were formed.	Repeat the crater formation activity to find out which objects make bigger craters. Use the Internet to research the first human landing on the Moon.	Some children read out their work; others make constructive criticisms. Finished work could be used in a wall display.	• Can explain how some of the craters on the Moon were formed.
LESSON 4	• To know what makes up our Solar System. • To know the order of the planets in our Solar System. • To know what a comet, an asteroid, a meteor and a meteorite are. • To know which planets have moons.	Show a video on our Solar System. Introduce the children to a variety of sources of information, including CD-ROMs and the Internet.	Find answers to questions about our Solar System. Find out information about each planet. Make pictures or models of the planets. Find out about comets or meteorites.	The children make up a nonsense poem to help them remember the order of the planets.	• Can name the nine planets of the Solar System. • Know which of the planets have moons.
LESSON 5	• To know what makes up our Solar System. • To know the order of the planets in our Solar System.	Play *The Planets* by Holst. Discuss how the music describes the planets. The children make scale models of the Solar System or paint pictures of the planet gods.		Children explain their scale models of the Solar System, or display and describe their paintings.	• Can name the nine planets of the Solar System.
LESSON 6	• To know about space exploration in the past. • To know about space exploration in the future.	Explain that the children will use a variety of sources of information to help them carry out research.	Groups research different aspects of space travel to answer given questions.	Groups present their findings to the class. Make a list of ways in which we can explore space.	• Know about the different methods that are used to explore space.
LESSON 7	• To think about space exploration in the future.	Use *The War of the Worlds* as a stimulus. The children write their own science fiction story and record it as a 'broadcast'.		Play some of the broadcasts to the class. The cassettes can be added to the class bookshelf or school library.	• Can use scientific knowledge to create a science fiction story.

ORGANISATION (8 LESSONS)

OBJECTIVES	ACTIVITY 1	ACTIVITY 2
● To review work on the Earth, Moon and Sun. ● To assess the children's knowledge about the Earth, Moon and Sun.	Use a range of resources (including ICT) to devise questions for a class quiz on the content of this unit.	Complete a written test on the content of this unit.

LESSON 1

OBJECTIVES
● To know that the Earth spins as it goes around the Sun, and that the Moon travels with the Earth and in orbit around it.
● To reinforce the relative sizes of the Sun, Moon and Earth.

RESOURCES

Introduction: Posters or pictures of the Earth (viewed from space), the Moon and the Sun; a version of the Icarus myth – for example, from the *Illustrated Dictionary of Mythology* (Dorling Kindersley) or *www.geocities.com/area51/labyrinth/8657/icarus.html*.
Main teaching activity: A TV and video, the *Our Earth* video (Channel 4 Learning; 217785); photocopiable page 191; a tray of spherical objects of different sizes (including poppy seeds, dried peas and a beach ball); calculators.
Group activity: Spherical objects, as above; the school field or other large open space.
Plenary: Photocopiable page 192.

Vocabulary

Earth, orbit, spherical, gravity, gravitational, rotate, axis

BACKGROUND

This lesson reinforces work that the children will have done in Years 4–5/Primary 6–7. It is important to revise these concepts, as children and many adults often get them confused.

The Earth is approximately spherical, and it rotates (spins) on its own axis. The axis is an imaginary line drawn through the centre of the Earth from the North Pole to the South Pole. One complete rotation takes 24 hours, which we call one day. The Earth's axis is tilted at a constant angle of 23.5° to the plane of its rotation. The side of the Earth facing the Sun is lit up, and we say it is 'daytime' on this side. The side of the Earth facing away from the Sun is in darkness, and so it is 'night-time' on that side. The Sun does not move (relative to the Solar System): the Earth moves around the Sun. It takes the Earth one year (365¼ days) to orbit the Sun. To take account of the extra quarter-day, the calendar has an extra day every four years (the 'leap year').

The Earth is held in orbit around the Sun by the Sun's gravitational pull. The Earth's tilt relative to the plane of the orbit causes the seasons. For half of its orbit, the tilt leans the northern hemisphere towards the Sun. Six months later, when the Earth is on the other side of the Sun, the southern hemisphere leans towards the Sun. In the hemisphere leaning towards the Sun, the Sun appears to rise high in the sky; the number of daylight hours is greater, and the air is warmer. This is summer. In the hemisphere leaning away from the Sun, the Sun appears to rise lower in the sky; the number of daylight hours is smaller, and the air is colder. This is winter.

The Sun is a star. All stars give out a large amount of heat, light and other forms of energy. The surface of the Sun is a seething mass of hydrogen, which acts as a fuel. The heat of the Sun is produced from nuclear fusion reactions in the middle, or core, of the Sun, where the temperature reaches many million degrees. At the surface, the temperature is only about 600°C.

Compared with other stars, the Sun is of average size and brightness. There are many larger stars (Betelgeuse is over 100 times larger), and many brighter stars (Rigel is 50 000 times brighter).

The Moon is a ball of rock that orbits the Earth and travels with it around the Sun. The Moon is held in its orbit by the Earth's gravitational pull. The Moon does not spin on its axis, so we always see the same side of it. All the planets in the Solar System, except Mercury and Venus, have moons. The Earth's moon is one of the largest; it is about one-quarter the size of the Earth. It takes 28 days for the Moon to orbit the Earth.

Further details can be found in the unit 'Earth, Sun and Moon' in *100 Science Lessons: Year 5/ Primary 6*.

is called the umbra, then point to the penumbra and explain that if you were in this area, you would see part of the Sun. If you are using an OHP, it might be useful to show what would happen to the shadow if the Moon were further away from the Earth.

Reinforce these ideas by showing a relevant video.

GROUP ACTIVITIES

1. Give out copies of page 193 and ask the children to complete them individually by labelling the diagram and filling in the missing words in the text.

2. Demonstrate an Internet search on the computer: use a search engine to search for the word 'Moon'. Ask the children to count how many hits were found. Now ask the children to use a search engine to search for the word 'Cornwall' and write down the number of hits found, then use another search engine for the word 'Eclipse' and then write down the number of hits found. Finally, they should search for 'Eclipse and Cornwall'. They should print what they have found in this final search, and mark key facts with a highlighter pen.

All the groups should be given the opportunity to carry out this ICT activity. When they have all completed the activity, they could share their findings. For example, if groups carried out the activity on different days, they can compare the number of hits in each search. Did the number of hits vary? If they did, why was this? Did they find the search helpful?

DIFFERENTIATION

1. Less able children could be given a list of words they can use to fill in the blanks on page 193. They (and/or more able children who have completed the sheet) could work on a poster or collage showing the Sun, the Earth and the Moon lined up to cause a solar eclipse. **2.** Less able children will need help with typing in the search words, skimming and selecting information.

ASSESSMENT

Note which children are able to: use a search engine correctly; print out information and highlight key facts; and explain what happens during a solar eclipse.

PLENARY

Ask the class: *Is the Moon the same size as the Sun? Why do the Sun and the Moon appear to be the same size? What does the Moon do to cause a solar eclipse? What would happen if the Moon were further from the Earth?* Once again, show the children the model of a solar eclipse.

OUTCOME

● Can explain how an eclipse of the Sun occurs.

LINKS

ICT: using the Internet to search for information.
Geography: visibility of a solar eclipse in different parts of the world.

OBJECTIVES

● To be able to describe the surface of the Moon.
● To know how the craters on the Moon were formed.

RESOURCES

Introduction: A source of Moon myths and legends, such as *Golden Myths and Legends of the World* by Geraldine McCaughrean (Orion).
Main teaching activity: A photograph of the Moon showing its craters (available from the NASA website – www.nasa.gov); a tray (the larger the better) with loose sand or flour to a depth of 5–10cm; a golf ball, a marble, pebbles of different sizes.
Group activities: 1. Trays of loose sand (these do not have to be as big as the tray used in the demonstration); golf balls, marbles, pebbles of different sizes; paper, pencils, rulers. **2.** Access to the Internet.

Vocabulary

Moon rock, Moon crater, mountain, asteroid.

BACKGROUND

Once the telescope had been invented, people drew detailed maps of the side of the Moon that faces the Earth. The Italian astronomer Galileo Galilei (1564–1642) built the most powerful telescope of his time: it could magnify things to about 30 times their real size. This meant that he could see the planet Jupiter and its four moons. In 1609, Galileo became the first person to make a study of the skies with a telescope. When he studied the Moon with his telescope, he saw craters and mountains that were invisible to the naked eye.

The Moon is a ball of rock that orbits the Earth and travels with it around the Sun. The Moon is held in its orbit by the Earth's gravitational pull. The Moon does not spin on its axis, so we always see the same side of it. All the planets in the Solar System, except Mercury and Venus, have moons. The Earth's moon is one of the largest: it is about one-quarter of the diameter of the Earth. It takes 28 days for the moon to orbit the Earth.

It is very quiet on the Moon: it has no atmosphere (air), so sound cannot travel and people could not breathe there unaided. If you look at the Moon through binoculars, you can see the craters in its surface. These are up to hundreds of kilometres wide. The dark patches that can be seen are flat areas of land called 'maria' or 'seas'. The lighter areas are mountains.

The craters are thought to have been formed around 4000 million years ago when rocks from the asteroid belt collided with the Moon. Asteroids are different-sized lumps of rock. Some are like specks of dust; others are a few hundred kilometres across. They were once thought to be the remains of another planet. The planets were formed thousands of millions of years ago when swarms of ice-covered bits of rock came together. Many bits were left over, and became asteroids. A large collection of them ended up circling the Sun in a broad band, between the orbits of Mars and Jupiter; these are known as the asteroid belt.

INTRODUCTION

Catch the children's imagination by reading to them one of the many myths and legends that relate to the Moon. Brainstorm words that describe the Moon on the board or flip chart; accept both scientific terms and descriptive language.

MAIN TEACHING ACTIVITY

Pass around the photograph showing the surface of the Moon. Ask the children to describe what they see. Compare their observations with the word list. Does the Moon look as they imagined? Discuss how the Moon looks, and explain what the light and dark patches are. Say that the larger craters are actually hundreds of kilometres wide. *Does anyone have any idea how these craters were formed?* Explain that they were formed by rocks hitting the Moon's surface.

To demonstrate crater formation, put a tray of dry sand or flour on the floor and ask a child to drop different-sized pebbles and marbles into it. This should create a similar effect to that seen on the Moon's surface.

GROUP ACTIVITIES

1. Groups of three or four children can repeat the crater demonstration for themselves. They should carefully remove each object from the sand, then draw the hollow or crater and measure its diameter and depth. Encourage them to answer these questions: *Which object makes a larger crater, a small object or a large one? Compare the craters you have made with those in the pictures of the Moon. In what ways are they similar? How were the craters on the Moon made?*
2. The children could use the computer to do some research into the first human landing on the Moon. They could think of key words relating to the information they want, use a search engine on the Internet, then print out the information and highlight key facts. They should use this

information to do a piece of creative writing, such as a journalistic account of the first Moon landing or an astronaut's account of visiting the Moon. Their account should include details such as how they got there, how long their journey took, how they felt when they first stepped onto the Moon, what they did there, what they saw, what they wore and how they moved about.

DIFFERENTIATION

2. Less able children may need more guidance with using the search on the Internet and skimming and selecting information. They might find it easier to list the relevant facts instead of doing a piece of creative writing. More able children could do some further research, using a search engine to find out about Galileo Galilei.

ASSESSMENT

Note which children are able to use a search engine to search for information about the first landing on the Moon; print out information and highlight key facts; describe how the craters on the Moon were formed.

PLENARY

Ask several children to read out their work. Invite responses from the class, including constructive criticism to help the children improve their writing. The children could redraft their work subsequently, and the finished accounts could become part of a display on 'Space'.

OUTCOME

● Can explain how some of the craters on the Moon were formed.

LINKS

ICT: using the Internet to search for information.

LESSON 4

OBJECTIVES

● To know what makes up our Solar System.
● To know the order of the planets in our Solar System.
● To know what a comet, an asteroid, a meteor and a meteorite are.
● To know which planets have moons.

RESOURCES

Introduction: A poster showing the planets in our Solar System (from Channel 4 Learning).
Main teaching activity: A video about the Solar System, such as *Our Solar System and Beyond'* (Channel 4 Learning); books, magazines and comics about space and the Solar System that give references to websites.
Group activities: Cards with group tasks written on them; card, paints, crayons, scissors; a computer and CD-ROMs such as *Eyewitness Space* and *Encarta*, access to the NASA website.

PREPARATION

Prepare sets of cards (enough for one card per group) with the four Group activities (see opposite) written on them.

Vocabulary

Solar System, comet, asteroid, meteor, meteorite, Mercury, Venus, Earth, Mars, Jupiter, Saturn, Uranus, Neptune, Pluto

BACKGROUND

The Universe is everything that exists. It includes many different solar systems and galaxies. A solar system consists of planets and other bodies orbiting a star. A galaxy is a system of stars held together by gravitational attraction. A hundred thousand million galaxies are known to exist. Our star, the Sun, is part of a spiral-shaped galaxy called the Milky Way.

Our Solar System consists of all the planets, asteroids and comets that orbit the star we call the Sun. They are arranged in this order: Sun, Mercury, Venus, Earth, Mars, asteroid belt, Jupiter, Saturn, Uranus, Neptune, Pluto. The Solar System was formed millions of years ago, when the Sun was born and the planets of the Solar System were formed from the material that was left over. The Sun was initially surrounded by a rotating disc of gas and dust. The dust came together to form rocks, which joined to form the first planets.

The number of Moons (rocky satellites) orbiting each of the planets in our Solar System is as follows: Mercury 0 moons, Venus 0 moons, Earth 1 moon, Mars 2 moons, Jupiter 16 moons, Saturn 18 moons, Uranus 15 moons, Neptune 8 moons, Pluto 1 moon.

Beyond Pluto's orbit are the remains of the cloud of dust that formed the Solar System. This cloud contains many comets. Comets have been described as 'giant dirty snowballs', because they are lumps of ice and rock that move towards the Sun. The ice melts and boils, forming an enormous head and a long tail. As the comet travels, it sheds bits of itself. From Earth, these are seen as showers of light called meteors or 'shooting stars'.

Meteors and meteorites are the same kind of body, but meteorites tend to be larger. They do not have an orbit: they just head towards the Earth, having drifted into its gravitational field. Most are the size of a fist, but some are larger. One landed in Arizona in the USA and produced a crater 1.3km across.

INTRODUCTION

Display a poster of the planets in our Solar System. Brainstorm what the children already know about these planets.

MAIN TEACHING ACTIVITY

Show a video that looks at the Solar System and beyond. Explain to the children that they will be working in small groups to find out things about our Solar System. Ask them to list where such information could be found. Hopefully they will suggest sources such as books, magazines, television, videos, CD-ROMs and the Internet. Show them some magazines or comics about space and the Solar System, and highlight the fact that these sources give website addresses to enable you to find out more information. Ask the children to look through these sources and find web addresses; make a list of these on the board for the children to choose from. Demonstrate how to find the NASA website, how to use a CD-ROM, and how to print a page off a website or CD-ROM.

Organise the class into groups of three or four. Allocate a Group activity card to each group, or let them choose. They have to find the information printed on the card using the Internet or a CD-ROM. Each working group should try to print out a page and highlight the text to show key information.

When the groups have completed their activities, they can feed back their findings to the rest of the class. A classroom display could then be made of the work done.

GROUP ACTIVITIES

1. The children could find information to answer the following questions: *What is the order of the planets moving away from the Sun? How far are the planets from the Sun? Which is the biggest planet? Which planet is nearest to the Sun? Which is furthest away? Which planets are larger than the Earth? Which planet is the coldest? Which is the hottest?*
2. The children could find out information about each planet: type of surface, average surface temperature, length of day, type of atmosphere, moons, rings.
3. The planets appear to be different colours. The children could find out what a planet looks like (colour, rings and so on), then paint a picture of it or make a 2-D model on card to hang in the classroom.
4. The children could find out about comets and/or meteors and meteorites, answering questions such as: *What is a comet? What names have been given to different comets? When have comets been seen? Who was Edmond Halley and what did he do? What are meteorites and meteors? How big are they? What did the Barringer meteorite do?*

DIFFERENTIATION

More able children could answer the extension question: *Why do you think Pluto was the last planet to be discovered?* They could write a story about 'A journey through the Solar System'. Less able children could work on a specially prepared worksheet, putting the names of the planets into the correct order and filling in missing words about the size of the planets, their temperature and their distance from the Sun.

ASSESSMENT

Note which children are able to access an Internet site chosen from a list; find relevant information on a website or a CD-ROM and print off the required pages; understand the printed information. These observations could form part of your ICT assessment.

PLENARY

Ask the children to write out the names of the planets in order, then make up a nonsense memory poem to help them remember the order.

OUTCOMES
● Can name the nine planets of the Solar System.
● Know which of the planets have moons.

LINKS
ICT: using CD-ROMs and search engines.

LESSON 5

Objectives	● To know what makes up our Solar System. ● To know the order of the planets in our Solar System.
Resources	A poster showing the planets in our Solar System (as for Lesson 4); a cassette or CD player, a recording of *The Planets* by Holst (such as *Journey To the Stars* in the 'Magical Music Box' series, IRDP); Plasticine, a grapefruit (or piece of card), a metre ruler or tape measure; paints, brushes, paper.
Main activity	Play excerpts from *The Planets*. Before each excerpt, tell the children which planet it is about. After each excerpt, ask the children what words they would use to describe the music. Discuss the fact that people used to believe each planet had a god. The music is meant to evoke the god of the planet and what the planet is like. 　Discuss the information from Lesson 4 about the order and size of the planets and their distance from the Sun. Copy the table shown below onto the board or flip chart. Ask the children to make a scale model of our Solar System. They can use a grapefruit, or a cardboard disc with a diameter of 11cm, for the Sun, then make a ball of Plasticine just 1mm across for the Earth, and use the information to make all the other planets to the same scale. Now they should hold the Earth 12m from the Sun and use the information for the other distances. On this scale, the nearest star would be another grapefruit about 3000km away. 　Other children could paint pictures of the planet gods, using the music they have heard and the words suggested for ideas.
Assessment	Note which children are able to work out appropriate scales for the different planets, and for their distances from the Sun.
Plenary	Ask the children to explain their scale models of the Solar System to the class. Other children can display and describe their paintings.
Outcome	● Can name the nine planets of the Solar System.

Planet	Me	Ve	Ea	Ma	As	Ju	Sa	Ur	Ne	Pl
Size (mm)	½	1	1	½		11	9	4	4	¼
Distance from the Sun (m)	5	8	12	18		60	110	220	350	460

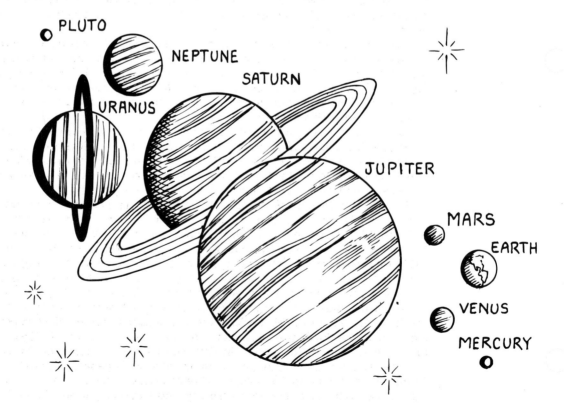

PLUTO
NEPTUNE
SATURN
URANUS
JUPITER
MARS
EARTH
VENUS
MERCURY

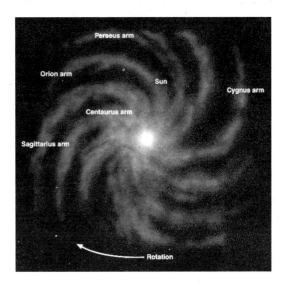
LESSON 6

OBJECTIVES

- To know about space exploration in the past.
- To know about space exploration in the future.

RESOURCES

Introduction: A telescope.
Main teaching activity: Books, magazines and comics used in Lesson 4.
Group activity: Cards from photocopiable page 194, computers, encyclopaedia CD-ROMs.

PREPARATION

Make sets of question cards (one card per group) by copying page 194 onto card and cutting it into sections.

BACKGROUND

Our Sun is a star. It is part of a huge galaxy called the Milky Way, which has a spiral shape and contains more than a hundred thousand million stars. Our Solar System is in one of the spiral arms (see picture above). The nearest other galaxy to us is Andromeda. Using modern telescopes, we can see millions of other galaxies. All the galaxies together and the space between them make up the Universe.

The first astronomer to use a telescope was Galileo Gallilei in seventeenth-century Italy. He discovered Saturn's rings and Jupiter's four large moons. In the last century, space exploration really took off! In 1903, a Russian schoolmaster called Konstantin Tsiolkovskii put forward the first scientific ideas on rocket propulsion. In 1926, an American engineer called Robert Goddard launched the first liquid fuel rocket. Since then, many space travel projects have allowed us to examine our Solar System in more detail.

Artificial satellites orbit the Earth and send back information about the weather or point out features such as mineral deposits on the Earth. Navigation satellites help ships or aeroplanes to pin-point their positions. In October 1957, Russia put the first artificial satellite (Sputnik 1) into orbit. It investigated the Earth's atmosphere from space. Sputnik 2, launched a month later, contained the first living thing to be sent into space: a dog named Laika.

Space probes are unstaffed spacecraft that investigate and report back information about our Solar System. Probe visits began in 1959, with a successful visit to the Moon by Luna 2 from the USA. In 1973, Mariner 10 visited Venus and Mercury. In 1976, Viking 1 and Viking 2 landed on Mars. In 1977, Voyager 1 and Voyager 2 were sent to Jupiter, Saturn, Uranus and Neptune. In 1985, five probes were sent to investigate Comet Halley. 1990 saw the launch of the Ulysses probe to fly over the poles of the Sun. In 1995, the Galileo probe entered Jupiter's atmosphere.

For centuries, humans have dreamed of travelling in space. In 1961, the dream became a reality when a Russian astronaut called Yuri Gagarin was rocketed into space and orbited around the Earth. On July 20th 1969, the American Neil Armstrong became the first person to walk on the Moon. In the 1970s, the Space Shuttle programme was launched. In 1983, Sally Ride became the first American woman in space; in 1991, Helen Sharman became the first British astronaut.

Astronauts can now stay in space stations. These are large satellites orbiting around the Earth, with room on board for people to live and work for months. In the future, space stations may be used as hotels where visitors can stay before travelling further in the Solar System, or before coming back to Earth. The first space station, Salyut, was launched from Russia in 1971. In 1973, the first American space station, Skylab, was launched. In 1983, the first purpose-built space laboratory, Spacelab, was launched. The largest space station, Mir, was launched in 1986.

INTRODUCTION

If you have a telescope (or can borrow one), it will be a useful prop to set the scene for this lesson. Ask the children what they think it is, what it does and what it has been made from. Have any of the children used one? Explain that Galileo Galilei was the first astronomer to make and use a telescope for observing the Moon and the planets. Explain what he discovered when he used the telescope (see Background). If any child in the class has a telescope at home, he or she could tell the rest of the class about using a telescope and what can be seen through it.

Now brainstorm what the children know about space travel. Use the board or flip chart to record key words, dates and events. Any space travel enthusiasts among the children may be happy to share their knowledge with the rest of the class.

MAIN TEACHING ACTIVITY

Ask the children to use the books, magazines and comics from Lesson 4 to find any relevant information they can on the following topics: telescopes, rockets, satellites, space probes, humans in space, space stations. Then ask them to see whether any website addresses are listed that are relevant to these topics. Record the topics and the relevant website addresses on the board.

Explain to the children that they are going to work in groups. Each group will be given a card with a title and a set of questions to answer. They will have to find the information they need, using the Internet or a CD-ROM. Each working group should print out a page and highlight the text to show the key facts.

GROUP ACTIVITY

Distribute the cards from page 194: give each group a card, or let them choose. The children work to answer each set of questions.

DIFFERENTIATION

Less able children may need help with reading through and highlighting the relevant information from the text they have printed. More able children could try any one of the following extension tasks (the one chosen will depend on which original activity they did):
- Write a short account of the life of Galileo Galilei.
- Find out about the Ariane rocket.
- Find out about the Topex/Poseidon satellite.
- Find out about the space probes that have been launched since 1995.
- Pretend you are Sally Ride. Record the adventure of your journey into space in a diary or journal.
- Design a space station.

ASSESSMENT

Note which children are able to access an Internet site chosen from a list; find relevant information on a website or a CD-ROM, and print off the required pages; understand the printed information. These observations could form part of your ICT assessment.

PLENARY

When the groups have completed their activities, they can feed back their findings to the rest of the class. With the children, list all the ways in which we can explore space. A classroom display could be made of the groups' work.

OUTCOME

- Know about the different methods that are used to explore space.

LINKS

ICT: using CD-ROMs and search engines.

LESSON 7

Objective	• To think about space exploration in the future.
Resources	A copy of *The War of the Worlds* by HG Wells (Orion); the musical version of *The War of the Worlds*, a CD player (if necessary), a cassette recorder and blank tape; ruled A4 paper, pens, pencils.
Main activity	Play part of the musical version of *The War of the Worlds*. Read part of the story to the children. Explain that this is a science fiction novel. In America in the late 1950s, this story was read over the radio as a series. When the first part was read out, many Americans actually thought that it was a news bulletin and that the Earth was being invaded by martians. Ask: *Why do you think there was such a panic? Do you think this could happen today?* If possible, it would be a good idea to take the children to visit a space exploration gallery – such as the London or Armagh Planetarium, or the National Space Centre – or to arrange for a Starlab to visit your school. This would reinforce the content of this unit, and the children would also be able to see what is planned for space exploration in the future. The children can work individually or in groups to write their own science fiction story, based on the information they have obtained from their work in this unit and/or from a visit to a space exploration gallery. They can then read their story as a radio broadcast. They could perhaps make up their own piece of music to add atmosphere to the story, and add sound effects as well. If possible, they should record the 'broadcast' on cassette for other classes to enjoy. They could draw or paint a picture for the cassette inlay card.
Differentiation	This lesson will appeal to children of all abilities. The less able may need help with structuring or writing out their story. The other children can be expected to produce a story and a broadcast that is appropriate to their ability.
Assessment	Note which children used their knowledge and imagination to predict future events in space exploration.
Plenary	Play some of the children's broadcasts to the class. The story cassettes can be added to the class bookshelf or the school library.
Outcome	• Can use scientific knowledge to create a science fiction story.

ASSESSMENT

LESSON 8

OBJECTIVES
• To review work on the Earth, Moon and Sun.
• To assess the children's knowledge about the Earth, Moon and Sun.

RESOURCES
1. Paper, pens, computers, relevant textbooks and software. **2.** Photocopiable page 195.

ASSESSMENT ACTIVITY 1
To review the work that they have done on the Earth, Moon and Sun, the children can devise a quiz (together with the answers). Each child or team should make a list of at least ten questions (together with answers). They can use textbooks, computer software and the Internet to help them come up with their questions. Ask the children to pose questions to each other, and help them to judge the appropriateness of the answers. If the class is split into teams, they could compete over several rounds.

Looking for levels
The children's questions and answers will reflect their understanding of the content of this unit. The notes on levels in Assessment activity 2 (below) may also be useful here.

ASSESSMENT ACTIVITY 2
Give out copies of page 195 and let the children complete this test individually. You may wish to mark the sheets yourself, or to swap them around the class and let the children mark each other's to encourage discussion of the questions and answers.

Answers
1. Spherical or sphere (1 mark). 'Round' is incorrect. 'Almost spherical' or 'a spheroid' is, strictly speaking, the correct answer.
2. 365¼ days or one year (1 mark).
3. 24 hours or one day (1 mark).

4. No (1 mark).
5. The Earth (1 mark). 28 days (1 mark).
6. No (1 mark).
7. For 1 mark, all three must be correctly labelled.

Sun

Moon

Earth

8a. Solar eclipse (1 mark). For 8b, 1 mark for each correct label (2 marks).
9. Sun, Mercury, Venus, Earth, Mars, asteroid belt, Jupiter, Saturn, Uranus, Neptune, Pluto (5 marks, deduct 1 for each error).
10a. Mercury and Venus (2 marks); 10b. Saturn (1 mark); 10c. The Milky Way (1 mark).
(Total possible marks: 20.)

Looking for levels

All the children should be able to describe the shape of the Earth and say how long it takes the Earth to make one journey around the Sun. They should also know that it takes the Earth 365¼ days to make one complete rotation on its axis, and that the Moon does not spin on its axis. (Questions 1, 2, 3 and 4.)

Most children should know that the Moon orbits around the Earth, and that this takes 28 days. They should also be able to label a diagram to show the relative positions and sizes of the Sun, Moon and Earth, and be able to put the planets in their correct order as you move away from the Sun. (Questions 5, 6, 7, 9.)

The more able children should know what happens in a solar eclipse, and what is meant by the terms 'umbra' and 'penumbra'. They should also know which planets have moons and rings and which don't. They should also know that our galaxy is called the Milky Way. (Questions 8 and 10.)

PLENARY

You may wish to go through the answers to the test with the children after you have collected in the work for marking.

There may be a question (such as question 8) that a lot of children get wrong. If this is the case, it is advisable to go over the concepts that relate to this question with the class, then ask them to work in groups on the problem. You may wish to use carefully chosen mixed-ability groups. It has been shown that if less able children are put with more able children, they can learn a lot. However, care must be taken over the mix of children, as sometimes more able children can be domineering and take over the whole show.

On the other hand, there may be a question that the majority of the children got right. In this case, it will be useful to give them an extension question or activity that covers the same concepts. For example, if all the children get question 1 right, you could ask them to answer the following questions: *Look around your school. How many objects can you find that are spheres? What is the largest sphere you can find? What is the smallest sphere you can find? How would you measure a sphere?*

Sun, Earth and Moon

	Approximate diameter (km)
Sun	1400 000
Earth	13 000
Moon	3 500

1. How many times greater than the Moon (in diameter) is the Earth?

_____

2. How many times greater than the Earth (in diameter) is the Sun?

_____

3. How many times greater than the Moon (in diameter) is the Sun?

_____

	Approximate distance (km)
Earth–Sun	150 000 000
Earth–Moon	390 000

4. If you were making a small-scale model of the Earth, Moon and Sun, how far apart would you put the models?

Name

Phases of the Moon

Keep an account of changes in the shape of the Moon.

1. Look at the Moon every night.

2. Draw the Moon's shape in one of the circles.

3. Here are some shapes you might see. Find out what they are called.

4. Colour the bright part of the Moon yellow in each of your pictures. When you cannot see the Moon at all, shade the circle black.

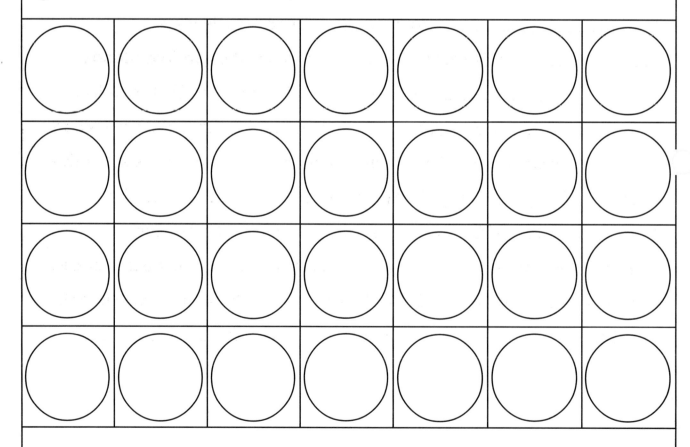

Name

Eclipse of the Sun

Label the diagram below with the following words:
Sun, Moon, Earth, umbra, penumbra.

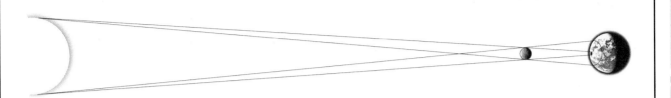

Fill in the missing words:

An eclipse of the Sun (_____ eclipse) happens when the Earth,

Moon and Sun line up in such a way that the Moon blocks the Sun's light

from the _____. A solar eclipse only occurs when the

_____ lies directly between the Earth and the Sun. The Moon's

shadow or _____ only covers a small area of the Earth's surface.

Anyone standing in this region will see the Sun totally eclipsed by the Moon.

Eclipses occur because the Sun and the Moon appear to be the same size

in the Earth's sky. In reality, the Sun is 400 times _____; but

because the Sun is 400 times further away, it appears Moon-sized.

If the Moon were _____ away from the Earth, it would not cast

such a large shadow on the Earth when it passed between the Earth and the

Sun. This is because the Moon is much smaller than the _____.

Space travel

Telescopes

Who was the first astronomer to use a telescope?

When was the telescope first used for observing the skies?

What is a telescope made of?

What did Galileo discover by using his telescope?

What is an observatory?

Find out about the Keck telescope.

Humans in space

Why is Yuri Gagarin famous? What nationality was he?

Who was the first person to set foot on the Moon? In what year did it happen?

Who was the first woman in space, and in what year? What nationality was she?

Why is Helen Sharman famous?

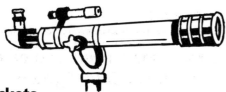

Rockets

What are rockets used for?

Where are rockets launched from?

Find out about Saturn V.

Who was Robert Goddard?

Space stations (1)

What is a space station used for?

Find out about Salyut.

Find out about Skylab.

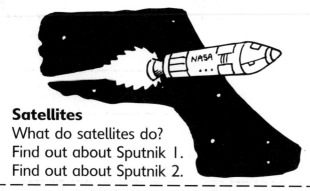

Satellites

What do satellites do?

Find out about Sputnik 1.

Find out about Sputnik 2.

Space Stations (2)

Find out about Spacelab.

Find out about Mir.

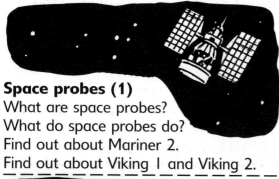

Space probes (1)

What are space probes?

What do space probes do?

Find out about Mariner 2.

Find out about Viking 1 and Viking 2.

Space travel in the future

Find out about plans for space travel in the future.

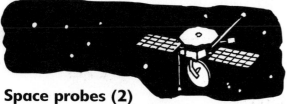

Space probes (2)

Find out about Voyager 1 and Voyager 2.

Find out about the Ulysses probe.

Find out about the Galileo probe.

Name

The Solar System

1. What shape is the Earth?

_____

2. How long does it take the Earth to make one orbit around the Sun?

_____

3. How long does it take for the Earth to make one complete rotation on its axis?

_____

4. Does the Moon spin on its axis?

_____

5. What does the Moon orbit around? How long does this take?

_____

6. Does the Sun move around the Earth?

_____

7. Label this diagram using the following words: **Earth, Moon, Sun.**

8. (a) What is happening in this diagram?

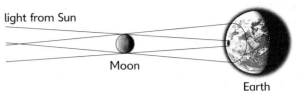

light from Sun

Moon

Earth

(b) Label the umbra and penumbra on the diagram.

9. The following planets and other bodies are in our Solar System: Venus, Earth, Mercury, Pluto, asteroid belt, Neptune, Mars, Uranus, Jupiter, Saturn. List them in the correct order, moving away from the Sun.

_____

_____

10. (a) Which two planets in our Solar System do not have moons?

_____

(b) Which planet in our Solar System is famous for its rings?

_____

(c) What is the name of our galaxy?

_____

National Curriculum in England

LINKS TO QCA SCIENCE SCHEME OF WORK

SC1 SCIENTIFIC ENQUIRY

1 Ideas and evidence in science

a that science is about thinking creatively to try to explain how living and non-living things work, and to establish links between causes and effects

b that it is important to test ideas using evidence from observation and measurement

2 Investigative skills – Planning

a ask questions that can be investigated scientifically and decide how to find answers

b consider what sources of information, including first-hand experience and a range of other sources, they will use to answer questions

c think about what might happen or try things out when deciding what to do, what kind of evidence to collect, and what equipment and materials to use

d make a fair test or comparison by changing one factor and observing or measuring the effect while keeping other factors the same

Investigative skills – Obtaining and presenting evidence

e use simple equipment and materials appropriately and take action to control risks

f make systematic observations and measurements, including the use of ICT for data-logging

g check observations and measurements by repeating them where appropriate

h use a wide range of methods, including diagrams, drawings, tables, bar charts, line graphs and ICT, to communicate data in an appropriate and systematic manner

Investigative skills – Considering evidence and evaluating

i make comparisons and identify simple patterns or associations in their own observations and measurements or other data

j use observations, measurements or other data to draw conclusions

k decide whether these conclusions agree with any prediction made and/or whether they enable further predictions to be made

l use their scientific knowledge and understanding to explain observations, measurements or other data or conclusions

m review their work and the work of others and describe its significance and limitations

SC2 LIFE PROCESSES AND LIVING THINGS

1 Life processes

a that the life processes common to humans and other animals include nutrition, movement, growth and reproduction

b that the life processes common to plants include growth, nutrition and reproduction

c to make links between life processes in familiar animals and plants and the environments in which they are found

2 Humans and other animals – Nutrition

a about the functions and care of teeth

b about the need for food for activity and growth, and about the importance of an adequate and varied diet for health

Humans and other animals – Circulation

c that the heart acts as a pump to circulate the blood through vessels around the body, including through the lungs

d about the effect of exercise and rest on pulse rate

Humans and other animals – Movement

e that humans and some other animals have skeletons and muscles to support and protect their bodies and to help them to move

Humans and other animals – Growth and reproduction

f about the main stages of the human life cycle

Humans and other animals – Health

g about the effects on the human body of tobacco, alcohol and other drugs, and how these relate to their personal health

h about the importance of exercise for good health

3 Green plants – Growth and nutrition

a the effect of light, air, water and temperature on plant growth

b the role of the leaf in producing new material for growth

c that the root anchors the plant, and that water and minerals are taken in through the root and transported through the stem to other parts of the plant

Green plants – Reproduction

d about the parts of the flower and their role in the life cycle of flowering plants, including pollination, seed formation, seed dispersal and germination

4 Variation and classification

a to make and use keys

b how locally occurring animals and plants can be identified and assigned to groups

c that the variety of plants and animals makes it important to identify them and assign them to groups

5 Living things in their environment

a about ways in which living things and the environment need protection

Living things in their environment – Adaptation

b about the different plants and animals found in different habitats

c how animals and plants in two different habitats are suited to their environment

Living things in their environment – Feeding relationships

d to use food chains to show feeding relationships in a habitat

e about how nearly all food chains start with a green plant

Living things in their environment – Micro-organisms

f that micro-organisms are living organisms that are often too small to be seen, and that they may be beneficial or harmful

SC3 MATERIALS & THEIR PROPERTIES

1 Grouping and classifying

a to compare everyday materials and objects on the basis of their material properties, including hardness, strength, flexibility and magnetic behaviour, and to relate these properties to everyday uses of the materials

b that some materials are better thermal insulators than others

c that some materials are better electrical conductors than others

d to describe and group rocks and soils on the basis of their characteristics, including appearance, texture and permeability

e to recognise differences between solids, liquids and gases, in terms of ease of flow and maintenance of shape and volume

2 Changing materials

a to describe changes that occur when materials are mixed

b to describe changes that occur when materials are heated or cooled

c that temperature is a measure of how hot or cold things are

d about reversible changes, including dissolving, melting, boiling, condensing, freezing and evaporating

e the part played by evaporation and condensation in the water cycle

f that non-reversible changes result in the formation of new materials that may be useful

g that burning materials results in the formation of new materials and that this change is not usually reversible

3 Separating mixtures of materials

a how to separate solid particles of different sizes

b that some solids dissolve in water to give solutions but some do not

c how to separate insoluble solids from liquids by filtering

d how to recover dissolved solids by evaporating the liquid from the solution

e to use knowledge of solids, liquids and gases to decide how mixtures might be separated

Lessons where curriculum content is the main objective are listed below. Lessons where content is included but is not the main focus are shown below in brackets.

Unit 1: Ourselves New beginnings	Unit 2: Animals & Plants Variation	Unit 3: The environment The living world	Unit 4: Materials Reversible and non-reversible changes	Unit 5: Electricity Changing circuits	Unit 6: Forces & motion Forces and action	Unit 7: Light & sound Light and sound around us	Unit 8: Earth & beyond The Solar System
–	UNIT 6A	UNIT 6A, 6B, 5/6H	UNIT 6C, 6D	UNIT 6G, 5/6H	UNIT 6E	UNIT 6F	–
1, 2		16	4, 7, 8			2	3
		14, 15	10	1, 2	1, 2	5	3
	6	1			1, 2	5	
	9	16		6		7, 9, 11	5, 6
	6, 7		6		1, 2	2	
	6, 7				7, 8	7, 13	3
		1, 7, 8, 14, 15	1, 4, 5, 6	1, 2	7	6, 10	
	4, 9	5, 6, 14, 15	7			6	
			2		1, 2	6, 13	3
(3), 7	1, 4, 8	5		8, (9), (10)	3, 4, 10, 11	1, 12	3
1, 5, 6	1, 2, 3, 5	3, 7, 14, 15	4, 5, 6, 7		3, 5	1, 2, 3, (4), 6	1, 2
	4	7	7, 8, 9		7, 8, 11	5	
					1, 6	8	3
(4)		14, 15		4, 5, 7		8, 13	
1, (2)		14, 15				7, 8	7, 13 3, (7)
4, 8							
1, 3, (8)							
4, 5, 6, 7, 8	(4)						
2, 3, (8)							
1, (0)							
	6, 7	(9)					
	(8)	9					
	3, 5, 9						
	2, 5						
	3						
		1					
		1, 3, 4, 5, 6					
		(1), 3, 4, 5, 6					
		2, 3, 8, 16					
		2, 3, (8), 16					
		2, 10, 11, 12, 13, 15					
	(1)						
			1, 2, 9, (23)				
			11, (23)				
			1, 2, 3, 4, 5, 6, 7, 8, (23)				
			3				
			9, 10, (15), (16), (17)				
			12, 13, (14), (18), (19), (20), (21), (22), (23)				
			2, 4, 5, 6, 7, 8				
			1				
Unit 1: Ourselves	Unit 2: Animals & Plants	Unit 3: The environment	Unit 4: Materials	Unit 5: Electricity	Unit 6: Forces & motion	Unit 7: Light & sound	Unit 8: Earth & beyond

SC4 Physical processes overleaf

National Curriculum in England (cont)

LINKS TO QCA SCIENCE SCHEME OF WORK

1 Electricity – Simple circuits

a to construct circuits, incorporating a battery or power supply and a range of switches, to make electrical devices work

b how changing the number or type of components in a series circuit can make bulbs brighter or dimmer

c how to represent series circuits by drawings and conventional symbols; how to construct series circuits on the basis of drawings and diagrams using conventional symbols

2 Forces and motion – Types of force

a about the forces of attraction and repulsion between magnets, and about the forces of attraction between magnets and magnetic materials

b that objects are pulled downwards because of the gravitational attraction between them and the Earth

c about friction, including air resistance, as a force that slows moving objects and may prevent objects from starting to move are pushed or pulled

d that when objects are pushed or pulled an opposing pull or push can be felt

e how to measure forces and identify the direction in which they act

3 Light and sound – Everyday effects of light

a that light travels from a source

b that light cannot pass through some materials, and how this leads to the formation of shadows

c that light is reflected from surfaces

Light and sound – Seeing

d that we see things only when light from them enters our eyes

Light and sound – Vibration and sound

e that sounds are made when objects vibrate but that vibrations are not always directly visible

f how to change the pitch and loudness of sounds produced by some vibrating objects

g that vibrations from sound sources require a medium through which to travel to the ear

4 The Earth and beyond – The Sun, Earth and Moon

a that the Sun, Earth and Moon are approximately spherical

The Earth and beyond – Periodic changes

b how the position of the Sun appears to change during the day, and how shadows change as this happens

c how day and night are related to the spin of the Earth on its own axis

d that the Earth orbits the Sun once each year, and that the Moon takes approximately 28 days to orbit the Earth

National Curriculum in Wales

1 The nature of science

the link between ideas and information in science

1 to apply their ideas and knowledge and understanding of science when thinking about and investigating phenomena in the world around them

2 to consider information obtained from their own work and also, on some occasions, from other sources

3 that scientific ideas can be tested by means of information gathered from observation and measurement

2 Communication in science

presenting scientific information

1 to report their work clearly in speech and writing using relevant scientific vocabulary

2 to use a range of methods, including diagrams, drawings, graphs, tables and charts, to record and present information in an appropriate and systematic manner

3 to use ICT to select and present a range of relevant information, when this is appropriate

4 to use standard measures and units handling scientific information

5 to search for and access relevant scientific information, using ICT to do so on some occasions

6 to recognise that it is useful to present and consider scientific information in an appropriate form, making use of ICT to do so when appropriate

planning an investigation

1 to turn ideas suggested to them, and their own ideas, into a form that can be investigated

2 that asking questions, and using their knowledge and understanding of the context to anticipate what may happen, can be useful when planning what to do

3 to decide what information should be collected

4 that in situations where the factors can be identified and controlled, a fair test may be carried out

5 to consider what equipment or other resources to use

6 to recognise the hazards and risks to themselves and others obtaining information

7 to use equipment or other resources correctly, taking action to control risks

8 to make careful observations and measurements and record them appropriately

9 to check observations and measurements by repeating them, when this is appropriate

10 to use ICT equipment and software to monitor changes

considering information

11 to make comparisons and to identify and describe trends or patterns in data

12 to use the results of their investigations to draw conclusions

13 to try to relate the outcomes of their investigation or their conclusions to their scientific knowledge and understanding

14 to review their work and suggest how their data could be improved

1 Life processes

1 that there are life processes, including nutrition, movement, growth and reproduction, common to animals, including humans

2 that there are life processes, including growth, nutrition and reproduction, common to plants

2 Humans and other animals

nutrition

1 how the teeth break up food into smaller pieces and the importance of dental care

2 that the body needs different foods for activity and for growth

3 that an adequate and varied diet is needed to keep healthy

circulation

4 that the heart acts as a pump

5 how blood circulates in the body through arteries and veins

6 that the pulse gives a measure of the heart beat rate

7 the effect of exercise and rest on pulse rate

movement

8 that humans and some other animals have skeletons and muscles to support and protect their bodies and to help them to move

growth and reproduction

9 the main stages of the human life cycle

Lessons where curriculum content is the main objective are listed below. Lessons where content is included but is not the main focus are shown below in brackets.

Unit 1: Ourselves New beginnings	Unit 2: Animals & Plants Variation	Unit 3: The environment The living world	Unit 4: Materials Reversible and non-reversible changes	Unit 5: Electricity Changing circuits	Unit 6: Forces & motion Forces and action	Unit 7: Light & sound Light and sound around us	Unit 8: Earth & beyond The Solar System
–	UNIT 6A	UNIT 6A, 6B, 5/6H	UNIT 6C, 6D	UNIT 6G, 5/6H	UNIT 6E	UNIT 6F	–
				1, 2, 4, 5, 6, 7, 8, 9, 11			
				1, 2, 11			
				3, 10, 11			
					1, 2, 11		
					2, 11		
					7, 8, (9)		
					4, 11		
					5, 6, (10), 11		
						1	
						1, (2), 8, 14	
						3, 5, 6, 7, 8, 14	
						4	
						9, 15	
						10, 15	
						11, (12), (13)	
							(1)
							1
							1
							1, (2), (3), (4), (5), (6), (7)

Unit 1: Ourselves New beginnings	Unit 2: Animals & Plants Variation	Unit 3: The environment The living world	Unit 4: Materials Reversible and non-reversible changes	Unit 5: Electricity Changing circuits	Unit 6: Forces & motion Forces and action	Unit 7: Light & sound Light and sound around us	Unit 8: Earth & beyond The Solar System
	6	1, 5			1	1, 13	
	4	1, 5		1, 4	1	1, 13	2, 4, 5
(2)	6	1, 5, 16	1	1, 4	1	1, 13	2
3, 7	(8)	1	7			3, 4, 9, 12	
	4	5	4		7, 8, 11	8	1
			4, 5				4, 6
			5				
2						9, 11	2, 4, 6
2			1			1	(7)
	6, 9	(5), 16	7		7, 8		3
		13	10			2	
	6, 9	16		8	10		
		13	4, 5, 6, 7			7, 13	3
	9			8		6	
		1, 5, 6, 8	1, 9			6	
		5, 6, 8				5, 6, 10	
	6, 9	7, 8		8	1, 2, 3	6	
	6				3		
1, (4), (5), (6)	1, 2, 3, 4, 5	6, 7, 8, 14	4	1, 2	4, 5, 6, 11	7	3
	4	1	5, 6	1		2	
	7		8		7, 8, 10		
1	7					2	
4, 8							
1, 3, (8)							
(1)							
4, 5, 6, 7, 8	4	(11), (12)					

Life processes and living things continued overleaf

LIFE PROCESSES AND LIVING THINGS (cont)

		health
	10	that tobacco, alcohol and other drugs can have harmful effects
3	**Green plants as organisms**	
		growth and nutrition
	1	to investigate the effect on the growth of plants of changing their conditions
	2	that plants need light to produce food for growth, and the importance of the leaf in this process
	3	that the root anchors the plant, and that water and nutrients are taken in through the root and transported through the stem to other parts of the plant
		reproduction
	4	the main stages in the life cycle of flowering plants including pollination, seed production, seed dispersal and germination
	5	about the process of pollination in flowering plants
	6	how pollen and seeds can be transported
4	**Living things in their environment**	
		adaptation
	1	to find out about the variety of plants and animals found in different habitats including the local area
	2	how animals and plants in two different habitats are suited to their environment
		feeding relationships
	3	that food chains show feeding relationships in an ecosystem
	4	that nearly all food chains start with a green plant variation
	5	how locally occurring animals and plants can be identified and assigned to groups, by making and using keys

MATERIALS & THEIR PROPERTIES

1	**Grouping and classifying materials**	
	1	to compare everyday materials, on the basis of their properties, including hardness, strength, flexibility and magnetic behaviour, and to relate these properties to everyday uses of the materials
	2	that some materials are better thermal insulators/conductors than others
	3	that some materials are better electrical conductors/insulators than others
	4	to describe and group rocks on the basis of appearance and texture, and soils on the basis of particle size and permeability
	5	to recognise differences between solids, liquids and gases, in terms of their properties.
2	**Changing materials**	
	1	to explore changes in materials and recognise those that can be reversed and those that cannot
	2	that dissolving, melting, condensing, freezing and evaporating are changes that can be reversed
	3	that irreversible changes result in a new material being produced, which may be useful
	4	that the changes that occur when most materials are burned are not reversible, and result in a new material being produced
	5	that mixing materials can cause them to change
	6	that heating or cooling materials can cause them to change
	7	that temperature is a measure of how hot or cold things are
	8	the part played by evaporation and condensation in the water cycle
3	**Separating mixtures of materials**	
	1	that solid particles of different sizes can be separated by sieving
	2	that some solids are soluble in water and will dissolve to give solutions but some will not, and that this provides a means of separating different solids
	3	that insoluble solids can be separated from liquids by filtering
	4	that solids that have dissolved can be recovered by evaporating the liquid from the solution

PHYSICAL PROCESSES

1	**Electricity**	
		simple circuits
	1	that a complete conducting circuit, including a battery or power supply, is needed for a current to flow to make electrical devices work
	2	to investigate how switches can be used to control electrical devices in simple series and parallel arrangements
	3	that the brightness of bulbs and the rotation of motors can be controlled by altering the current
	4	ways of varying the current in a circuit, including changing the power supply, and changing the length of conductor in a circuit
	5	how to represent simple circuits by drawings and diagrams, and how to construct such circuits on the basis of drawings and diagrams
2	**Forces and motion**	
		behaviour of forces
	1	to measure forces between objects and find out how the forces change in size
	2	that forces act in particular directions
	3	that forces con make things speed up, slow down, or change direction
		types of force
	4	that there are forces of attraction and repulsion between magnets, and forces of attraction between magnets and some materials
	5	that the weight of an object is the force of the Earth on the object and is measured in newtons
	6	about friction, including air resistance, as a force between surfaces which slows moving objects and may prevent them from starting to move
	7	that objects that are stretched or compressed exert a force on whatever is changing their shape
	8	that the change in shape of a spring is used in force meters for measuring forces
3	**Light and sound**	
		everyday effects of light
	1	that light travels from a source
	2	that we see light sources because light from them travels to and enters our eyes
	3	we see objects because light falling on them is reflected
	4	that most of the light falling on shiny surfaces and mirrors is reflected
	5	that light cannot pass through some materials, and that this leads to the formation of shadows
		vibration and sound
	6	that sounds are made when objects vibrate but that vibrations are not always directly visible
	7	that the pitch and loudness of sounds produced by some vibrating objects can be changed
	8	that vibrations from sound sources can travel through a variety of materials
4	**The Earth and beyond**	
		the Sun, Moon and planets
	1	that the Sun, Earth and Moon are approximately spherical
	2	the relative positions of the Sun, Earth and other planets in the solar system
		periodic changes
	3	how the position of the Sun appears to change during the day, and how shadows change as this happens
	4	that the Earth spins around its own axis, and how day and night are related to this spin
	5	that the Earth orbits the Sun once each year, and that the Moon takes approximately 28 days to orbit the Earth

Lessons where curriculum content is the main objective are listed below. Lessons where content is included but is not the main focus are shown below in brackets.

Unit 1: Ourselves New beginnings	Unit 2: Animals & Plants Variation	Unit 3: The environment The living world	Unit 4: Materials Reversible and non-reversible changes	Unit 5: Electricity Changing circuits	Unit 6: Forces & motion Forces and action	Unit 7: Light & sound Light and sound around us	Unit 8: Earth & beyond The Solar System
2, 3, (8)		(15)					
	6, 7	(6)					
	6, 7						
	(8)						
	(2)	1, 3, 4, 5, (6), 9					
		(1), (4), (6), 9					
		2, (10), (13), (14), (15), 16					
	3, 5, 9	2, 16					
		(1)					
	(1)						
			3, 4, 5, 6, 7, 8, (23)				
			9, 15, 16, 17, (23)				
			12, (13), (14), (18), (19), (20), (21), (22)				
			9				
			11				
			5				
			(3)				
		1					
		4, 23					
		1, 10					
		2					
				1, (7)			
				4, 5, 6			
				1, 2, 11			
				8, 9			
				3, 10			
					1		
					1, 5, 6, 10, 11		
					1, 10		
					1, 2, 11		
					3, 11		
					7, 8, 9		
					4		
					3, 4, 11		
						1	
						4	
						3, 7, 14	
						5, 6, 7, 14	
						2, 7, 8, 14	
						9, 15	
						10, (13), 15	
						11, 12, 15	
							1, (3)
							2, 4, 5, (6), (7)
							1, (2)
							1
							1
Unit 1: Ourselves New beginnings	Unit 2: Animals & Plants Variation	Unit 3: The environment The living world	Unit 4: Materials Reversible and non-reversible changes	Unit 5: Electricity Changing circuits	Unit 6: Forces & motion Forces and action	Unit 7: Light & sound Light and sound around us	Unit 8: Earth & beyond The Solar System

The Northern Ireland Curriculum

Pupils should be encouraged to adopt safe practices when undertaking science and technology activities. They should be made aware of potential hazards and the appropriate actions necessary to avoid risks.

INVESTIGATING AND MAKING IN SCIENCE AND TECHNOLOGY

Planning

a recognise a fair test

b suggest ideas which can be investigated and make predictions

c choose appropriate materials and components when planning what to make

d suggest how to carry out a fair test

e plan what they are going to make and talk about the materials and components they could use

f design a fair test

Carrying out and making

a reinforce measuring skills using non-standard measures and progress to using standard measures

b develop manipulative skills using a range of materials and tools

c record what they have done or observed using appropriate methods

d make decisions about what, when and how to measure

e carry out a fair test

f make observations and measurements, taking account of the need for care and accuracy

g develop competence in the safe use of appropriate tools and techniques to cut, shape and join materials

h record findings choosing appropriate methods

i construct working models which incorporate an energy source and which can be controlled

j carry out a fair test that they have designed and record results systematically in tables

Interpreting and evaluating

a present their findings using appropriate methods

b relate what happened to what they predicted

c talk about what they have made in terms of materials, colour, size or shape and make suggestions for improvement

d choose appropriate methods to present results and make a record of their conclusions

e use results to draw conclusions or make comparisons

f evaluate what they have made, in terms of appearance and fitness for purpose, and suggest improvements

g use results to identify patterns

h evaluate a model that they have made bearing in mind their original intentions

KNOWLEDGE AND UNDERSTANDING OF SCIENCE AND TECHNOLOGY

Living things

Ourselves

a find out about themselves, including how they grow, move and use their senses

b identify major organs, including brain, heart, lungs, stomach, liver, bladder, small and large intestines, kidneys, and place these organs on an outline of the human body

c learn about factors that contribute to good health including diet, exercise, hygiene and develop an awareness of the safe use of medicines and the harmful effects of tobacco, alcohol and other substances

d develop an awareness of puberty-related changes, through discussion with the teacher or other professionals, for example, discuss with the teacher the changes that occur in their bodies during puberty

e investigate how basic life processes including circulation, simple respiration and digestion relate in order to maintain healthy bodies

f understand that humans have skeletons and muscles to support their bodies and help them move

Animals and plants

a find out about other animals, including how they grow, feed, move and use their senses

b observe similarities and differences among animals and among plants

c discuss the use of colour in the natural environment

d find out ways in which animal and plant behaviour is influenced by seasonal changes

e investigate a local habitat, including the relationship between the animals and plants found there, and develop skills in classifying animals and plants by observing external features

f find out about the main stages in the life cycle of some animals including a butterfly and a frog

g investigate the conditions necessary for the growth of familiar plants including light, heat and water

h learn about the life cycle of a flowering plant including how pollen is taken from the stamen into the stigma, fertilised in the ovule and a seed produced which is dispersed in a variety of ways

i order living things in a simple food chain and understand the dependency of one on the other

Materials

Properties

a investigate similarities and differences in materials and objects and sort them according to their properties

b find out about the origins of materials and learn that some are natural and others are manufactured

c investigate the properties of materials and how these relate to their uses

d investigate the distinctive properties of solids, liquids and gases as exemplified by water

Change

a investigate which everyday substances dissolve in water

b know that when materials are changed this may be desirable or undesirable

c investigate the changes of state brought about by heating and cooling everyday substances

d relate changes of state to the water cycle

e understand that when new materials are formed, change is permanent

f investigate how rusting can be controlled

Environment

a find out how human activities create a variety of waste products

b find out that some materials decay naturally while others do not

c understand that some waste materials can be recycled and that this can be of benefit to the environment

Physical Processes

Forces and energy

a find out about the range of energy sources used in school and at home

b find out the sources of energy in a variety of models and machines

c investigate how forces can affect the movement and shape of objects

d investigate the effect of friction on the movement of objects

e understand the differences between renewable and non-renewable energy resources and the need for fuel economy

Electricity

a know about the safe use of mains electricity and its associated dangers

b construct simple circuits using components, such as switches, bulbs and batteries

c investigate materials as to whether they are insulators or conductors

d investigate the effects of varying current in a circuit to make bulbs brighter or dimmer

Sound

a investigate how sounds are produced when objects vibrate

b investigate that sound travels through a variety of materials

Light

a explore how light passes through some materials and not others

b find out that when light travelling from a source does not pass through materials, shadows are formed

c investigate the reflection of light from mirrors and other shiny surfaces

EMU and cultural heritage Pupils should have opportunities to develop an understanding of themselves and others by exploring similarities and differences between themselves and other children, and developing a sense of their own individuality. They should appreciate the environment around them, the need to

Lessons where curriculum content is the main objective are listed below. Lessons where content is included but is not the main focus are shown below in brackets.

Unit 1: Ourselves New beginnings	Unit 2: Animals & Plants Variation	Unit 3: The environment The living world	Unit 4: Materials Reversible and non-reversible changes	Unit 5: Electricity Changing circuits	Unit 6: Forces & motion Forces and action	Unit 7: Light & sound Light and sound around us	Unit 8: Earth & beyond The Solar System
						7, 13	3
			1, 4		1, 2	1	
	6	13	7, 8			7, 13	3
						10, 11	1
	6, 7	13	7, 8		7, 8	7, 13	3
					1		1, (5)
	1, 2, 3	1, 5, 6		2		1, 5	
				1, 2		6	
	6	13	5, 6, 7, 8		7, 8	7, 13	3
	1, 2, 3, 4, 5	1, 5, 6, 7	5, 6, 7, 8		3, 4	6	
						10, 11	
	7	8				6	
			5, 6, 7, 8	8			3
1			4, 5			8, 9, 12	1, (4)
	6, 7	13	1, 4	1, 2	1, 2	6	3
1, 2, 3, (4), (5), (6)			5, 6			3, 4	
	4, 6, 7, 9	1, 5, 6, 7, 9, 14	5, 6	5	4, 5, 6, 11	2, (8), 13	
7				6		10, 11	
	4			1, 2		2, 6	3
							1, (2), 5
1, 2, 3, (8)		(11), (12), (14)					
(4), (5), (6), (7), (8)							
	6, 7, 8	(3), (8)					
	(1), 2, (3), 4, 5	4					
		(1)					
		(1)					
	(1), 2, 3, 4, 9	1, 5, 6, (7), 9, 10					
		2, (10), (13), 14, 15, 16					
			1, 4, 5, 6, 7, 8, 10, (23)				
			15, (23)				
			2, 3, 11, 17				
			(2), (3)				
			9, 12, 13, (14), (23)				
			15, 16, (23)				
			18, 19				
					1, 2, 3, 4, 5, 6, 10, 11		
					7, 8, 9		
		19, 20, 21, (22)					
				1, 7, (10), (11)			
				1, (3), 4, 5, 6			
				(8), (9)			
				2, (8), (9), (11)			
						9, (10), 15	
						11, (12), (13), 15	
						(1), 14	
						1, 2, 14	
						3, (4), 5, 6, 7, 8, 14	

take care of it and how human activities can upset the natural environment. They should consider how some toys and devices work and know that the technology which drives them has been developed over a period of time.

National Guidelines for Scotland

SKILLS IN SCIENCE: INVESTIGATING

Preparing for tasks
Understanding the task and planning a practical activity. Predicting. Undertaking fair testing.

C
- suggest a question for exploration and decide how they might find an answer
- make reasoned predictions about a possible outcome
- suggest some ways of making a test fair

D
- identify two or three questions to investigate
- provide reasons for planning decisions
- include fair testing in planning by changing one factor
- show awareness of the significance of variables

E
- identify a number of questions to investigate
- plan a valid and reliable test for a given hypothesis

Carrying out tasks
Observing and measuring. Recording findings in a variety of ways.

C
- select and use appropriate measurement devices or make appropriate observations
- record findings in a greater range of ways

D
- make an appropriate series of accurate measurements
- select an appropriate way of recording findings

E
- select and use appropriate forms of graphical presentation

Reviewing and reporting on tasks
Reporting and presenting. Interpreting and evaluating results and processes.

C
- make a short report of an investigation, communicating key points clearly
- explain what happened, drawing on their scientific knowledge
- make links to original predictions

D
- make an organised report of an investigation using appropriate illustrations
- provide explanations related to scientific knowledge
- draw conclusions consistent with the findings
- identify limitations of the approach used

E
- write a structured report of an investigation using appropriate illustrations and vocabulary
- establish links between the results and the original hypothesis
- suggest improvements to the approach used

EARTH IN SPACE

Earth in space
Developing an understanding of the position of the Earth in the Solar System and the Universe, and the effects of its movement and that of the Moon

C
- describe the solar system in terms of the Earth, sun and planets
- link the temperature of the planets to their relative positions and atmospheres

D
- relate the movement of planets around the Sun to gravitational forces
- give some examples of the approaches taken to space exploration

E
- explain day, month and year in terms of the relative motion of the Sun, the Earth and the Moon

Materials from Earth
Developing an understanding of the materials available on our planet, and the links between properties and uses

C
- describe the differences between solids, liquids and gases
- give some everyday uses of solids, liquids and gases

D
- describe the internal structure of the Earth
- describe the processes that led up to the formation of the three main types of rock
- give examples of useful materials that we obtain from the Earth's crust
- describe how soils are formed
- name the gases of the atmosphere and describe some of their uses

Changing materials
Developing an understanding of the ways in which materials can be changed

C
- describe changes when materials are mixed
- describe how solids of different sizes can be separated
- distinguish between soluble and insoluble materials
- describe in simple terms the changes that occur when water is heated or cooled

D
- describe what happens when materials are burned
- explain how evaporation and filtration can be used in the separation of solids from liquids
- describe the effect of burning fossil fuels

E
- describe the effect of temperature on solubility
- describe what happens when metals react with oxygen, water and acids

ENERGY AND FORCES

Properties and uses of energy
Developing an understanding of the energy through the study of the properties and uses of heat, light, sound and electricity

C
- link light to shadow formation
- give examples of light being reflected from surfaces
- link sound to sources of vibration
- construct simple battery-operated circuits, identifying the main components
- classify materials as electrical conductors or insulators and describe how these are related to the safe use of electricity

D
- distinguish between heat and temperature
- describe in simple terms how lenses work
- give examples of simple applications of lenses
- use the terms 'pitch' and 'volume' to describe sound
- construct a series circuit following diagrams using conventional symbols
- describe the effect of changing the number of components in a series circuit

E
- construct a parallel circuit following diagrams
- use the terms 'voltage', 'current' and 'resistance' in the context of simple circuits

Conversion and transfer of energy
Developing an understanding of energy conversion in practical everyday contexts

C
- give examples of energy being converted from one form to another
- describe the energy conversions in the components of an electrical circuit

D
- give some examples of energy conversions involved in the generation of electricity
- describe how electrical energy is distributed to our homes
- name some energy resources

E
- explain the difference between renewable and non-renewable energy resources

Lessons where curriculum content is the main objective are listed below. Lessons where content is included but is not the main focus are shown below in brackets.

Unit 1: Ourselves / New beginnings	Unit 2: Animals & Plants / Variation	Unit 3: The environment / The living world	Unit 4: Materials / Reversible and non-reversible changes	Unit 5: Electricity / Changing circuits	Unit 6: Forces & motion / Forces and action	Unit 7: Light & sound / Light and sound around us	Unit 8: Earth & beyond / The Solar System
	2, 5		4, 5, 6, 7, 8	1, 2	4	1, 5	
		(1)	4, 5, 6, 7, 8	1, 2	7, 8	6	3
	6, 7	5, 6	4, 5, 6, 7, 8, 15, 16	8			3
			(4), (5), 6, 7, 8				3
	6, 7		4, 5, 6, 7, 8		4	6	3
	6, 7		4, 5, 6, 7, 8, 15, 16	8	8		3
	6, 7		4, 5, 6, 7, 8		7, 8		3
	7		16		7, 8		
	(6), 7		6, 15, 16	4, 8	4	(6)	3
	4	(1)	4, 5, 6, 7, 8, 10, 12	1, 2	1, 5, 6	1, 5, 7	(2)
	4		4, 5, 6, 7, 8			6	3
	4, 6, 7	8	4, 5, 6, 7, 8		1, 4, 8	6	
	4, 6, 7	5, 6	4, 5, 6, 7, 8, 15, 16		1	6	
	4, 6, 7	5, 6	5, 6, 7, 8	8			
1, 2, 3, 4	1, 2	8		1, 2, 4	5, 6	1, 5, 9, 11	1, 4, 6
		(1)	4, 5, 6, 7, 8, 10	1, 2	4		3
			4, 5, 6, 7, 8	1, 2		6	3
	4	5, 6	4, 5, 6, 7, 8, 15, 16		7	6, 9, 11	1, 4, 6
			4, 5, 6, 7, 8		7		3
	6, 7		4, 5, 6, 7, 8		4		3
		5, 6	6, 7, 8, 15, 16				
	6, 7	5, 6	7, 8				3
	6, 7	5, 6	7, 8				3
	6, 7		7, 8, 15, 16				
							(3), 4, 5
							(4)
							4, 5
							6, 7
							1, 2, 8
		(7), (8)					
			(1), 9, 10, (17)				
			(1)				
			1, 2				
			(3), 11				
			12, 13				
			1, 2, (3)				
			18, 19				
			4, 5, 6, (7), (8)				
			(15)				
						1, 2, 8, 14	
						(3), (4), 5, 6, 7, 8	
						9, (11), (12), 15	
				1, 2, 4, 5, 6, (9)			
						(4)	
						9, 10	
				3, 10			
				1, 2, 8, (9), 11			
				(3)			
				(3), (7), 8, 9, 10			
			18	1, 5			
			(18)	1, 5			
			19				
			(19)				
			18				
			20, 21				

ENVIRONMENTAL STUDIES 5—14 SCIENCE

ENERGY AND FORCES		**Forces and their effects** Developing an understanding of forces and how they can explain familiar phenomena and practices
	C	• give some examples of friction
		• explain friction in simple terms
		• describe air resistance in terms of friction
	D	• give examples of streamlining and explain how this lowers resistance
		• describe the relationship between the Earth's gravity and the weight of an object
	E	• describe the effects of balanced and unbalanced forces
		• explain how gravity on other planets and the Moon affects the weight of an object

LIVING THINGS AND THE PROCESSES OF LIFE		**Variety and characteristic features** Developing an understanding of the characteristic features of the main groups of plants and animals, including humans and micro-organisms.
	C	• give some of the more obvious distinguishing features of the five vertebrate groups
		• name some of the common members of the vertebrate groups
		• name some fo the common animals and plants using simple keys
	D	• give the main distinguishing features of the major groups of flowering and non-flowering plants
	E	• give the main distinguishing features of micro-organisms
		• create and use keys to identify living things
		• give examples of inherited and environmental causes of variation
		The processes of life Developing an understanding of growth, development and life cycles, including cells and cell processes.
	C	• name the life processes common to humans and other animals
		• identify the main organs of the human body
		• describe the broad functions of the organs of the human body
		• describe the broad functions fo the main parts of flowering plants
	D	• describe the role of lungs in breathing
		• outline the process of digestion
		• describe the main changes that occur during puberty
		• describe the main stages in human reproduction
		• describe the main stages in flowering-plant reproduction
	E	• identify, name and give the functions of the main organs in the human reproductive system
		• identify the raw materials, conditions and products of photosynthesis
		Interaction of living things with their environment Developing an understanding of the interdependence of living things with the environment. The conservation and care of living things are also considered
	C	• give examples of living things that are very rare or extinct
		• explain how living things and the environment can be protected and give examples
	D	• describe examples of human impact on the environment that have brought about beneficial change, and examples that have detrimental effects
		• give examples of how plants and animals are suited to their environment
		• explain how responses to changes in the environment might increase the chances of survival
	E	• construct and interpret simple food webs and make predictions of the consequences of change
		• describe examples of competition between plants and between animals
		• give examples of physical factors that affect the distribution of living things

DEVELOPING INFORMED ATTITUDES	Pupils should be encouraged to develop an awareness of, and positive attitudes, to:
	A commitment to learning
	• the need to develop informed and reasoned opinions on the impact of science in relation to social, environmental, moral and ethical issues
	• working independently and with others to find solutions to scientific problems
	Respect and care of self and others
	• taking responsibility for their own health and safety
	• participating in the safe and responsible care of living things and the environment
	• the development of responsible attitudes that take account of different beliefs and values
	Social and environmental responsibility
	• thinking through the various consequences for living things and for the environment of different choices, decisions and courses of action
	• the importance of the interrelationships between living things and their environment
	• participating in the conservation of natural resources and the sustainable use of the Earth's resources
	• the need for conservation of scarce energy resources and endangered species at local and global level

Lessons where curriculum content is the main objective are listed below. Lessons where content is included but is not the main focus are shown below in brackets.

Unit 1: Ourselves New beginnings	Unit 2: Animals & Plants Variation	Unit 3: The environment The living world	Unit 4: Materials Reversible and non-reversible changes	Unit 5: Electricity Changing circuits	Unit 6: Forces & motion Forces and action	Unit 7: Light & sound Light and sound around us	Unit 8: Earth & beyond The Solar System
					7		
					7, 8, 9		
					3		
					(4), (5), 6, 10, 11		
					3		
	(1), 2						
	2						
	3, 5, 9						
		(8), (10), (11), (12), (13), (14), (15)					
	3						
	(4)						
(1), 4							
	(6), (7), (8)						
(4)							
4, 5, 6, 7, 8							
5, 6, 7, 8							
	7, (8)						
		8					
		(1), 4, (5), 8, 9					
		(2), (3), 16					
		(4), 5, 6, 16					
		(5), (6), (9)					
1, 2, 3, 8		10, 11, 12	14			13	
		8		7		13	
		8, 9					
			(18), (19), 20, 21, 22		(2)		
			(18), (19), 20, 21, 22		(2)		

Series topic map

Year/Primary	YR/P1	Y1/P2	Y2/P3	Y3/P4	Y4/P5	Y5/P6	Y6/P7
Unit 1: Ourselves	This is me!	Me and my body	Keeping healthy	Teeth and food	How I move	Growing up healthy	New beginnings
Unit 2: Animals & plants	Looking at animals and plants	Growing and caring	Growing up	The needs of plants and animals	Different sorts of skeletons	Life cycles	Variation
Unit 3: The environment	Out and about	Environments and living things	Life in habitats	How the environment affects living things	Habitats and food chains	Water and the environment	The living world
Unit 4: Materials	Exploring materials	Properties of materials	Materials and change	Natural & manufactured materials	Warm liquids, cool solids	Gases, solids and liquids	Reversible and non-reversible changes
Unit 5: Electricity	Making things work	Using and misusing electricity	Making circuits	Electricity and communication	Switches and conduction	Making and using electricity	Changing circuits
Unit 6: Forces & motion	Pushing and pulling	Introducing forces	Making things move	Magnets and springs	Friction	Exploring forces and their effects	Forces and action
Unit 7: Light & sound	Looking and listening	Sources of light and sound	Properties and uses	Sources and effects	Travelling and reflecting	Bending light and changing sound	Light and sound around us
Unit 8: Earth & beyond	Up in the sky	Stargazing	The Sun and the seasons	The Sun and shadows	The Sun and stars	Sun, Moon and Earth	The Solar System